Tom Wright, until recently Bishop of Durham, is currently Research Professor of New Testament and Early Christianity at the University of St Andrews and is a regular broadcaster on radio and television. He is the author of over fifty books, including the For Everyone guides to the New Testament, the best-selling *Simply Christian* and *Surprised by Hope*, and the magisterial series entitled Christian Origins and the Question of God.

Twelve Months of Sundays

Years A, B and C

Biblical meditations on the Christian year

— ≋ —

Tom Wright

Twelve Months of Sundays: Year A first published in 2001 and reprinted once
Twelve Months of Sundays: Year B first published in 2002 and reprinted twice
Twelve Months of Sundays: Year C first published in 2000 and reprinted twice

First published in Great Britain as *Twelve Months of Sundays,
Years A, B and C: Biblical meditations on the Christian year* in 2012

Society for Promoting Christian Knowledge
36 Causton Street
London SW1P 4ST
www.spckpublishing.co.uk

British Library Cataloguing-in-Publication Data
A catalogue record for this book is available from the British Library

ISBN 978–0–281–06581–3

First printed in Great Britain by Ashford Colour Press
Subsequently digitally printed in Great Britain

Produced on paper from sustainable forests

Contents

— ≈ —

Contents

Contents

Preface

——— ∾ ———

This book brings together my reflections based on the weekly biblical readings in the official lectionary now in use in the Church of England. The pieces first appeared in the *Church Times*; the encouraging response to them suggested that they should be made available in a more permanent form.

The lectionary offers a three-year cycle of readings, set out in *The Christian Year* (Church House Publishing, 1997). This volume of reflections covers Years A, B and C. No attempt has been made to cover the readings for the various Saints' Days that may from time to time fall on a Sunday. Every possible regular Sunday, however, has been covered, including the extra 'Propers' provided after Epiphany when Easter is late and after Trinity when Easter is early. I have used the 'continuous' set of readings for the Sundays in Ordinary Time after Trinity, rather than the 'related' set in each case.

Where the official lectionary suggests a 'passage' consisting of clumps of verses selected out of a longer paragraph or chapter, I have sometimes simply listed, and commented on, the entire passage. I am well aware that it is often impossible to read as much Scripture during the course of a well-ordered liturgy as the integrity of the text might seem to require. But it is important that the serious reader, let alone the preacher, be aware of the whole from which the parts are taken, and interpret those parts in the light of that whole.

I assume that the reader will have the biblical texts to hand, preferably in more than one good modern translation. These pieces are not, of course, a full commentary on the passages. They are personal reflections designed to stimulate fresh thought. If they prompt the reader to his or her own exploration, understanding and love of the text, and of the God of whom it speaks, my purpose will have been more than accomplished.

My thanks are due to Paul Handley, Editor of the *Church Times*, and to the editorial assistant Yolande Clarke, for the invitation to write these reflections in the first place and for the patient encouragement which has kept me to the task. I am grateful, too, to SPCK for accepting the project, and to Joanna Moriarty and Mary Matthews who have helped bring it to completion.

Tom Wright

YEAR A

Advent

The First Sunday of Advent

— ∽ —

Isaiah 2.1–5
Romans 13.11–14
Matthew 24.36–44

With the lectionary's new year comes St Matthew, with warnings about the days of Noah. Noah's solitary gospel cameo; he doesn't feature much in the epistles, either. Why not?

The point about Noah's days is that they were *ordinary*. Eating, drinking, family life as usual; no signs, no hint of what is to happen. This contrasts with the previous verses, where detailed signs herald Jerusalem's destruction; some suggest that this is a different 'day and hour', the second coming itself, which might occur at any time, not necessarily after a generation. Alternatively, these warnings too can be interpreted as relating to Jerusalem's fall, but as referring narrowly to the specific moment of calamity.

From early days, however, Christians have read this text as referring to the ultimate future, the day for which even AD 70 was just a rehearsal, the day when some will be 'taken' (in judgement) and others 'left' (in mercy). If we wish to read the text this way, however, we must temper it with the emphasis of Paul: do not suppose that you are at the moment simply in darkness, with nothing to do before the great day arrives. The day has already begun to dawn with the coming of Jesus, so that Jesus' followers are *already* people of the day. The promise – and warning – of God's future is meant to inculcate neither helplessness nor complacency, but rather energy to work as day-people in a world that thinks it's still night.

Paul has his own detailed agenda of what this will mean. No night-behaviour: many of the sins he lists in v. 13 may have been nocturnal in Rome, but his point is clearly meta-phorical, since quarrelling and jealousy keep no special hours. Those who clothe themselves with the Lord of the day must renounce all such behaviour; sinful practices, par-ticularly those of the flesh, will shriek that it's unnatural to say 'no' to them, but once the day has dawned the shadows cannot dictate to the sunlight, nor the nightmares to the morning's tasks.

For Paul, then, the great event for which Israel had longed had already arrived in Jesus. This means that prophecies like Isaiah 2 are already brought to birth in God's reality. Paul saw his own mission to the Gentiles as the fulfilment of Isaiah's promise: the nations were already coming in to God's people, to hear the message of salvation that the creator God had entrusted to the Jews, and had fulfilled in the Jewish Messiah. Isaiah's promise of universal peace must therefore be read, like Paul's call to personal holiness, as our present agenda. We must neither look helplessly at a dark and sleeping world, nor think complacently that we, the church, are all right as we are. We must wake people up to the fact that the sun is already shining, and that the judge of the nations is at the door, longing to see his justice and peace enfold the world in a single embrace.

The Second Sunday of Advent

— ◦≈◦ —

Isaiah 11.1–10
Romans 15.4–13
Matthew 3.1–12

'His delight shall be in the fear of the Lord' (Isaiah 11.3). Yes, no doubt, but the Hebrew word for 'delight' actually means 'smell'. This may be just a metaphor, borrowed perhaps from the cultic contexts in which God delights in the pleasing odour of sacrifices, but the reason for taking it thus is our modern, Western downgrading of the sense of smell as the most accurate judge of situations and people. It may sound absurd to us, but to this day in several cultures there are people who stand at the doors of churches, and for that matter mosques, and refuse people admission on the grounds that they carry with them a scent of evil. Some animals, of course, can arrive at accurate judgements of people on similar grounds.

The point of this surprising comment in Isaiah is that the Messiah, when he comes, will judge with fine-honed accuracy. Eyes may deceive; ears may listen to powerful voices; but the Messiah's justice will have a sense of smell, attuned by the fear of the Lord, through which wickedness will be identified and dealt with. Out of this sharp-edged judgement, cutting through the fuzzy half-truths with which so much of our human discourse is saturated, will come the time of peace, of harmony, of wolves lying down with lambs, of the earth being full of the knowledge of the Lord as the

4

waters cover the sea. (And how do the waters cover the sea? They *are* the sea.)

The passage from Romans is a hangover from the old Bible Sunday readings (see 15.4 in particular), but it happily echoes Isaiah's theme anyway. Paul swaps the prophet's animals for humans: instead of wolves and lambs, Jews and Gentiles are brought together in harmony. All is based on the work of the Messiah, who has fulfilled the promises to Israel (v. 8) precisely in order that the whole world might now glorify God for his mercy. Despite the persistent idea that the gospel message to Gentiles had to be de-Judaized, Paul sees that what the world needs is precisely the Jewish message that the creator God is bringing his justice to bear on the world by fulfilling his promises to Israel. This is, of course, precisely what the previous fourteen chapters of Romans are about: the messianic work through which God's justice/righteousness (I'm still waiting for offers of a word which carries both meanings) is brought to bear on all creation.

Isaiah again, this time in Matthew 3. The 'voice' was to prepare the way for YHWH to come, back through the desert from Babylon or wherever else he had hidden, back to Israel in justice and redemption. And there in the wilderness was John preparing the way for the Messiah who would come and separate the wheat from the chaff. The waters that would flood the world with the knowledge of the Lord must first sweep over Israel in cleansing and mercy.

The Third Sunday of Advent

— ⁓ —

Isaiah 35.1–10
James 5.7–10
Matthew 11.2–11

One of the recently edited Dead Sea Scrolls (no. 521 of the Cave 4 collection, if anyone out there wants the reference) contains a portrait of the coming Messiah that, like Matthew 11, looks back to Isaiah 35: 'He will . . . free prisoners, giving sight to the blind, straightening out the twisted . . . and he will heal the wounded and make the dead live, he will proclaim good news to the meek, give to the needy, lead the exiled and enrich the hungry.' These ideas were clearly 'in the air' at the time of Jesus: when the Messiah came, the lavish programme of healing and restoration outlined by Isaiah would be put into effect.

Nobody knows, of course, just how literally people took it. Scholars debate whether, for instance, the Qumran community expected the literal resurrection of the dead. But nor can anyone doubt that Jesus' reply to John was about as clear a messianic claim as could be made without spelling it out explicitly inch by inch. (John had heard in prison, says v. 2, of 'the deeds of the Messiah', not 'what Christ was doing'; making 'Christ' a proper name here neatly misses the point of the whole paragraph.)

But why would Jesus want to be reticent? The rest of the passage makes it clear: there was already a king of the Jews, and the house of Herod had a bad track record, to put it

6

mildly, when it came to tolerating other would-be kings. John, from whom the question had come, was after all in Herod's prison at the time.

So why was John still there? If Jesus really was the Messiah, why didn't he free prisoners like John as well as giving the blind their sight? There is a dark mystery here, to do with the now-and-not-yet of the gospel, both in Jesus' ministry and after his death and resurrection. Hence James's call to Advent-style patience: yes, the Judge is already known, and is even now at the doors, but precisely for that reason do not expect to see everything sorted out in the present. That is both the glory and the frustration of Advent.

But it's no reason for not implementing as much of the agenda as we can here and now. The New Testament writers believed that Isaiah 35 was in principle fulfilled in Jesus, who brought the ransomed of the Lord back from the Babylon of death itself, opening up the new day whose watchword is 'Be strong! Don't be afraid!' His healings, and his call to a new and joyful holiness, have set up the highway to the true Zion, and he invites all and sundry to follow him along it. Don't follow the Herods of this world; they are just reeds shaking in the wind (Herod Antipas had chosen a Galilean reed as the symbol on some of his coins). Follow the prophetic pointings of Isaiah and John, and come to the kingdom that transcends them both.

The Fourth Sunday of Advent

— ∽ —

Isaiah 7.10–16
Romans 1.1–7
Matthew 1.18–25

We were taught in college, and many repeat in the pulpit, that the word *'almah* in Isaiah 7.14 doesn't mean 'virgin', but 'young woman'. It's not that easy, actually: the word is rare, and the other uses, all compatible with virginity, don't finally settle the issue. Nor does the more common word *bethulah* necessarily mean 'virgin'. In Genesis 24.16 Rebekah is described as 'a *bethulah*, neither had any man known her'. The Greek translation of Isaiah 7.14, which makes it unambiguously 'virgin', is not necessarily changing the original meaning, simply making things more explicit.

Why does all this matter (as it clearly does, considering how frequently the question is raised – indeed, one sometimes gets the impression that *'almah* is the only Hebrew word some people know, and even that they get wrong)? Is it to suggest that Matthew (or his source) has invented the story of Mary's virginal conception in order to cook up pseudo-'events' that just happen to 'fit' or 'fulfil' prophecy? Matthew is of course very concerned, not least in these early chapters, with all sorts of prophetic fulfilments; but if that were the origin of the story, how might we explain Luke's account, where Isaiah 7 is not mentioned? Or the sneer about Jesus' illegitimacy in John 8.41? It looks, rather, as though things worked the other way round: Matthew, faced with a deeply puzzling story

8

about Jesus, found a biblical text that might shed some light upon it. Like Joseph, Matthew knew well enough what people would say. He was right: they still do.

In Isaiah, the fact of the *'almah* being with child was given as a sign to the unbelieving king Ahaz, that un-David-like Davidic descendant, that God would rescue Judah from the northern threat, and would do so very soon, before the child reached an awareness of good and evil (when this moral maturing was supposed to take place is not clear). Eight centuries later Paul would write of another son of David through whom God's rescue was assured, and the issue of good and evil settled: the one whose birth and resurrection now formed the summary of 'the good news', itself an Isaianic term.

Paul gives us the earliest written evidence that the phrase 'son of God' was acquiring, within developing Christianity, the meaning of 'one who was from the beginning with the father', without losing, as clearly in Romans 1 it has not lost, the meaning 'Messiah' which was one of its connotations in the Hebrew Scriptures. The 'good news' for which Paul has been 'set apart' is that God's son has come to be of David's seed, and has been publicly marked out as God's son through the resurrection. Birth matters; resurrection matters more. Without Easter, nobody would ever have told the Christmas story. Ponder that when battling with seasonal mammon-worship, in which, as Marx wryly noted, purchasable commodities become the incarnation of the rival god. Mammon doesn't raise the dead.

Christmas

The First Sunday of Christmas

— ❦ —

Isaiah 63.7–9
Hebrews 2.10–18
Matthew 2.13–23

More Isaianic translation problems. Fortunately here the meaning is not in doubt. 'In all their affliction he was afflicted, and the angel of his presence saved them'? – or is it 'He became their saviour in all their distress; it was no messenger or angel, but his presence that saved them'? Either way, the underlying point is that YHWH, Israel's God, did not send someone else to rescue his people when they were in their deepest need. He came and did it himself. He could (the second version implies, echoing the debate between God and Moses in Exodus 32—34) have sent a lesser being, but was eventually persuaded to accompany Israel in person, consistent with his action when he heard their cry in Egypt and came to save them. The prophet looks back to the Exodus to invoke this same compassionate, grieving, personally present God for his own day.

Egypt forms the link with today's gospel (our nicely non-sensical calendar means that we get the Flight into Egypt before the Epiphany). Again, this is hardly likely to have been invented simply on the basis of Hosea 11.1, quoted in v. 15; nor is Matthew unaware that God's 'son', for Hosea, was of course Israel itself (compare Exodus 4.22). Jesus specifically takes on the role of Israel, doing as an unwitting baby what

12

Isaiah said YHWH had done, coming to where the people were in distress, recapitulating the story.

The house of Herod, who hover balefully in the background throughout Matthew's Gospel, are introduced in this chapter for the first time (does Matthew's genealogy, sweeping down the royal line from Abraham to David to Jesus, owe its existence to Jews who kept the true Davidic hope alive during the Hasmonean and Herodian years?). First the old man, bitter, ill and paranoid, lashing out, as we know from Josephus he regularly lashed out, at anything that might conceivably be a threat. Then his son Archelaus, the new 'king of the Jews', who lasted ten years until popular dislike ousted him, to be replaced by direct Roman rule. Antipas, another son, will appear soon enough. Matthew's story reminds us vividly that the good news of God's personal redeeming activity had from the first to make its way in the disorderly and dangerous real world of violence and conspiracy.

This is exactly the point made by Hebrews. These readings nullify any Christmas sentimentality, and insist that, from the first, Jesus embodied the living, saving God, personally present with his people. Like us in every respect, suffering and being tempted, he is able to help. That's another contrast between the true God and the idols; they are able to thrill, but they can't help. They can excite, but they can't rescue. There is only one God who can. To believe in the incarnation is not to perform a mental conjuring trick, but to swear allegiance to the God who had always acted like that, whose love would be satisfied with nothing less.

The Second Sunday of Christmas

— ⁓ —

Jeremiah 31.7–14
Ephesians 1.3–14
John 1.1–18

C. S. Lewis said that it sometimes seemed an anticlimax to move from the broad poetic sweep of the Old Testament to the narrow focus and seemingly mundane concern of the New. No chance of that this week; but the readings show well enough why the problem occurs.

Early Christian writers were faced with a towering challenge. They believed that the events concerning Jesus were the fulfilment, the filling-full-ment, of the long and winding story of Israel. The hopes and fears, the laughter and tears, of all the years of Israel's story, and the world's story, met together in Jesus in Bethlehem, Galilee, Jerusalem, Calvary, the empty tomb. How can you write that into story after story? How can you say, and get your readers to take it in, that this birth, this death, this new life, were the reality towards which the prophetic signposts all pointed?

One obvious answer is more poetry; and that, in a sense, is what both Paul and John offer here. The Ephesians passage is a sweeping retelling of Israel's story: God's choice of his people, the redemption from Egypt, the unveiling of God's wider purpose, the revealing of his will, and the personal presence of God as his people journey to the land of promise. Only it has all happened fully and finally – in Jesus the Messiah. Try reading the passage with the emphasis on 'him' each time, to bring out the surprise: it is *in him* that all this has happened, not in some other Jewish moment or movement, not in the rule of Caesar or any other feature of world history. The story is familiar, the hero unexpected. Open your ears, says Paul, and hear how the songs of the prophets have at last come round into the major key. Learn to listen for the echoes. Watch the picture come up in three dimensions, or maybe even more.

John 1 suffers from carol-service repetition. It becomes audible wallpaper: the headmaster's drone tells the school only that it's nearly time for mince pies. Almost worse: it is usually cut off at v. 14, producing the literary and theological equivalent of leaving the spire off a cathedral.

Try taking one image and seeing the whole Johannine poem reflected in it. In the beginning . . . You are standing in the dark looking eastwards out to sea. The stars flicker overhead. The first signs of light, and of life: grey pre-dawn sky, seabirds around the breaking waves. Grey turns to green, then gold. Curtains still closed inshore, oblivious to the wakening glory. Stars fade, sea and sky catch fire, and the bright, overpowering disk emerges. Too radiant to look at, but in its light you can see everything else. The heavens declare God's glory, new every morning: was Psalm 19, along with Genesis 1 and Exodus 32—34, among the many passages in John's mind?

New Year resolution: read the New Testament while the Old is still echoing around the mind's rafters.

Epiphany

The First Sunday of Epiphany

— ∽ —

Isaiah 42.1–9
Acts 10.34–43
Matthew 3.13–17

John's baptism can easily seem a mere introduction, the soon-to-be-forgotten starting point. The early Church clearly didn't see it like that, since John continues to haunt the story in all four Gospels and Acts. This wasn't just surreptitious polemic against John's continuing followers. It was positive: John was the heaven-sent prophet through whom the Messiah was to be revealed. Mentioning him reinforces Jesus' messiahship.

This is particularly striking in the Cornelius story. Peter, speaking to a Gentile, makes no attempt to de-Judaize his message. It is essentially a messianic statement, as indeed the title 'Jesus Christ' in v. 36 indicates: Jesus is the anointed one, whose works of healing were the signs that 'God was with him' (a phrase used of David among others). The resurrection demonstrates that Jesus' death was messianic, despite appearances; and now this Jesus is to be judge of living and dead, the dispenser of divine forgiveness. All of this sustains the claim that Jesus, the Messiah, is Lord of all the world – a title which, as Cornelius would recognize, was claimed by his own boss. There lies the true challenge to the non-Jew: to see the Jewish king as the world's true Lord.

The story of Jesus' baptism in Matthew's Gospel, therefore, is both a further challenge to Herod – here is God

18

anointing his true king under the nose of the old one, some-what like Samuel anointing David with Saul still on the throne – and the beginning of the confrontation with, as well as the welcome for, the whole world. It explains why the foreign kings (if that's what they were) brought him gifts. It explains why another centurion, in Matthew 8, knows that he possesses authority. If he is the anointed Messiah, he is Lord of all. The mere announcement of this messiahship, as Acts 10 bears witness, is the thing that carries the power of the Spirit. It declares that Israel's God has brought his people's long story to its strange moment of truth. The whole world is now to be addressed by the one who is both Israel's representative and God's own son ('Son of God' is a messianic title before it is a trinitarian one).

But the large agenda set before the servant-Messiah in Isaiah 42 is accomplished only by implication in the Gospels. Matthew clearly believed that Jesus fulfilled Isaiah 42, and that his death was the primary achievement of the task there set out. But if he knew in his day that the good news still needed to be carried to all the nations, would he not say in ours too that 'the coastlands [still] wait for his teaching' (42.4)? If it is true that the Messiah will not faint or be discouraged until he has established justice in the earth, how is that steady, tireless programme to be implemented by those who, today, claim to be anointed by his own royal Spirit to proclaim him as Lord of all?

The Second Sunday of Epiphany

— ∽ —

Isaiah 49.1–7
1 Corinthians 1.1–9
John 1.29–42

Our question to Isaiah is always, 'Who is the Servant?' Israel, replies the prophet (Isaiah 49.3). But the far harder question is, 'Who is Israel?'

To this, Isaiah gives three concentric answers. The nation as a whole, the people abhorred by the nations (v. 7). Those whose task it is to raise up the tribes of Jacob, and to restore the survivors of Israel (v. 6). And also one who stands over against both nation and remnant (50.10: the remnant are those 'who hear the voice of the servant'). Nation, remnant, individual form a lasting pattern.

As Christians we want to add: Jesus, naturally; and the apostles (Paul often uses Isaianic servant-language to describe his own work). Worryingly, the New Testament also adds: 'ordinary' Christians (not that there are any such, but you know what I mean). We can't get off the hook of the demanding servant-vocation by supposing Jesus has done it all. The Isaianic pattern still awaits fulfilment: if God's justice and salvation are to reach to earth's bounds, it will be through servants, equipped with the spirit of the Servant.

This is the basis of Paul's appeal to Corinth. Before he launches into the letter's many problems, he lays down a foundation. God's people in Corinth are summoned to be saints and worshippers (v. 2); great grace has been poured out on them (v. 4); God has given them many gifts of speech and knowledge (vv. 5–7). God is faithful, and will now give them strength (vv. 8–9). They belong to the *koinonia* the partnership, of God's Son, King Jesus, the Lord (v. 9).

But that partnership is not just a dining club where one can settle down and enjoy fellowship. It is a business partnership with a purpose: to address the sin and pain of the world with the love of God unveiled on the cross. Paul is about to call the Corinthian church to model and implement the genuine new humanity through which alone God will overturn the wisdom and power of the world. This is the servant-vocation, first-century style. It remains the servant-vocation still.

The fluidity of Isaiah's servant-concept therefore has nothing to do with the prophet's being unable to make up his mind or to bring the picture into clear focus. It has to do with God's continuing determination to work *through* his created order, *through* his chosen people. *Through* Jesus, yes, as the true Israelite, the firstborn of all creation, but also now through those who belong to Jesus; lest, salvation having been accomplished in Jesus, the world and the human race be merely passive thereafter. So, in John's account of Jesus' baptism and the first disciples, Andrew's announcement ('we've found the Messiah!') is matched, balanced, by Jesus' comment ('Simon, eh? I'm going to call you Mr Rock'). When, through the window of God's revelation, you recognize the unique Servant, you will also glimpse your own reflection in the glass.

21

The Third Sunday of Epiphany

— ⁓ —

Isaiah 9.1–4
1 Corinthians 1.10–18
Matthew 4.12–23

Was Jesus waiting for a signal?

The Gospels agree that he didn't begin to announce the Kingdom until he heard that John had been arrested. Something about that sinister moment told him that the time had come. He had fought with the powers of darkness, and had overcome. Now one of their earthly representatives had closed in on the Baptist, the one who had prepared the ground for the Kingdom message. Jesus could wait no longer. The darkness had reached its height; it was time for the great light to shine.

The precedents, echoing down the history of Israel, pointed in this direction. Isaiah addressed the problems of his own day by referring back to the Midianite crisis. The enemy power grew stronger, and God saved Israel through an unexpected deliverer. Isaiah's theme of the coming child (omitted from today's reading) provides his own equivalent. Whatever threats the powers of darkness may provide, a child will be born through whom God's zeal will shine the true light in 'Galilee of the nations' (then, as in Jesus' day, Jewish territory permeated with foreign influences). Matthew, invoking Isaiah, draws on this millennium-old tradition in order to say: now at last the story reaches its complete fulfilment.

The very first thing Jesus did, according to Matthew, was to call followers. The beginning of a community, the Kingdom people; the first sign, earlier even than the remarkable healings, that something new was afoot. They left jobs, they left family – both vital symbols of who they were – and became part of that something new, without knowing where it would lead.

This Kingdom people, called into existence by Jesus' announcement and invitation, grew quickly into the twelve, and has grown from that into a great multitude which no one can number. But it is still the same family, formed by the Kingdom proclamation and its accompanying summons, formed of people who have seen the light shining in the darkness and have chosen to follow the path it illuminates.

It was out of concern for that family that Paul wrote 1 Corinthians. We cannot now tell which, if any, of the subsequent problems in the letter were connected to the warring personality cults in the young Church; but the existence of such groups was itself a first-order disaster. Confused and muddled, the Corinthian Christians seem to have lined up Paul, Apollos and Peter with Jesus Christ himself as cult-figures into whose entourage one might be initiated. Paul insists that his role is simply that of the herald, announcing Jesus, the crucified king of the world. That strange message has created a new family out of nothing, a family whose very existence, and particularly whose unity, was supposed to be shining God's great light into the dark culture around.

As we prepare to celebrate Paul's own conversion, and to keep the Week of Prayer for Christian Unity, 1 Corinthians provides a salutary lesson. What are we waiting for? Is the world not dark enough yet?

The Fourth Sunday of Epiphany

— ∾ —

1 Kings 17.8–16
1 Corinthians 1.18–31
John 2.1–11

The third day; it would be. John does nothing by accident. New creation bursts in upon a village wedding, itself a sign of hope. Wine is to water as the new world is to the old; bubbling up, taking people by surprise, confounding expectations, raising questions, raising the dead.

Other overtones crowd in too. Jewish purification rites belong with the old creation, but Jesus belongs in the new. 'Woman, what is there between us? My hour has not yet come'; then, when the hour had truly come, 'Woman, behold your son.' Jesus' glory was there already, for those with eyes to see; though they only really acquired such eyes when they saw his glory, crowned as it had been with thorns, on, yes, the third day.

From then on, the challenge was to see that glory in the shame of the cross. The message of the crucified King of the Jews and Lord of the world burst upon an unsuspecting world, not least through Paul's proclamation, and was a rude shock to the system. Jews were looking for signs of the Kingdom, but what sort of a sign is a crucified King? The pagan world was yearning after wisdom, but what wisdom is there in the stark message that yet another rebel leader has met a messy and untimely end? How can this message contain anything that anyone in their right mind will want to hear? Pour the water into these vessels, though, and then pour it out before the world, and watch it bubble up with transforming power. The gospel, says Paul elsewhere, is God's saving power, God's dynamite. Part of its point is precisely that it is, in the world's eyes, upside down and inside out.

This statement of the gospel's power to up-end human expectations, set alongside last week's passage about personality cults among the Corinthian Christians, provides an introduction to the main thrusts of the letter. The Corinthians were eager to turn the rich wine of the gospel back into water again, back into another version of the philosophies they were used to. Paul will have none of it. Unless the stewards at the feast are looking astonished, the party hasn't really begun. Unless the wrong people are crowding into the kingdom, it isn't God's Kingdom. If it's wine you want, pour water from these vessels. If it's boasting you want, boast of the Lord – Jesus, the vessel that contains all wisdom, and all else besides.

Elijah's multiplication of meal and oil, like Jesus' remarkable multiplications and transformations, was not just a matter of providing for people in need. It was a sign of hope, of new creation, at a time of famine and drought. More: as Jesus himself would indicate in Luke 4, it was a sign that God was at work beyond the borders of Israel. New life was bursting out all over the place. But it took faith to see it. 'Make me a little cake first.' Now there's a challenge.

Ordinary Time

Proper 1

— ∾ —

Isaiah 58.1–12
1 Corinthians 2.1–16
Matthew 5.13–20

Isaiah's stinging rebuke contains the seeds of the Sermon on the Mount. True piety must be part of the outward movement to share your blessing with the world. Fasting is useless if injustice goes unchecked. Look after the poor, and your light will rise like the dawn. God will be present when you call him.

Jesus' challenge to be the salt of the earth and the light of the world was not simply an agenda for his followers at the time or the Church of the future. It was a direct Isaianic challenge to the Israel of his day. They were called to be the light of the world. God's purpose for Israel was that through them he would bring his justice and mercy to bear upon the nations. The city set on a hill, unable to be hidden, is Jerusalem, where the nations would come to learn God's law.

Yet Israel in Jesus' day was refusing this vocation. Of course there were many wise and devout Jews; but the nation as a whole, as Josephus records, was bent not on bringing God's light to the pagan world but on bringing it God's swift judgement, especially that part of it that was currently ruling the Middle East with casual brutality. Understandable, but unfaithful.

Jesus' call is far more than a set of abstract moral lessons. It is a summons to Israel to *be* Israel, while there is still time. This is what the law and the prophets pointed to. And if Jesus' way meant abandoning some of the interpretations (Pharisaic or whatever) which at the time seemed part and parcel of the law, so be it. The call to the higher righteousness corresponds to Isaiah's summons to an outward-looking piety in which Israel will at last be God's people for the world.

In one sense, the call was unsuccessful. Capernaum, Chorazin, Bethsaida – the towns around the Mount – by and large resisted Jesus' bracing challenge. The early Church took it up again later. But in the meantime it was Jesus himself who followed his own programme. He became salt for the world around. He acted as the light-bringer to the nations. He became, when all others had rejected him, the one set on a hill who could not be hidden, embodying in himself what Jerusalem was meant to be but had not been, drawing all peoples to himself. The sermon was an agenda which Jesus himself carried out.

That is why his death was the defeat of the powers. The rulers of the world wouldn't have crucified him if they had known what they were accomplishing: they were signing their own death warrant. From now on, true power comes, as Paul discovered, not through the wisdom or force of the world but through the gospel of Christ and him crucified. If the Spirit is at work through this gospel, law and prophets alike will look on and declare that this is what they had in mind all along.

Proper 2

— ∾ —

Deuteronomy 30.15–20
1 Corinthians 3.1–9
Matthew 5.21–37

A real choice with real consequences. The great temptation today is not so much to cast off all moral restraint – few would actually advocate that, though many act from time to time as though that were the norm – as to imply that there are so many different ways of being human, and of being Christian, that our choices in this life are not that important, and that God will sort it all out in some great (and at present unknowable) future.

This view is often coupled with a clever parody of the Sermon on the Mount. What matters, says Jesus, is not so much that you don't commit murder, adultery and the rest, but that your heart is right. God is looking (as in Deuteronomy; this isn't a Christian innovation over against a Jewish background) for an obedience which goes through and through a person, resulting in an integrity between heart and action. But today, with romanticism and existentialism as our hidden teachers, we 'naturally' think that, as long as we are acting from the heart, what we do outwardly doesn't matter so much. 'His heart's in the right place' is usually said as an *excuse*.

We apply this selectively, of course. Nobody excuses murder on the grounds that it was most sincerely meant. But it goes unnoticed elsewhere that the antithesis between outward and inward observance is never meant, in either Testament, as a way of abolishing the commandments themselves. It is a way of saying that the truly mature, integrated follower of Jesus will be someone for whom it is no longer a moral effort to keep the commandments. They will do so because they deeply want to. That, I suspect, shows what a steep mountain most of us still have to climb.

But, to recapitulate, the choices are real. It won't do to say, 'But we thought we were supposed to do what came naturally.' Not to choose – to go with the flow, whether of the insidious pressures from around or the whispered suggestions from within – is still to choose, namely, to choose to disobey. Part of growing up as Christians is to realize that a tough choice is being asked of us. Jesus, after all, didn't say 'If anyone would come after me, they should go with the flow and do what comes naturally.' The next part is to pray for that change of heart, that total reform and redirection from within, through which alone that obedience can become, as we say, second nature. That, according to both Deuteronomy and Jesus, is the way of life.

One sign of maturity and integration within a Christian community will lie, as Paul knew only too well, in its attitudes to its leaders. Going with the flow of natural instincts had produced personality cults in Corinth, a sure sign of spiritual immaturity. The Church is called to grow beyond what comes naturally to humans, and to embrace instead what comes as the fruit of the Spirit and faith.

Proper 3

— ∿ —

Leviticus 19.1–2, 9–18
1 Corinthians 3.10–11, 16–23
Matthew 5.38–48

There are two basic mistakes people make about the command to love your neighbour as yourself. The first is to forget the last two words. We aren't told to love our neighbour with all our heart, mind, soul and strength; only God has that absolute claim. We are to love our neighbour no more, but no less, than we love ourselves.

This will vary according to whether we are naturally selfish people, who pamper ourselves, or of an ascetic temperament, rebuking and restricting our fleshly desires. It might be fun, for a while, to be loved by the first sort of person as they loved themselves; the second sort, obeying the commandment, might be uncomfortable neighbours.

But here the second mistake kicks in. We are not left without guidance as to how we should love ourselves. True, the lectionary does its best to shield us from the sterner parts of that instruction, as the omitted verses from 1 Corinthians 3 reveal. Verses 12–15 are vital and unique, speaking of the future judgement which will be passed, not on non-Christians, but on Christians themselves, indeed, on Christian *workers*. Paul uses imagery not just from house-building but from temple-building: he is, after all, building the new temple, the community in which God's Spirit truly dwells. Sooner or later fire will test that building, and only the proper materials will last. Builders who have used wood, hay and stubble – jerry-builders who haven't really taken the trouble to do properly the work to which they were called – will discover too late that it all goes up in smoke.

With warnings like this, a proper self-love cannot afford to be complacent. Self-respect, yes, as long as it doesn't become an excuse for sloppy thinking or behaviour ('this is just the way I am'); self-care, yes, as long as it is appropriate and not pampering or greedy. But above all, respect for one's own outward-looking vocation: not, how can I feather my own nest, but how can I be true to what God has called me to be for his Church and world? And if that's what self-love looks like, love of neighbour must be the same: neither an easy-going tolerance of everything a neighbour may do, nor a confrontational bossiness. Leviticus commands a string of practical measures which, culturally translated, give vivid clues to the true approach.

Matthew 5, in turn, suggests a cheerful, almost playful approach (granted that most neighbours today won't strike us on the cheek or pressgang us into carrying military equipment for a mile). Jesus is not asking us to be doormats, but to find creative non-violent ways forward in difficult situations. Ultimately, both self-love and neighbour-love derive from love of God: the steadfast, devoted gaze at our creator and redeemer through which we discover the pattern for those made in his image. If we are called to be God's holy temple, nothing less will do.

The Second Sunday Before Lent

— ∽ —

Genesis 1.1—2.3
Romans 8.18–25
Matthew 6.25–34

The project was all set up and ready to go. Creation was more like a perfect studio than a finished painting; everything was there, paints, canvas, artist, and all. It had its own inbuilt rhythm and drama, its own sources and signs of life: notice the emphasis on the seed in vv. 11–12, and on the command to be fruitful in vv. 22, 28. Paradise it may have been, but it was just the start, the opening scene of the play.

Part of it seems play in a different sense. What sort of a skittish God makes giraffes and chilli peppers, sun and moon and sesame seeds? But the six-day sequence ends with solemn glory. Into the studio the creator places a working model of himself. These creatures are to carry forward the project, to paint the picture. They are to act out the creator's intention, reflecting into the rest of the new-made world the play and the purpose, the very image and likeness, of their maker.

Has the lectionary turned over a new leaf? Do we really get the whole story? A glance at Lent indicates that this is no flash in the pan . . .

But you need more than a whole chapter to get the point of Romans 8. We come crashing in at the climax, like somebody turning on the radio just as *Nimrod* states its theme for the last time. Paul has spent eight chapters preparing for just this moment. Jesus the Messiah has been obedient to God's

34

Israel-shaped play and purpose. Israel's mistake had been to suppose the play was all about herself. It wasn't. Israel's task was to redeem the rest of the world; Jesus has accomplished it. God forgive us, we have often supposed that the plan, the play, was all about us humans. It wasn't. The human task was to reflect God's image into the whole of creation, painting on God's canvas the living signs of powerful, sovereign love. So when Jesus accomplished his great saving act, humans were delivered from death; and when humans then share God's solemn glory, creation itself will be set free for its original purpose. It can't wait.

Underneath all this is a principle that cuts deeply across some current assumptions. Creation was made to flourish when looked after by humans. Humans were made to reflect the image of the creator into the world. Freedom isn't throwing off all constraint. It's finding what you were made for, and being obedient to that and nothing else. It will always be costly; that's part of the point, part of reflecting the image of God now seen in Christ (v. 29).

Inside this again, waiting to be rediscovered by our rushing, restless age, is the strange glory of the sabbath. Look at it this way: if even *God* took a day off, why do you need to worry? Look at the signs of God's relaxed pleasure – the lilies, the birds – and learn to reflect that too.

The Sunday Next Before Lent

— ⪼ —

Exodus 24.12–18
2 Peter 1.16–21
Matthew 17.1–9

The mountain, the glory, the fear. The old story thunders around the crags of scripture, and we hear it echoing from every side, rolling on down the valleys. Moses on the mountain with God. Joshua ('Jesus' in Greek) there with him. Jesus on the mountain with Moses and Elijah. Peter on the mountain with Jesus and Moses and Elijah. We beheld his glory, as of God's only son. The prophetic word made more sure. The cloud and the fire. The booths in the wilderness. No one has seen God; this one has revealed him.

Whatever else it means, it means we have to listen to the thunder and ponder what it says. Peter implies that the way to faith is to hold firm to the great old stories, and treat them with the respect they deserve. They are a candle to see you through the night; attention to them will be rewarded as day breaks (always slightly later than you thought, or wanted) and the morning star rises in your hearts. Eager for the day, we often spurn the candle, and wonder why we bump into things while waiting for light to dawn.

Today's candle flickers to and fro. Themes glint and sparkle. God's glory rests on the mountain for six days; on the seventh Moses is summoned. Is the giving of the law a new creation? Yes and no: forty days and nights on the mountain, alone with the glory, and meanwhile Aaron and Hur are left behind to keep charge – but did they? Maybe this is like a new Genesis 1 *and* Genesis 3? Jesus waits six days, and on the seventh takes Peter and James and John up the mountain. Who meets whom? What did it mean for Moses and Elijah? The candle sets light to time and space, the devouring fire blazes out like the sun, the cloud swallows them up, and the word echoes around the disciples' hearts ever afterwards.

There are strange old stories, and some not so old, of those who watched the candle, and then the morning star, with such intensity that their own faces started to change. Sometimes it's in the eyes. Sometimes, perhaps, the whole face. Our Western consciousness, and perhaps self-consciousness, denies us so much. Transfiguration was not meant to be a private experience for Jesus only. When he appears, we shall be like him; we shall see him as he is.

The Israelites saw the cloud and fire. Aaron saw it. And yet . . . Peter saw Jesus' face shine like the sun. He heard the words. And yet . . . Memory is a great antidote to temptation. Whatever mountain you have to climb in the coming forty days, whatever words you have to hear, remember where you came from and where you are going. Remember how the thunder sounded. Remember what you saw in the candle's flickering light. Joshua was with Moses. He saw, and remembered. 'As I was with Moses, so I will be with you.' And so . . .

Lent

The First Sunday of Lent

— ∽ —

Genesis 2.15–17; 3.1–7
Romans 5.12–19
Matthew 4.1–11

Students set to translate Romans 5 often despair: some of its 'sentences' have neither subjects nor verbs nor objects, but are just collocations of indirect phrases. Paul at his most oblique: 'So then – through the trespass of the one – unto all people – unto condemnation, so also – through the righteous act of the one – unto all people – unto the verdict of life!' Perhaps this too is quite deliberate, the linguistic form that reverence takes when alluding to the deep and strange work of God.

It is also something to do with the fact that this paragraph sums up the previous four and a half chapters and looks on to the next three – and the next three, and the final five. This is the craggy ridge from which, unless you suffer from vertigo, you can look out in both directions – and, indeed, at Genesis 3 and Matthew 4. With a view like that, you don't expect the path to be gentle.

The point of the Adam/Christ comparison is to emphasize that the human project begun in Genesis, the key part of the creator's project for the whole creation, has been put back on track. Paul doesn't offer a full 'doctrine of sin' here, but merely summarizes what he had said in 1.18–32 (which doesn't usually make it into the lectionaries). Enough for the moment to know that sin involves disobedience, failure

40

of loyalty, a fracturing of the creator's intention, which, because it is a turning away from the source of life, cannot but bring death.

The parallel is unbalanced (that is the point of vv. 15–17) because Jesus did not start where Adam started; he began where Adam ended up. The 'obedience' of the Messiah is his obedience to the whole saving plan of God, the Israel-shaped plan to which Israel had herself been disobedient; hence the double task, not just to lift the weight that Adam failed to lift but first to catch it as it fell. And the result of that abounding grace (v. 15) is the firm platform on which Christ's people now stand. 'By his knowledge shall the righteous one, my servant, make the many to be accounted righteous, and he shall bear their iniquities'; Isaiah is never far from Paul's mind, and the echoes here are plain.

Dense doctrinal statements are, of course, shorthand ways of drawing together a larger world of narrative. Romans was written, so far as we know, before the Gospels, but it presupposes the sort of story we find in Matthew 4. Jesus offers God not merely the obedience which Adam refused, but that redeeming obedience which Israel refused in the wilderness. Jesus faced the 'if . . .' of the tempter with courage, with Scripture, with loyalty to the one who had called him. Interestingly, he thereby chose the way Eve had thought to avoid, the way of death, the naked death of the cross. But the tree he chose was the tree of wisdom, the tree of life.

The Second Sunday of Lent

— ∿ —

Genesis 12.1–4a
Romans 4.1–5, 13–17
John 3.1–17

'Leave country, kin and home, and go.' And Abram went. The call was like that other word, to leave and cleave, spoken before the Fall: a marriage vow, a challenge and a pledge of loyalty. Like, too, the older word to image-bearing Adam, and to Eve: be fruitful, multiply, and tend the garden. Now: I'll make you fruitful – bless, through you, the world of thorns and thistles. Abraham, father of us all.

Paul's question, then, is not 'what Abraham gained', or 'found'. Repunctuate (there were, of course, no marks, or even spaces, in the early texts): 'What shall we say? Have we found Abraham to be our forefather in terms of flesh?' Paul's question comes, of course, from his insistence that God's faithfulness is now unveiled, fulfilled, in Jesus Christ. Does this mean, then, that those who come to faith in Christ must join the fleshly, ethnic family founded by Abraham?

No. This family is not marked out by works of Jewish law. The law, as Paul made clear, discloses only sin, leading to wrath. The promise stands outside that scheme, opening the wider world before the patriarch long before the giving of the law. Paul's mind leaps over the intervening scheme of Torah, holy land, ethnic restriction, seeing instead the glittering promise in the early dawn of Israel's ancestry. 'He would inherit the *world*: a line drawn from this point reaches right into Romans 8.

And how would Abraham's family attain their promised land? Through Exodus, marking them out as liberated slaves, God's freedom-people (Genesis 15).

The good news, then: Abraham is father not of one nation merely, but of all, all who now share his faith in God the life-giver. 'The father of us all': 4.16 (which doesn't need a bracket, as some versions think) gives the climactic answer to the question of verse 1. With this, Paul's argument is nearly done: this is how the one true God has been, in Christ, faithful to what he'd promised. From here, he too will journey on, through water (chapter 6) and Spirit (8) to the larger promised land. When, finally, he opens up the sight of cosmic liberty, creation free at last from death, part of the point is 'This, then, was what God promised Abraham'.

What then of Jesus, and his night encounter with the puzzled teacher? 'New birth', in Jewish ears, meant a new family: leaving the old, cleaving to something new. Abraham's family redefined, out-nomading the old nomad. Water and Spirit, baptism and faith. Israel took its shape from Exodus and Sinai, sea and fire, its healing from the strange bronze serpent. Now, a new covenant: the love of God, not Israel's private boast, but for the world. All is revealed in one who left his father's home and went where he was told. 'So must the Son of Man be lifted up.' God is now newly working: everyone, all who believe, will share the glory of the age to come.

The Third Sunday of Lent

— ⟨≈⟩ —

Exodus 17.1–7
Romans 5.1–11
John 4.5–42

John's great sprawling story (what an excellent move to have some of Jesus' Johannine encounters in full during Lent) offers food for thought at every level. The antipathy between Jews and Samaritans was not just a cold stand-off: then as now, if you travelled through Samaria from the Dead Sea region to Galilee, you could expect trouble. Josephus tells of violent riots, a few years after Jesus' time, when Jewish pilgrims tried to make the journey. Try telling someone in the Middle East today that, while 'salvation is from the Jews', in God's design there will be no such thing as a holy mountain. That's fighting talk.

The dialogue is a long string of double meanings and misunderstandings (did John actually intend it, perhaps, to sound funny, a semi-comic scene with a serious point hidden among the to-and-fro of the repartee, like some of Shakespeare's clown scenes?). Jesus offers living water (the regular phrase for 'running water', as opposed to still or stagnant), and the woman reminds him he hasn't got a bucket. Is Jesus greater than Jacob, the original giver of the well (notice the '*our* father Jacob', and the long memory of water rights – again, today, a sore point in the same region)? She can't, of course, cite Exodus, since the Jews claim that as their text – but there, too, water is all-important, and a cause of strife between the wilderness people, their leader, and their God. When Jesus responds with the promise of a water that slakes thirst for ever, she is suddenly submissive. She probably doesn't know what it is he is really offering (did she think he was making advances?), but she wants it.

As in his response to the rich young ruler, Jesus puts his finger on the point where her life is most sorely in need of living water. Repartee again: 'Call your husband.' 'Haven't got one.' 'No – five down, one to go.' Oops, change the subject . . . 'Are you a prophet by any chance? We have this thing about which mountain we should worship on.' ('Oh, you're from that church, are you? My granny said we should go to this one.' Always a good distraction.) Objection over-ruled. 'Spirit, not mountain, is what matters; and the one God is looking for Spirit-people right now.' 'Oh, very inter-esting – of course one day the Messiah is coming. He'll explain all that complicated stuff.' Phew. Let's not get too far with this.

Pause. No way off the hook. Jesus holds her gaze. *Ego eimi, ho lalon soi*: 'I am, who am speaking to you.' Messiah, and . . . 'I am'? End of repartee. Time for action. Sower and reaper are about to rejoice together.

The extension of Jesus' ministry to the Samaritans, even during his lifetime, is a foretaste of that full extension which Paul celebrates throughout Romans. The Messiah's death demonstrates the love of God, undercutting all regional or ethnic claims and boasts, and creating a new people, Spirit-people, worship-people.

The Fourth Sunday of Lent

— ❧ —

1 Samuel 16.1–13
Ephesians 5.8–14
John 9.1–41

Don't miss the sinister moment towards the end of John's great story. We were told from the beginning that the blind man's condition from birth had nothing to do with previous sins, whether his own or his parents'. That possibility, so prevalent in folk-religion (and in some more sophisticated systems), is alien to the Judaeo-Christian tradition. The Bible regularly refuses to ask 'why?', but rather 'what?' Our instinct is to look for a 'solution' in terms of a theory about the cause or origin of suffering (which might then mean we wouldn't need to do anything further). God's is to provide a solution by working towards new creation.

The Pharisees, however, don't see it like this. Jesus is a sabbath-breaker; he can't be the Messiah. His mighty works must have a different origin. He is deceiving the people. When pushed in discussion, they give the answer Jesus rejected to the question with which the chapter began: 'you were born entirely in sins' (v. 34). Your condition proves that you, and your parents, were in fact 'sinners', so you can't teach us. There is a distant echo of Psalm 51.7, but they can't be thinking of that (it would apply to them too).

The notion of purity in some sectarian Jewish groups (the Dead Sea Scrolls have the same idea) includes physical wholeness. It was this symbolic world, claiming to be the

46

true observance of the Jewish law, that Jesus opposed with his fresh vision of that very Jewish vocation, to be the light of the world (v. 5). His healings, with all their own rich symbolic value, posed a deep-level challenge: is this not what it means to be loyal to the God of Israel, to be doing his work of salvation and new creation? If this is so, to cling to the symbols of a different world, a hard, exclusive system, is to be truly blind. It is to call down on oneself the very judgement one has pronounced on others (v. 41).

God sees, then, in a different mode to how we see, as Samuel discovered when examining Jesse's sons – every bit as subversive an action, granted that Saul was still king, as that of Jesus in healing on the sabbath. Christian obedience can be categorized, as a result, in terms of learning to see differently. The image of light flickers and flashes through Ephesians 5: you *are* light, you are children of light, so your role (unfashionable though this may be) is to shine into the dark corners of life and show up what is going on. In doing so, you are acting as agents of Christ himself, the world's true light, summoning the dead to life, to wake up to God's new day. This message is all the more important at a time when our culture seems to have forgotten the meaning of shame. Take the reading back a couple of verses: 'Let no one deceive you with empty words.'

The Fifth Sunday of Lent
(Passiontide begins)

— ∽ —

Ezekiel 37.1–14
Romans 8.6–11
John 11.1–45

'Resurrection' began as a metaphor for the return from exile. Ezekiel's surreal vision was an image of Israel, 'dead' in Babylon, being restored to her own land. It goes with the promises of the previous chapters, promises of covenant renewal, of cleansing from sin, of God's gift of a new heart, a new spirit. The God who breathed into human nostrils at creation will do so again. Covenant renewal will mean new creation.

After Easter, metaphor and history changed places. 'The resurrection' should have happened to all God's people at the end of time, not to one person in the middle of history; Jesus' followers explained Easter in terms of return from exile, the long-awaited new Exodus. Romans 8 is the classic passage: what God did for Jesus he will do for all creation, liberating it from its present slavery to corruption. Those whose bodies are heading for death, but who are indwelt by God's Spirit, are assured that what God did for Jesus as an individual he will do for all the Messiah's people. (Notice how Paul moves between the name and the title: 'Jesus' is the individual, 'Christ' the one who represents God's people.)

A preacher who needs help with John 11 is in bad shape.

48

But the story has oddities as well as obvious, indeed spectacular, moments of glory. Jesus heard that Lazarus was ill,
and therefore (vv. 5–6) he stayed where he was two days
longer. This is only partially explained by vv. 4 and 14: Jesus
has something in mind through which God's glory will be
revealed, and the disciples' faith strengthened (perhaps not
only the disciples', either?). Jesus is the bearer of Israel's
destiny: he doesn't just teach about the great Return, the
new Exodus, he is embodying it. Then the exchange in vv.
39–42: Martha, characteristically anxious, warns about the
smell from a three-day corpse; Jesus commands that the stone
be removed, and then thanks the Father for having heard his
prayer. We must presume that *there was no smell*: Jesus had
prayed for Lazarus's death to be temporary, and the prayer
had been answered.

The life and light of this story are framed by a dark
background. The Judaeans (not 'the Jews' as in most translations) include many who want to do away with Jesus, and
this supreme sign – the sixth in John's sequence, pointing on
to the coming completion of Jesus' work – will only exacer-
bate their opposition. Jesus' prayer and action for Lazarus
looks ahead to his own coming ordeal. The resuscitation of
Lazarus into the same sort of body partially anticipates the
greater event of Easter, when the Messiah will go through
death and out into the unmapped new land beyond. But, as
Lenten pilgrims know, the road to Easter lies along the way
of the cross. Was Thomas doubting, or was he believing,
when he said 'Let's go too, so that we may die with him' (v.
16)?

Palm Sunday
(Liturgy of the Passion)

— ∼ —

Isaiah 50.4–9a
Philippians 2.5–11
Matthew 26.14—27.66

C. S. Lewis, writing as a literary critic, proposed a test for good writing: how often does it deserve to be read? Cheap magazine stories come at the bottom (once you know what happens, you don't read them again), and the great novels and plays near the top (I once knew an octogenarian who read through Shakespeare every year). Thus measured, the passion narratives score highly. The action is swift, the dialogue terse and pregnant. A dozen brilliant human cameos: Jesus and Judas; Peter; Caiaphas; Pilate (and his wife); Barabbas; Simon; the bandits; the mockers; the centurion; the women; and Joseph – each one deserving careful mulling over. The whole drama swirls to and fro with friendship betrayed, new worlds evoked, justice denied, empire appeased, faith insulted, innocence abused. And still we are only in the foothills, aware of the crags looming above us, of the drama's central character, of the questions he posed for his contemporaries and still poses for us, of his strange words and even stranger silences. Tales of torture and death are always ugly and awesome; this torture, and this death, still provoke thunder and lightning. When Matthew tells us of the earthquake, we somehow feel that nothing less would do.

If these events were not pivotal to human destiny, what else could take their place? How can we not reread this tale without ceasing?

The story brings to its head the tale of the strange prophet-Messiah from Nazareth. This itself, in the evangelists' telling, brings to its climax the entire drama of Israel – which, in Scripture, is the focal point of world history. Here we are offered that which unmakes and remakes the world, ourselves included. Here, could we but scale the crags, is the answer to our deepest questions, our most agonizing longings. And it comes, not as a theory, not as an explanation, but as a story which opens up to embrace or perhaps engulf us, sweeping us off our feet like a giant wave, carrying us off, out of our depth, away on the dark sea of God's passion. And still the figure at the centre beckons, woos, disturbs, frightens and compels us. Like the Psalms, this story contains all that we are and feel, and lays it bare before the presence of an overmastering love.

Paul, echoing Isaiah, speaks of Jesus' obedience (to the plan of God; to Adam's call, and Israel's) and vindication. Isaiah himself pictures a strange teacher, called to listen, to sustain the weary, and to undergo suffering. Elsewhere (e.g. Romans 8.31–39), Paul with considerable daring applies this same passage to Christians. Those who tell, and live by, the story of the cross may learn to hear between its lines the story of the martyrs, ancient and modern, and the call to take our own share of this world-changing, world-healing, passion. Those who go this way may have to face and suffer much. But they will not be put to shame.

Easter

Easter Day

— ∼ —

Jeremiah 31.1–6
Colossians 3.1–4
John 20.1–18

Again you shall plant vineyards; the planters shall plant, and shall enjoy the fruit. Jeremiah echoes Deuteronomy's promise of covenant renewal, and points forward to John's Easter garden. Mary was on the right track, mistaking Jesus for the gardener. In typical Johannine irony, he was indeed the gardener (though not the way Mary thought), the true Adam, planting again the vineyard of Israel, bringing God's people home from the exile of death and sowing them like seed in their new land.

Only imagery like this can begin to do justice to the reality of Easter. Too often the story and its meaning are flattened out into subsidiary truths: a belief in life after death (which most of Jesus' Jewish contemporaries held anyway), or the truth that Jesus is still alive, and we can come to know him. John's poetic genius tells a larger story through hints and allusions. Easter is the beginning of God's new creation, new covenant, God's whole new world. John's readers are invited to live in that new world, to become partners in the new covenant, to be under-gardeners in the new creation. With the rolling away of the stone, a great door has swung open in human history, and we are summoned to go through, to make our own the undiscovered country on the other side.

Scarcely surprising, then, that the story is full of puzzles.

54

Where were the angels when Peter and John (if it was John) went into the tomb? Could only Mary see them, and if so why? Why did John describe the linen cloths and the head-piece so carefully? And – perhaps most perplexing – why did Jesus forbid Mary to hold on to him? What does his explanation ('I have not yet ascended') mean, and how does it relate to his subsequent invitation to Thomas to touch him and see?

The only way of coming to terms with all this is to grasp the nettle. Easter invites us to recognize a new level of being, a new mode of existence. Jesus' resurrection (unlike Lazarus's) was not a mere resuscitation. It was a transformation into a new sort of physicality, catching up the old within it but going far beyond. This is a body that somehow lives in earth and heaven simultaneously (easier to imagine when you remind yourself that, in biblical thought, they are complementary and overlapping spheres of God's created order), though it is sometimes more appropriate to think of it as basically inhabiting one or the other. It is the beginning of that new creation which will only be complete when heaven and earth are finally married. The fact that we are obviously at the borders of language here is no shame. Where else should you be on Easter morning?

Part of the strange truth of Easter is that it is about us, too. 'Your life is hidden with Christ in God.' You are already a citizen of the heavenly world. So why still behave as though you weren't?

The Second Sunday of Easter

— ∼ —

Acts 2.14a, 22–32
1 Peter 1.3–9
John 20.19–31

Jesus' resurrection scattered new meanings all around, like light reflecting a thousand ways off a priceless jewel. The first thing was *the validation of Jesus' messianic ministry*. His powerful deeds had commended him to Israel, but not everyone had believed that God was at work in him. The resurrection unveiled the truth; and the way of getting a handle on it was to tell the scriptural story and to show that it had now reached its dramatic conclusion. The story of David, culled here from various psalms, pointed the way. Nobody could have supposed that the crucified Jesus was the Messiah (despite what some have suggested, there is no pre-Christian evidence that any Jews believed in such a thing); but the resurrection declared, before anything else, that Jesus really was, and is, the Messiah. His life really had been messianic, and God had validated it. Early Christianity was messianic to the core; the explanation was that God had raised Jesus from the dead.

The second meaning that quickly followed was that *the Messiah's followers now shared in God's new world*. We too easily read 1 Peter 1 in terms simply of a supernatural 'salvation', the heritage which is 'kept safe in heaven for you'. But the image is not of us going to heaven to experience it, but of heaven as the celestial cupboard where God keeps the wonderful things that will one day be brought out for all to see. The resurrection has opened up the vista of a whole restored creation, under the saving lordship of the Messiah. This is the heritage that can never go mouldy. And those who belong to the Messiah discover that the new creation has already infected them; the new stirrings of faith, hope and above all joy within them are the signs of this new life, new birth, so that they are simultaneously out of tune with the way the world still is and joyfully in tune with the new world that will appear when Jesus is 'revealed'. Peter, like Paul in some passages, thinks here of Jesus as present though invisible. The risen Lord will one day be seen again, as he was in the upper room, and those who now love him will find their true selves (their 'souls', v. 9, though the word to a Jew hardly carried the disembodied sense it has for us) rescued from the trials that beset them in the present.

John's resurrection accounts are full of fresh meaning, but the key to this passage is *the new commission* that follows from the vision of faith. 'As the Father sent me, so I send you': the messianic life of Jesus is to be replicated through Jesus' people, as, with the breath of new creation in their nostrils, they go out with the message of forgiveness, and warning too. Thomas' cameo appearance sums up the paradox of faith from the whole gospel: touching is possible, seeing is enough, but believing is best of all.

The Third Sunday of Easter

— ∽ —

Acts 2.14a, 36–41
1 Peter 1.17–23
Luke 24.13–35

Today's readings bubble over with the excitement of the new moment that has dawned in Israel's story, in the world's story, with the resurrection. It isn't merely that God is offering a new kind of spiritual experience, or that there is now a new belief in life after death (which most Jews believed in anyway). It is the sense that something has *happened*, as a result of which everything is different.

But the thing which had happened was emphatically not what was expected. Theories about 'cognitive dissonance', that highfalutin pseudo-medical term used by some to say that the disciples were so overwhelmed with disappointment at Jesus' crucifixion that they simply went on believing what they had believed anyway, simply won't do. 'We had hoped', say the two on the road to Emmaus, 'that he was the one who would redeem Israel.' But (the implication runs) they crucified him, so obviously he wasn't. Everybody knows that a crucified Messiah is a contradiction in terms. We are just another failed messianic movement.

They were like people on a hillside, watching eagerly for the sunrise. (This image works better in the tropics where there's no twilight.) Disoriented, they are facing the wrong way. The expected moment comes and goes, and nothing happens. Then they become aware that, though the sky they are scanning remains dark, light seems to be shining anyway. With a strange excitement they turn around, to see the sun shining in full strength in the very place they least expected it.

It was the Scriptures, not least (we must assume) the Davidic promises, that warmed their hearts with the thought that they had been looking in the wrong direction, and nudged them to turn around and face the real dawn. The biblical story was all about God bringing redemption, new life, *through* death and out the other side. To expect the ransoming of Israel in the sense they had cherished was to look in the wrong direction. The ransoming (an Exodus word, of course) had indeed occurred, but it was the deep, ultimate act that freed human beings from 'futility' (1 Peter 1.18: a human life that, failing to reflect God, decays and self-destructs). The new creation brought to birth at Easter would now be born within human lives, creating love, trust and hope. The transforming power lay precisely in God's word (1.23).

Peter's challenge to the Pentecost crowd contains perhaps the earliest 'theology of the cross' in the New Testament. (You may need to include some extra verses to get the full thrust.) Jesus' dying and rising has broken through into a new way of being Israel, a new way of being human; so, urges Peter, turn quickly from your headlong flight into ruin, share in the new-Exodus life of which baptism is the sign and seal, celebrate God's one-off act of forgiveness, and pass it on to everyone else. Now there's a message as urgently needed today as ever it was.

The Fourth Sunday of Easter

— ∽ —

Acts 2.42–47
1 Peter 2.19–25
John 10.1–10

A student of mine spent a long vacation working with local churches in central Africa. Next term, the College Head asked him, in my presence, what he wanted to do with his degree. 'Work in third world development,' he replied. 'Then why', asked the Provost, an economist himself, 'aren't you reading Politics and Economics?' The student didn't even blink. 'Because Theology is so much more relevant,' he shot back.

Read Acts 2 and see why. Jesus had launched the new-covenant movement. His followers, like the Qumran community, believed that they, the renewed Israel, should live as a *family*. They belonged to each other, as brothers and sisters; and close families, in that culture at least, shared a purse. (This, by the way, is why it's so misleading when non-sexist translations render 'brothers' as 'friends' and the like. Why not 'family'?) If God had now acted to bring forgiveness at every level, how could they not forgive debts as they had been forgiven?

The so-called primitive communism of the early Church had little to do, then, with a belief that the world was coming to an end, and a great deal to do with the sense of fulfilment: the world of debt, the world of injustice, *had* come to an end on Calvary, and they were modelling the new world of forgiveness. They weren't so concerned with the last days of the old world as with the first days of the new one. Politicians and economists can't sort out third world debt, but the gospel, and its message of Jubilee, just might. If 'teaching, fellowship, bread-breaking, prayers', let alone 'theology' (remember Harold Wilson and 'the theology of the Common Market'?) sounds boring to some, maybe it's because we've forgotten that each of the four aspects of the early Church's daily life stood the world's values, not least its systemic injustices, on their head.

Abundant life, then: that's what Jesus has on offer, not the thin, hang-on-like-grim-death approach that you find in some churches. The 'shepherd' parable in John 10, which really continues to v. 30, explores the intimate relation between shepherd and sheep, with the emphasis on the shepherd's desire that the sheep be led in the right direction, fed and watered, and kept secure for ever. And the point throughout is that Jesus is contrasted with other would-be Messiahs: thieves and brigands, he calls them. There were plenty of those in Jesus' world, leaders of marauding gangs on the one hand and 'holy brigands' (fundamentalist terrorists, we would call them) on the other. Jesus' way of leadership, of founding the new movement, was totally different, and totally relevant to his day and ours. A different style, an upside-down ambition, a self-giving love that, as Peter saw, would then be imitated by his followers – the world waits to see what can happen when wandering sheep, brought home by the Shepherd's love, then start to live by the same pattern.

The Fifth Sunday of Easter

— ∾ —

Acts 7.55–60
1 Peter 2.2–10
John 14.1–14

I'm never quite sure what Jesus meant when he said 'you will do greater works than these, because I am going to the Father'. But I'm quite sure he did not mean 'you will do *lesser* works than these'. An old cliché; but those who used to say 'expect great things from God; attempt great things for God' had John on their side far more than those who, by implication at least, simply want a place on the sidelines where a few little Christian activities can take place without causing a fuss. As the world continues to reveal its powerlessness in the face of evil, is it not time to take Jesus at his word?

The promise is flanked by others, equally remarkable. Many dwelling-places, furnished and ready. Knowing the Father – *seeing* the Father, even, something nobody expected to do and live – is found through looking at Jesus. And the simple and overwhelming promise about prayer: whatever you ask in my name, I will do it. Much standard Christianity, in all sections and parties of the Church, has adjusted the focus just enough so that, instead of seeing all this clearly, we get the general picture but it's all rather blurred. We aren't really sure about our final destiny. We don't really expect to attain the vision of God by looking long and hard at Jesus (or why would we do anything else?). And we don't pray for solid, substantial definite things that will bring the Father glory in the Son.

62

The great statements earlier in the chapter are likewise at a discount in our half-hearted, lukewarm-blooded Christianities. Jesus, we are told, couldn't have said that he was the way, the truth and the life. Many now make that denial the shibboleth of a new orthodoxy. (What this amounts to, of course, is the statement that the Enlightenment, or perhaps postmodernity, is 'the way, the truth and the life'; is that any less 'arrogant', the charge normally advanced against John 14.6?) We don't want our own worldview disturbed by someone telling us that Jesus has upstaged it all.

Which was, of course, what Stephen did with the worldview of the chief priests and the hardline Pharisees. The Temple is under judgement, he said; Israel has always rejected its heaven-sent rulers, and has now done so again, once and for all. That would have been arrogant, fighting talk if it weren't for the fact that it was *Jesus* he was talking about; as it was, it was suffering, *forgiving* talk. In the great Jewish tradition of martyrdom, the dying called down curses on their persecutors; the first Christian martyr followed his Lord in praying for their forgiveness. But forgiveness wasn't what they wanted (despite the fact that this was what the Temple stood for!); they wanted their worldview left intact. That's the stuff that stonings are made of. But God has laid in Zion the true corner stone, precious beyond imagining to those who believe.

The Sixth Sunday of Easter

— ∼ —

Acts 17.22–31
1 Peter 3.13–22
John 14.15–21

In a spectacular (and presumably heavily abbreviated) speech, Paul takes on culturally sophisticated Athens with the new upside-down wisdom. He begins on their own territory, with the altar to the Unknown God: even the Athenians had left a window open, a gap in their well-worked-out theology, where fresh air could blow in from an unexpected quarter. Some of the poets, too, had pointed towards a God who was both other than the world and yet intimately involved with it.

Yet Paul is not simply finding points in the local culture he can affirm, as though Christian mission simply pats people on the back for being as they are. Affirmation is more than balanced by confrontation. Even today, if you stand on Mars Hill, where the highest court of the city used to meet, you have a wonderful view of the Acropolis, with the Parthenon and the other temples clearly in view, the pinnacle of a culture and its theology. Paul, against that backdrop, tells them it's all a waste of time: the creator of all doesn't live in houses like that. Nor does he need the whole paraphernalia of the sacrificial system. Nor – despite what not only traditional Athenians but also the pre-Christian Paul would have said – does he make any ultimate distinctions between one race of humans and another. Paul may have found an open

64

window in the culture, but what's blowing through it is a hurricane that will turn the room upside down.

In particular, Paul takes on the Epicureans and Stoics with whom he'd been debating in the marketplace. Epicureans, like Deists, thought of the gods as remote and detached, happily unconcerned about our world. Stoics, like some other pantheists, thought of God as the inner divine essence within our world. Both can lead, and sometimes do, to atheism (the gods are either so distant that they might as well not exist, or they turn out to be simply a metaphorical projection of our feelings of wonder) or at least to relativism (the gods are so far away that all religions are just vague approximations; or they are so present that all religions are different expressions of 'the divine'). Both are confronted head on by Paul's message of one God, the creator, who is both different from the world and compassionately involved with it. Both, in particular, are confronted, as is all atheism and relativism, by the fact of Jesus' resurrection, and the message which it brings: the God of Israel is the one true God, who is bringing to the world the justice for which it longs.

Paul knew, as did Peter, how unwelcome this announcement would be. Yet the consequent suffering of Christians is itself to be part of the witness, because the justice proceeds from self-giving love. And the witness itself, as John would remind us, proceeds from the Spirit, God's wind blowing fresh spring air through whatever windows, in whatever culture, may happen to be open.

The Seventh Sunday of Easter (Sunday after Ascension Day)

— ∾ —

Acts 1.6–14
1 Peter 4.12–14; 5.6–11
John 17.1–11

'When his glory is revealed.' The ascension gives us a glimpse in advance of the great truth which will one day be unveiled – or rather, the glorious Person who will one day be revealed. It is as though the universe is throbbing with the secret knowledge that Jesus, the Messiah, is its true Lord, a knowledge that cannot yet be spoken, that would not be understood. To be a Christian is to be privy to this secret, to have it indeed engraved into one's life; because the other side of the secret is the Christian call to suffer. The transformation of suffering is a further key part of the meaning of the ascension.

The 'suffering' that comfortable Western Christians endure often seems small in comparison with that which our brothers and sisters still face day by day in (for instance) the Sudan. Much of it – the stresses of contemporary life and all that they produce – is partly self-caused, at least at a societal level. But there is a deep suffering, unquantifiable and hence impossible to compare, which comes from living as one who believes that the crucified Messiah is the world's true Lord, in the midst of a world that lives by the rule of force, or pleasure, or wealth. We are called to be out of tune with the world's orchestra, swimming against the world's wind and tide. Not merely cross-grained and awkward; rather, in tune with God's hidden music, buoyed up by the submerged swell of his love.

It is therefore vital to remember that the ascended Lord is precisely the one who was crucified. In John's Gospel, indeed, reaching something of a climax in the great prayer of ch. 17, crucifixion and exaltation seem to be merged together, so that the ascension, when it is promised in John 20.17, does not 'reveal his glory' any more fully than the cross itself.

Without this, Acts 1 would simply be a triumphalist rant. In Luke's readers' world, the way Roman emperors were formally declared divine after their deaths was to have someone declare that they had seen him ascend into heaven. Ascension was the instrument of power and glory: the power of the Roman state to keep subject peoples controlled with religious, as much as military, threat; the glory of the imperial system and the all-powerful person at the top of it.

For Luke, however, as the whole of Acts makes clear, the fact that it was the crucified Jesus who was now exalted to share the throne of the one true God (he has Daniel 7 in mind as well, of course) means that the mission of his followers will carry power, and indeed glory, but of a very different sort. It will be the power, and the glory, of suffering love. When Jesus speaks of the glory the Father had given to him being shared with his followers (John 17.22), this seems to be central to what he has in mind.

Day of Pentecost

— ∼ —

Numbers 11.24–30
Acts 2.1–21
John 7.37–39

Jesus, quoting Scripture, says that rivers of living water will flow out of the believer's heart. But no Old Testament text says exactly that. Which Scripture is he referring to, then?

Isaiah 55, of course, issues God's invitation to all who are thirsty to come and drink. This, however, is not the part of Jesus' saying that carries the phrase 'as scripture says'. No: the 'rivers of living water' seem to evoke the great river which flows out of the restored Temple in Ezekiel 47, to make even the Dead Sea fresh. The image goes all the way back to the second chapter of Genesis; to call it up indicates the renewal of creation. And it goes all the way on to Revelation 22 – though where the river flows to there is not clear, since the sea, symbolizing the forces of chaos and evil, has been abolished altogether (21.1). Jesus takes this wide-ranging and powerful image and gives it a further twist.

There is a place in the Scottish Highlands where the broad and tranquil River Dee is funnelled in a swirling and seething foam through a gap in solid rock, narrow enough for a foolish teenager to jump across. (Don't ask me how I know that.) So it is here. The four great rivers that flowed from the garden, the great new river that will stream from the Temple, are to come rushing and churning into, and (equally importantly) out of, the one who believes in Jesus. All the new life of God's new creation is to be focused on, and channelled through, each believer.

To invoke or invite the Holy Spirit, then, is not simply to hope for a gentle nudge from time to time, a quiet sense that things are going to be all right after all, though that (thank God!) is often how the Spirit's presence is known. It is to take the risk of having all that wild, untameable energy sweep through us. The resulting transformation can be dramatic, something which Christians of many years' standing can easily forget. But the rivers of living water have a purpose. They are not bubbling and whirling around for the sake of it. They are designed, not simply to satisfy our thirst (though they will more than do that), but to irrigate the land beyond us. If the rock is worn into a new shape in the process, so be it. If the expected, even the official, channels seem to be bypassed, as with Eldad and Medad, so be it.

Peter's speech on the day of Pentecost was an attempt to explain how God's wind had come to blow in this way, how God's fire had escaped from the fireplace of the Temple and was striking flames all over the place. It was nothing short of the promised new creation, undoing the effects of the fall and of Babel. Don't trivialize Pentecost. Think how the Spirit-imagery works. Water, wind and fire are not tame.

Ordinary Time

Trinity Sunday

— ∽ —

Isaiah 40.12–17, 27–31
2 Corinthians 13.11–13
Matthew 28.16–20

The doctrine of the Trinity used to be caricatured as a piece of irrelevant theory: learned people using human philosophy to make simple things overly complex. The charge often rebounds on those who make it. The beginnings of trinitarian thinking, in the New Testament, are powerful and relevant, designed to help in time of need, to bind us together in love, to send us out on our mission.

People often puzzle, reading Matthew's conclusion, over Jesus himself offering his followers the first-ever 'trinitarian' formula as their baptismal symbol. Actually, the whole passage is implicitly trinitarian; if there wasn't a trinitarian formula somewhere we'd have to supply one to make sense of it all. What does it mean to say that all authority, in both created realms (heaven and earth), has been given to Jesus? What does it mean to say that he is truly the Emmanuel (1.23), with his followers to the close of the age? The Trinity is, paradoxically, a doctrine about *Jesus*: it safeguards the reality of his humanness, then and now, as the true and final revelation of the one true God. It simultaneously unites him with, and distinguishes him from, the unseen source of all, on the one hand, and the breath of life that sustains us now, on the other. And the point of it all is mission: the God revealed in Jesus is the missionary God, sending his healing love into the

72

world in Jesus, and now, under Jesus' authority, sending Jesus' followers out with that same healing love, of which baptism is the sign and seal.

So also in Paul. The trinitarian blessing is not bolted on to 2 Corinthians as an afterthought. It arises from the inner logic of the whole letter, as Paul wrestles with the grace of Jesus as the motive for his work (e.g. 8.9), learns to live by the love of God in good times and bad (e.g. 1.3–7), and celebrates the Spirit through whom he and his diverse, often difficult, congregations learn to see Christ in one another (e.g. 3.1–18). It all comes down to very practical and basic matters, as 13.11 makes clear: sort things out, pay attention to what you are told, agree together, live in peace. 'The God of love and peace will be with you'; the Emmanuel promise again, guaranteed by the God-with-us person, Jesus, and renewed in daily reality by the God-with-us Spirit.

Behind it all stands the God of Isaiah, the God of creation and covenant. Since the very heart of his incomparable greatness is self-giving love, the more one contemplates his power and glory the more one discovers that it is strangely available, shared not least with those who are weary and exhausted. To understand the Trinity, ask yourself, as you read Isaiah 40—55, addressed to those in dire need: what might this God look like if he were to become human?

Proper 4

— ∾ —

Genesis 6.9–22; 7.24; 8.14–19
Romans 1.16–17; 3.22b–28 [29–31]
Matthew 7.21–29

'These words of mine.' No wonder they thought Jesus was claiming an authority of his own, superior to that of the scribes. They would never have claimed anything for their own words, merely for those of the text they were expounding.

The house on the rock, arguably, is another picture of the Temple – which Herod Antipas was still building, and against which Jesus addressed some of his sternest words. The whole Sermon has constituted a claim that the way things are going in Israel is a mistake, a disobedience, and that this is the last chance to get back on track, to be the light of the world. Failure now will mean the destruction of the Temple and all that it stood for. The Sermon on the Mount balances Matthew's final discourse (chs 23—25), where these warnings reach their height.

Jesus, meanwhile, is warning sternly against an easygoing discipleship which, while keeping companionship with him, fails to take seriously the challenge of the gospel, the absolute demands for God-centred holiness and renewed integrity. How easy, then and now, to be around Jesus, to enjoy something of his influence, but to keep options open when it comes to actual choices about behaviour and life direction. Easy, maybe, but about as useless as trying to learn to swim while keeping one foot on the bottom for safety. That won't do you any good when the floods come.

As come they will. Jesus' warnings of judgement call up the image of Noah and his ark. Among the many lessons of that wonderful story is God's promise never again to destroy the earth in such a fashion; but, as Jesus makes clear, this doesn't mean that God is now taking a more easygoing attitude as far as wickedness is concerned. It still defaces his good creation, and he still hates it as much as ever. We may want to be generous in speaking of judgement in relation to others, but for ourselves we do well to be sober and sanguine. There is such a thing as being close to Jesus but never truly knowing him, and a more terrible discovery it is hard to imagine.

The lectionary makes a Nijinsky-like leap from part of the introduction to Romans into part of its second main section. The result is like a doctor giving a prescription without anyone knowing what the disease is. Only when we have fully appreciated the scale of human wickedness, infecting God's people as much as everyone else, can we understand just how breathtaking it is to be told that because of Jesus' sacrificial death God now justifies, freely, by grace alone, all who believe the gospel. Only those who appreciate that the flood – both Noah's, and that about which Jesus is warning – is God's sober and proper reaction to human rebellion, neither capricious nor malevolent, can appreciate what it means for God's saving, world-healing righteousness to be unveiled in the message of Jesus Christ.

Proper 5

— ∿ —

Genesis 12.1–9
Romans 4.13–25
Matthew 9.9–13, 18–26

Abraham's call (Abram, actually, at this stage; but just as we say the Archbishop was born in 1935, even though he wasn't Archbishop then, so we don't need to fuss about giving the patriarch the right name all the time). Abraham's call to go out into the unknown is a fitting start for the long stretch of Sundays after Trinity. Equipped with the new vision of God in Jesus and the Spirit, we are to follow in obedience, knowing only who it is that leads us, and the purpose of the journey.

Abraham was promised the land; Abraham's family was promised the earth. Or rather, the whole world was promised God's blessing in and through Abraham's family. That, after the curse of Genesis 3 and 11, was the point of Abraham's call in the first place. God now makes a new start, absurd and scandalous as it seemed and still often seems, to create a new creation from within the old, a new human family from within the old, to give new life in the midst of death. Abraham, as far chronologically before Jesus as we are after him, was gripped by the strange presence of the one God doing a new thing. His descendants have been haunted by that presence, that purpose, ever since, especially when it turned into flesh and blood, into wind and fire.

But his descendants are no longer defined, as far as the

New Testament is concerned, by flesh-and-blood generation. Romans 4, completing the argument which began in 3.21, explains God's righteousness, God's covenant faithfulness, in terms of God's strange fulfilment of the promises to Abraham in Genesis 12—18, focusing especially on ch. 15. This fulfilment has happened in Jesus Christ, and in the creation through him of the worldwide family promised to Abraham in the beginning. The emphasis of the whole chapter is that Abraham is the father, not of one nation only (as though, as the Galatians thought, one now had to become a fully-fledged Jew in order to belong to God's covenant family), but of the many nations spoken of in Genesis 17. Romans 4.17 is therefore not, as in some translations, an aside, to be placed in a bracket; it is the climax of the chapter. Through the sin-forgiving death of Jesus and his life-giving resurrection, the covenant God has created a new, single family of Jews and Gentiles together, whose sole badge of identity is their faith, specifically their faith in Jesus' resurrection (4.24), which shows that they share the faith of Abraham himself (4.19–22).

As so often, the grandeur of the Old Testament, and the fine-tuned arguments of Paul, are distilled into the gospel's small-scale but sharp-edged human drama. Life comes, in place of death, to a Galilean home (and one synagogue ruler at least, we may assume, followed Jesus ever after). Matthew, like Abraham, obeys the call to follow, he knows not where.

Proper 6

— ◇ —

Genesis 18.1–15
Romans 5.1–8
Matthew 9.35—10.8 [9–23]

Take the gospel reading (the longer version) and lay it, like a template, over the life of the average parish. What do you find?

I know, I know. We don't live in the first century; we aren't peasants; Jesus' mission was unique; the disciples' mission predated Calvary, Easter and Pentecost; the special and urgent ministry to Israel (10.6, 23) was later transformed, by Jesus himself (Matthew 28.19) into the wider and more long-lasting mission to all the nations.

All this I know. But it remains disturbing that the only point of contact between what Jesus told his twelve followers and what the average churchworker does with most of her or his waking hours is that we wander around like sheep among wolves. We know that Jesus told us to be wise as serpents and innocent as doves, but most of us, being after all busy people, find it advisable to specialize.

Of course you can't lift culturally specific instructions off the page and plonk them down elsewhere. But when did anyone last make the effort to get inside this passage and wrestle with the question: what would be the functional equivalent, the necessary re-application, of Matthew 10 in today's Church? The fact that we haven't done this (when did you last, metaphorically, shake the dust off your feet when leaving a house or town?) may of course explain the fact that our gospel, our lifestyle, threatens no one; no one arrests us for doing our job, no one betrays us to the authorities. Unless, of course, certain newspapers count as authorities.

The shock of facing up to these questions is the characteristic shock of the gospel. Life is supposed to be *different*. Sarah will have a son; yes, it's impossible, yes, she did laugh, and yes, it's going to happen anyway. When the great rolling wave of God's love comes at you, don't try to fight it; launch out and let it knock you off your feet. That's what Paul is talking about in Romans 5 (the paragraph ends at verse 11, by the way). God's action begins with love and ends with celebration, taking in suffering en route; a good trinitarian thought for this time of the year, echoing with memories of the three who visited Abraham.

The narrative of Genesis is effortlessly subtle. Is 'the Lord' one of the three men (they have become two angels in 19.1, while 'the Lord' has been talking to Abraham)? Or somehow all three together? As in the Emmaus scene, God's self-revelation is set in the context of hospitality, in this case the lavish and generous care of a Bedouin host forgetting his status and acting as servant, giving, as he has received, freely. Do Jesus' instructions to his followers, though, somehow imply that they are also to be like the three men, going about with great promises and great warnings? Dare we take that seriously as a model of the Church and its mission?

Proper 7

— ∾ —

Genesis 21.8–21
Romans 6.1b–11
Matthew 10.24–39

The prince of peace comes with a sword. To that theological oxymoron we must add the sad, and still tragic, story of Abraham, Hagar and Ishmael. Go down into the Genesis story, down the dark staircases of imagination, and even then you will perhaps never plumb the depths of Hagar's misery, of Abraham's dilemma, of Sarah's memories, of Ishmael's destiny. The next chapter, Isaac's nightmare, belongs closely with this one, but that hardly constitutes an explanation. If God is to heal the world appropriately it must be through the obedient covenant people. But what if the covenant people are themselves disobedient? They themselves must share the pain of the healing process. The fact that it is also God's pain does not make it easier.

Jesus' challenge here is not that his followers should be anti-social for the sake of it, but that they should live out of a new identity, in comparison with which the normal Jewish identity, based tightly upon kinship, is to be set aside. Deep kinship loyalty is not normally our problem; where then are our deep loyalties, and how does this call of Jesus put us on the spot? Why did they call Jesus 'Beelzebub'? Why don't they call us that? We must ask, too, what we are most truly afraid of, and whether that squares with v. 28 – which I persist in taking to refer to Satan, not God (God can be trusted with the hairs of your head; he's not out to get you).

Paul's appeal in Romans 6 is likewise based on a new sense of identity. Underneath the whole argument of chapters 6—8 lies the Exodus narrative, emerging triumphantly into the daylight halfway through ch. 8 itself. As in 1 Corinthians 10, Paul sees the Christian life in the light of the wilderness wanderings of God's people. They have left Egypt by coming through the waters of the Red Sea; in other words, they have left the territory of sin and death in their baptism into the Messiah. They will then come, not to Sinai to be given the law, but to the new Pentecost, the giving of the life-giving Spirit (7.1—8.11). That Spirit will be for them the pillar of cloud and of fire, leading them home to their promised inheritance, which turns out to be the entire redeemed creation (8.12–30).

Paul's concern, therefore, is that in appreciating who they are in Christ his hearers should no longer regard themselves as 'in Egypt', constrained by the old order of sin and death. 'Reckon yourselves to be dead to sin', v. 11; this is not a matter of 'if you make a big enough mental effort it'll become true', but 'do the mathematics and you'll see that this is who you are'. Like the children of Israel, we often hanker for the leeks and melons of Egypt. We need, instead, to be encouraged by the fruit brought fresh from the promised land.

Proper 8

— ∽ —

Genesis 22.1–14
Romans 6.12–23
Matthew 10.40–42

Perhaps precisely because it is one of the darkest of all Bible stories, the tale of Abraham and Isaac on Mount Moriah has left deep imprints in Judaism and Christianity. Child sacrifice was as abhorrent to pre-Christian Jews as it is to us.

So the old questions arise: did God really tell Abraham to kill Isaac? Did Isaac really consent (as one Jewish tradition claimed), so that his readiness for martyrdom became a kind of proto-atonement? Our own day has added other questions: what would that experience do to Isaac? What did Sarah feel about it? And, once again, what is this story saying about God?

Part of the answer, as often, lies in the larger narrative. Ishmael has just been banished; is this chapter part of God's response? Is it, in other words, not so much a sudden arbitrary demand, but rather a way of ascertaining whether Abraham is really interested in founding a pure clan of his own rather than trusting God to fulfil the promises in his own way?

Early Christian tradition offers answers from other angles, too. Abraham's faith, says Hebrews, was a kind of resurrection-faith, believing that he would receive Isaac back from the dead (Paul, interestingly, doesn't use that argument in Romans 4, where you might expect it). But supremely, of course, the early Christians saw that the odd, shocking thing God was calling Abraham to do was the long-range, and certainly ambiguous, signpost to the thing that God himself would do, not sparing his own dearly beloved son. 'God will provide,' said Abraham; Christianity began on the basis that he had, finally and fully. And, lest anyone therefore accuse God, as some are doing today, of 'cosmic child abuse', we must insist, with the New Testament writers, that God himself was personally and intimately present and involved at Calvary. The only full answer to the mystery of Abraham and Isaac is the far greater mystery of the Trinity.

Out of the death of ambition, pride, all that gives the word 'self' its unpleasant ring, there emerges freedom. Abraham is promised a superabundant blessing, a huge family (vv. 15–18). Those who obey the call of God to lay on the altar everything that belongs to the old life, the life that was crucified with Christ, discover the new freedom that points the way to 'eternal life'. And, as Romans 8 will make clear, this eternal life consists precisely in the large-scale fulfilment of the promise to Abraham: the whole world will be set free to share the freedom of the glory of God's redeemed children.

Meanwhile, if God was in Jesus on Calvary, God is in Jesus today; and Jesus is in those who go in his name. This brief gospel reading is not primarily a command to give hospitality to those who preach the gospel; it is an encouragement to wandering missionaries, a reminder that as they go about their work God will provide once more.

Proper 9

— ≈ —

Genesis 24.34–38, 42–49, 58–67
Romans 7.15–25a
Matthew 11.16–19, 25–30

An American sent me a strange book the other day. Jesus, he argued, was an alcoholic. Roused from his drunkenness by the preaching of John the Baptist, he struggled to kick the habit, and finally made it. Telltale 'evidence' is provided by Matthew 11: did they not say that Jesus was 'a glutton and a drunkard'?

Well, yes, they did, and the early Church wouldn't have made it up. But the book (which may be a source of hope to some, though I doubt it) misses the point here as much as elsewhere. 'Glutton and drunkard' is what, according to Deuteronomy 21.20, the parents of a rebellious son will say of him to the elders of Israel. It is part of a capital charge. Jesus knew that his celebration of the Kingdom with all and sundry was incurring the righteous indignation, and even the condemnation, of the respectable and religious. He was out of line. The Torah had things to say about people like him.

So it did, indeed; but the Torah, the Jewish Law, plays a deeply ambiguous role within the work of Jesus and the subsequent theology of Paul. Romans 7, which is hard enough to get your tongue around, never mind your mind, is the point par excellence where Paul wrestles with the question of why God gave the Law and what its role had been. Here the understanding I seek often eludes me; the misunderstandings I try to avoid come back to haunt me. The best explanation I know runs like this: when Paul says 'I' here, he is speaking, with Christian hindsight, of Israel as a whole, Israel under Torah. Israel is right to embrace and celebrate Torah; it is indeed God's Law, holy and just and good. But Israel, being also 'in Adam', innately sinful, finds that the Law condemns. Paul may also be alluding to well-known sayings from pagan moralists about the weakness of the human will. Even the God-given Law cannot rescue Israel from being trapped in sin, just like Aristotle, Ovid or Epictetus.

Paul does not stop with diagnosis. He offers treatment. 'Thanks be to God, through Jesus Christ our Lord!' The Law's condemnation has fallen on sin; this has happened in Jesus' own flesh (Romans 8.3). Today's gospel is one more indication of what that meant in practice. Wisdom, said Jesus, is justified by her deeds.

This is what gives Jesus' invitation to the weary and anxious its peculiar and powerful comfort. It is precisely in his standing alongside the ungodly, the gluttons and drunkards, the outcasts and sinners, precisely in his bearing their condemnation, that the Son chooses to reveal the Father's very heart, to offer the easy yoke and the light burden. The story of Abraham's servant, faithful to his master and his master's God, finding a bride for Isaac, is full of that comfort and hope. The lonely road across the desert can still be the right way to the destination.

Proper 10

— ∾ —

Genesis 25.19–34
Romans 8.1–11
Matthew 13.1–9, 18–23

The next chapter of Genesis offers a striking echo to this parable: Isaac sowed seed, and reaped a hundredfold, for the Lord blessed him (26.12). But the key background, I think, is Isaiah 40.6–8 and 55.10–13. All flesh is grass, but God's word will last. It will not return to him empty, but will accomplish his purpose, making the desert blossom like the rose.

The Sower, in other words, is not simply an earthly story with a heavenly meaning, a moral lesson about listening carefully (though it is that too; there are many Esaus in today's Church, despising their birthright of hundredfold blessings through hearing and understanding the word). It is full of the music of the Kingdom, the new song of God after the long silence of the exile. It encapsulated Jesus' challenge to his contemporaries to *be* Israel, because God was at last 'sowing' them again; and the warning that if this final word was not heeded the alternative would be catastrophe.

Note carefully what the lectionary's omissions might lead us to ignore: the 'interpretation' is given to the disciples, not the crowds. This isn't a 'story with a moral'. It is a prophetic word. It performs that of which it speaks. You only say 'If you have ears, then hear' after something which is cryptic because, if stated explicitly, it would be explosive. Jesus' hearers were presumably listening to him that day, benefiting from the natural acoustic properties of the Galilean shoreline, because they had already seen the Kingdom at work in what he was doing. Now he was telling them, in the only way possible, that this Kingdom was breaking into their world not simply to solve their problems, to endorse their agendas, but to do God's strange work of judgement and mercy. They couldn't take it for granted. They couldn't hijack it for their own purposes. That's dangerous talk.

Take this picture of Jesus as himself the sower, sowing God's powerful word, and transpose it into the Pauline key. The Son of God is sent into the world to accomplish the Father's will; and (an easy transition in Jewish thought) the word that goes forth to implement this work is the powerful breath of the Spirit. Romans 8, that most noble of Pauline passages, stresses here the new-Temple theme, another powerful image from Israel's hope of restoration. The Spirit 'indwells' the people of God, as the Glory had dwelt in the wilderness tabernacle and the Jerusalem Temple.

Here, too, there are warnings against presumption, against the Esau-attitude of 'those who have the mind of the flesh'. But here, supremely, is the promise of all promises. What the Torah could not do, God has done in Jesus' death and the power of the Spirit. He has given life and peace. In a world of death and war, God's human temples have an awesome responsibility. If you have ears, then hear. And if you have breath, then speak.

Proper 11

— ❦ —

Genesis 28.10–19a
Romans 8.12–25
Matthew 13.24–30, 36–43

To get the full flavour of the Pauline passage, hold in your mind the story of the children of Israel on their way through the wilderness, having left Egypt but not yet having arrived in the promised land. Paul's vision of the Church in the present age is frequently informed by this picture (compare, for instance, 1 Corinthians 10). The crossing of the Red Sea is picked up in his thinking by the death and resurrection of Jesus; baptism, in which the Christian shares in that dying and rising, is the sign and seal of our liberation from slavery, and the starting point for the pilgrimage to our promised inheritance. This is one of the key ways in which Paul envisages the Christian life as both *already* and *not yet* re-deemed: 'we were saved', he says (past tense), 'in hope.'

Those 'in Christ' are thus 'the children of God'; 'Israel is my son, my firstborn', says God through Moses to Pharaoh. They are led through the present wilderness by the personal presence of God himself in the Spirit, just as the Israelites were led by the pillar of cloud and fire. Instead of the Law on Sinai, they are given the personal, intimate prayer, Abba, Father (notice how the Lord's Prayer occupies the centre of the Sermon on the Mount, Matthew's New Sinai). And instead of a geographical territory as their 'inheritance', they are given – the world. All things belong to you, says

Paul in 1 Corinthians 3.21. The entire cosmos will have its own Exodus (8.21), and will be your true inheritance.

Among the dozens of important lessons from all this, one of the most significant for today's Western Christians is that we unlearn the idea that our destiny, our 'inheritance', is simply 'heaven', conceived in entirely otherworldly terms. The present world is good, and will be redeemed, just as our bodies are; notice that Paul distinguishes between 'body', which is more or less what we mean by 'person', and 'flesh', which is corruptible, rebellious, and will die for good. The imperatives of 8.12–15, seen from within the Exodus theme, mean 'Don't even think of going back to Egypt'; the point is that if the body will be redeemed, what you do in and with it in the present time matters. In the same way, if creation is going to be redeemed, rather than abandoned as in much sub-Christian thought, what we do in and with it here and now matters more than we have usually thought.

This setting explains well enough why the Christian pilgrimage involves suffering. We are not yet home, not yet shining like the sun, and the weeds still grow among the wheat. Like Jacob, we go out into the threatening unknown, with the vision of the risen Lord, promising us the inheritance, to inspire us on the long road ahead. And every place where the angels meet us becomes another house of God, another gate of heaven.

Proper 12

— ❧ —

Genesis 29.15–28
Romans 8.26–39
Matthew 13.31–33, 44–52

'All things work together for good to those who love God.' Probably not the first thought that sprang to Jacob's mind the morning after his wedding, on discovering how his father-in-law had succeeded in marrying off both daughters and gaining an extra seven years' work in a single blow. Yet in the long perspective of Genesis part of the point is to see God's hand in the duplicity and half-faith of the patriarchs. Jacob himself, after all, was no stranger to trickery.

The Pauline claim is always a statement of faith, part of that faith in the creator God which, looking at Jesus' resurrection, deduces both God's steadfast commitment to the original creation and his determination to rescue it from its bondage to decay.

Paul's enormous claims about the victory that has already been accomplished in Christ regularly, in my experience, raise the question: how can you say that, granted the mess the world is still in? Romans 8 supplies part of the answer, and the parables of the Kingdom in Matthew 13 take it back even further, to Jesus' own facing of the equivalent question during his ministry.

Paul's statement about being 'more than conquerors' is made in the teeth of persecution, famine, nakedness, peril and sword. He wasn't in jail when he wrote this letter but he had been not long before and would soon be again. It must have looked to the outward eye as though the rulers, the powers, and everything else in creation were having it all their own way, and that the purposes of God, entrusted to this strange little man with his fanatical mission, had been stopped in their tracks. But the gospel events of the death, resurrection and intercession of Jesus the Messiah meant that he could look them in the face. These events unveil, and make real and present to the believer, a love which goes deeper than all the forces in the universe. Faith, hope and love are not deductions from our day-to-day experience; they are rooted in God's faithfulness, God's purposes, and above all God's own love, seen and known in Jesus and in the strange presence of the Spirit (vv. 26–28).

Jewish onlookers from Jesus' days until now have always questioned how the Kingdom of God can be in any sense present as long as the world remains the way it does. Look out of the window, they say, and it's obvious the Kingdom hasn't come. The little parables in Matthew 13 are all, in their different ways, answers to the question, perhaps the only sort of answers we can ever give. The tiny seed will grow. The leaven will work through the lump. The treasure is at present hidden, but those who find it will know its worth. One day the multiple and peculiar fish in the net will be sorted out. The Kingdom is truly here; one day it will be obvious. Like Jacob, we are called to patience.

Proper 13

— ∾ —

Genesis 32.22–31
Romans 9.1–5
Matthew 14.13–21

A well-known bishop wrote a book not long ago called *Limping into the Sunrise*. It was, of course, alluding to this story of Jacob; which was all very well, except that at the time Jacob was travelling westwards . . .

He was coming home after fourteen years of exile. Time enough to acquire two wives (and two not-quite-wives), eleven children, and more flocks and herds than his father-in-law cared to think. Enough time for his brother Esau to forgive and forget? Nobody knew. But the God of Bethel had kept his promise up until now, and Jacob's last request was to return in peace. So everything is set up: processions, presents, and a last night to wrestle with vocation, with past and future, with God.

Who knew then, and who knows now, what happened that night? Was it an angel? Was it a human being? Was it indeed the one God? As sceptics like to ask about the empty tomb, if there had been a video-camera there, what would it have seen? At one level, it was obviously a very physical experience, leaving Jacob's family with a new food taboo (tastefully omittted by the lectionary). At another, it was the most profound and potent moment of Jacob's long and twisting spiritual pilgrimage, at the close of which he would call God his 'shepherd' (Genesis 48.15). Jacob knew what being a shepherd involved. Lost, puzzled and frightened sheep can be quite a handful. He wasn't the only one to be tired after that night.

Jacob's homeward crossing of the stream resonates down the Jewish traditions, incorporated within the larger theme of Red Sea and Jordan, until it meets a prophet immersing people as a sign of the final great homecoming. John's symbolic actions, and his fearless denunciations of the Herodian regime, cost him his life. Jesus' reaction, on hearing the news, is twofold. He wants rest; when that proves impossible, he too does something deeply symbolic, again something for the video-cameras to squabble over. He feeds the crowd in the wilderness. He too is a desert prophet, a herald of the Exodus, who must wrestle with God and with humans until he hangs in mid-air between them. And when he crosses the water, he will have his own sovereign way of doing so.

Paul, planning his own westward journey, stands at the crossroads of Jewish history. His siblings – perhaps, who knows, some very near and dear – regard him as a traitor, a birthright-thief. This list of Israel's privileges, after all, summarizes all he has said in the previous eight chapters as being true of the Messiah, and of all his people, Gentile as well as Jewish. His response is to wrestle with God, with the gospel, with the Messiah, and with his kinsfolk according to the flesh. Unlike worldly happiness and sadness, godly grief (Romans 9) coexists with true joy (Romans 8). That, it seems, is what wrestling with God is all about.

Proper 14

— ❦ —

Genesis 37.1–4, 12–28
Romans 10.5–15
Matthew 14.22–33

A recently published letter from Qumran (4QMMT) helps us
to see what Paul is talking about here. It mostly contains
priestly regulations. But the last part is a fresh telling of the
story of Israel, from the great promises of Deuteronomy
28—30 to the author's own time. Deuteronomy 30 is read
as a prophecy of what is happening now, as God is at last
renewing the covenant. Disobedience has brought about the
covenantal curse; now at last the time of blessing is beginning.

Paul's theology is a kind of second cousin to that view;
Romans 9—10 as a whole corresponds to that story: 9.6—
10.4, one of the most vital parts of the whole argument, tells
the story of Israel from Abraham to the Messiah, pulling out
of the rich tapestry the single dark thread that ran on to the
Messiah's own casting away. God's purpose in having a
'chosen people', it seems, was that they should be the
place and the means whereby the sin and sorrow of all the
world would be brought to a head, so that the world might
be saved. All this was to become, alone and uniquely, the
destiny of the Messiah. 'Christ is the goal of the Law, so that
covenant membership may extend to all who believe' (10.4).

We are therefore now, Paul declares, in the time foretold
by Deuteronomy 30: the time of covenant renewal, of bles-

sing now that the curse has been exhausted. God is even now creating, through the gospel, a single worldwide family in whom God's intended 'doing of the Law' is accomplished – even if, being Gentiles, they have never heard of the Law. What the Law could not do, enabling people to live from the heart according to God's will, God has now done. There is therefore now a Gentile mission: Paul, telling the story of God's ways with his people, has reached his own day, his own vocation.

Joseph, too, told the story of God's people in a highly controversial fashion, with himself at the heart of it. The spoiled child has delusions of grandeur – or were they the voice of God? If so, they would pass through a severe test, with Joseph anticipating in his own person the whole story of the Exodus, being sold as a slave and then wonderfully released and exalted. The misery of his fate, ten times worse because of who it was that caused it, never shook his faith: 'you meant evil against me,' he would say much later, 'but God meant it for good' (Genesis 50.20). Who knows how different Joseph, the ruler of Egypt, must have been because he had once been a slave himself?

The same pattern, of the raging waters doing their worst and the people of God emerging surprised but safe, is acted out in the gospel scene. Who dares step out of safety on to the waters of God's turbulent purposes, trusting only the call of Jesus?

Proper 15

— ∽ —

Genesis 45.1–15
Romans 11.1–2a, 29–32
Matthew 15.10–28

Look at the word *God* in Genesis 45. All these years later, with plenty of free time to ponder his brothers' evil deeds and build up resentment, what comes out of Joseph's mouth is a doctrine of providence strong enough for eleven men to stand on.

There was no question, of course, of having the story of Joseph, or indeed the whole majestic sweep of Romans 11, read aloud all in one. But the depth and subtlety of character, plot and motive (study Judah some time and you'll see what I mean) are unsurpassed. Why not a dramatic reading, with a couple of actors from the congregation – not least to remind people of the story behind the musical? The theme, which the musical glimpsed but never quite grasped, is God ... God ... God. The strange but ultimately trustworthy, and even beautiful, ways of God. The Gospel reading is all about God doing things which were utterly unexpected, overturning the taboos that kept the Jews a cut above their neighbours. Unexpected, yet with hindsight they made a lot of sense.

Paul was addressing the same question. How can we go on trusting God when he behaves like this? Within the logic of Romans, indeed of his thought as a whole, he sooner or later had to address the question: what then about his non-believing kinsfolk according to the flesh? It's not just personal; the faithfulness of God, the foundation of chs 1–8, is at stake. Yet Romans 9–11 is not simply a long footnote. It is one of the main things he wants to say to the Roman Christians.

Claudius had expelled the Jews in the late 40s, possibly because of riots over the arrival of Christianity in the capital. For the next few years, Christianity in Rome was exclusively Gentile, a new and dangerous state of affairs. Granted the strong pagan anti-Judaism, Gentile Christians could easily think, as Joseph might have of his brothers, that the Jews were simply a lost cause, heading for judgement. Paul saw that Marcionite heresy coming over the horizon seventy years in advance. Had he been heeded, other more recent heresies, and tragedies, might have been averted.

Claudius died in 54, Nero became Emperor, and the Jews returned. What was the Church to do? Keep its nose in the air and have nothing to do with them? Far from it. They were to learn the wisdom of Joseph. Paul has been as it were sent on ahead, suffering and in tears, into the land where there is food to be had. He now longs to bring his family to be with him. Yes, he says (v. 23), 'if they do not persist in unbelief, they will be grafted back in'. They are the natural branches of the tree; you Gentiles are the odd ones out. How easily inverted snobbery takes hold, in theology as in the rest of life. And how strong a doctrine of providence it takes to uproot it.

Proper 16

— ∼ —

Exodus 1.8—2.10
Romans 12.1–8
Matthew 16.13–20

How do slaves get free? By living the present in the light of the future. The midwives, and Moses' mother, act out of defiant hope. Moses, destined to lead Israel through the Red Sea, begins his own life being snatched from a watery grave. Future freedom rushes into present slavery and transforms it.

Screwtape pointed out to Wormwood that effective tempters don't put things into people's heads; they keep things out. Learn to think straight, urges Paul, about where you are in God's purpose, what time it is, what role you have in Christ's one body. Straight thinking isn't a matter of unaided reason. Here in Romans it is about the mind's transformation: the slave mentality of the present age is to be abandoned in favour of the freedom of God's children, who, knowing themselves to belong to the new age that has come to birth with the Messiah, learn to live in the present in the light of that future.

The mind has to travel, as it were, ahead of the rest ('body' in 12.1, as often in Paul, doesn't just mean 'your physical self', but more what we mean by 'person', or even 'personality'). As the mind is renewed, so it must lead the way into the future, producing acts of will, and hence sacrificial acts of the whole person, which discover, test out in practice, and celebrate in performance, the behaviour which will bring delight to God.

Why is God delighted? Because the divine image is restored. Imagine a great queen, whose royal likeness had been defaced on the coins of the realm, discovering with joy that the coins themselves had chosen to be reworked into a true likeness. Or think of the Oxford don who, objecting to a gargoyle carved in his likeness, provoked the sculptor to produce instead one that would resemble him in forty years' time, so that he was forced to look every day at the haggard wreck he was increasingly becoming. Stand that story on its head, and you have the sequence of re-humanization that overarches Romans from 1.18 to 12.2, via 8.29. God has carved, in Christ, the true likeness that by grace we shall one day bear. We, by our liberated and thoughtful choosing, are to become in the present what God designs that we shall be in the future. That, rather than a new system of casuistry or 'ethics', is the foundation of Christian behaviour.

Peter glimpsed God's future, and declared Jesus to be Messiah. But Jesus gave Peter, too, a future which had to be brought into present reality. The idea that Peter, and hence the papacy, was the church's foundation 'rock' was a sixteenth-century innovation. The Messiah himself is the foundation of the new Temple. Recognizing Jesus as Messiah meant, for puzzled Peter, learning to think in the straight line that led from God's eventual future, through the cross, and on into a present more challenging than he had suspected.

Proper 17

— ❧ —

Exodus 3.1–15
Romans 12.9–21
Matthew 16.21–28

Peter, like Moses, hid his face, afraid to look upon God. He wanted to see God's messianic movement launched, but not like this; Moses had wanted to see Israel liberated, and had indeed begun his own one-man project to that effect, but was not prepared for the God whose chosen symbol was the burning bush. So much easier to do things one's own way, to fight evil with evil, to overthrow violence with violence. So much harder to stand before the fire and then before Pharaoh. So much harder to follow the way of the cross.

But only thus is God's name revealed – in so far as ever it is. Not simply 'The Lord', a bland and perhaps remote deity, but YHWH, challenging imagination and pronunciation alike. 'I am who I am'; 'I will be what I will be'; the deepest source, the highest court, the final cause, the One Who Is, the Person behind all personality. Moses stood before the flame to learn God's name and then to speak it to give hope to God's oppressed people. Peter had spoken Jesus' new name – God's Messiah, the hope-bringer – but still had to learn what it meant, and didn't like the first lesson. The God of Abraham is not like the gods of the Egyptians. The true Messiah does not belong in the line of warrior kings. The prince comes disguised as a beggar: God's wisdom as human folly, God's power as weakness, God's anointed as an outlaw.

Peter must go to Jerusalem, Moses to Pharaoh, both following the God whose ways and thoughts were other than theirs. The alternative is to gain the whole world but to forfeit one's deepest and truest self, the self found only in self-abandonment.

This upside-down vocation characterizes what at first appear the rather obvious exhortations in Romans 12. After the complex earlier theology, it is easy to suppose that we are left simply with a few straightforward dos and don'ts. Thus we read v. 9: hate the evil, cling to the good; basic morality, we think, common ground between Paul's readers and the wider Roman world.

But Paul goes much further. The theme, following directly from the preceding theology, is the *victory* of good over evil, and the way in which that victory is to be implemented in the lives of God's people. This is the theology of the cross at work in the world. Like Moses or Peter, we must abandon our normal ways of doing good, our careful calculation of moral balances, of rights rewarded and wrongs paid back. Generous, self-giving, overflowing love, meeting the other where they are, and always with blessing and peace; no cursing, no pride, no vengeance, but the quiet confidence that the God of the cross and burning bush has triumphed over evil and will at the last put all wrongs to rights. This is the way of the cross. It is also, when followed, a new burning bush for surprised desert wanderers.

Proper 18

— 〰 —

Exodus 12.1–14
Romans 13.8–14
Matthew 18.15–20

Jesus' followers are to struggle to live by the law of reconciliation. It's always a struggle, but it's always a law. Some say, of course, that Jesus couldn't have spoken, as in Matthew 18, about a 'church', because there wasn't one then; but, conversely, only in Jesus' lifetime would the saying about Gentiles and tax-collectors mean what it does here. The word translated 'church' can, in fact, refer to the gathering of Jesus' followers, such as might well take place within a village or town where he had passed, preached, healed and taught. Jesus was establishing little cells, loyal to himself, within the kingdom of Herod. The striking rule by which they were to live was that of forgiveness and reconciliation.

But it is always a hard-won reconciliation. Appropriate confrontation is the necessary prelude: reconciliation does not come by sweeping things under the carpet, or by pretending that nothing is really wrong. Equally, confrontation that does not aim at reconciliation is worse than useless. The model of Matthew 18, which has both in balance, is conspicuous by its absence in many church circles, where people prefer to associate with the like-minded rather than, so to speak, the like-faithed. What if our faith is precisely faith in God's costly reconciliation?

If Jesus was planting cells of loyal followers within

Herod's kingdom, Paul was planting and maintaining such groups under the very nose of Caesar. The letter to Rome takes the risk, joyfully, of marking out how one such group might live in loyalty to Jesus as Lord in the capital whose major theme was that Caesar was Lord. The last great section of Romans is all about how to live as the Jesus people, modelling the new way of being human which demonstrates who this new Lord is. Again, the central law is love. This does not mean that anything goes as long as you feel good about it, as a degenerate form of situation ethics might suggest. Rather, the love which wells up from within the Spirit-filled heart is known precisely by its joyful obedience to the commandments which protect us from wronging, and being wronged by, one another.

Commandments may help, but knowing what time it is helps even more. The signs of dawn are around us; as daytime fast approaches, nocturnal behaviour is no longer appropriate. The little community in Rome is to live out of the future, the future whose name is Jesus the true King, the true Lord, and to model the way that shows, against the dark backcloth of pagan nocturnal behaviour, that there is a path in which human being and human living is ennobled, enhanced, honourable. The note of urgency creeps in at this point: dawn is almost breaking, and we cannot put off the task of living the Jesus-way, the truly human way. As Passover people, redeemed people, the Church is commanded to flee with haste from whichever Egypt still beckons with its seductive slavery.

Proper 19

— ∾ —

Exodus 14.19–31
Romans 14.1–12
Matthew 18.21–35

The tidal wave struck, and we were unprepared. Comfortable liberal civilization, in which we were OK and they were OK – the corporate version of the street-level feel-good philosophy of the 60s – wasn't expecting post-Cold-War tribalism. Ideologies based on blood and turf have spilled blood, and dug fresh turf for mass graves, in Africa, central Europe, the Middle East, and of course Northern Ireland. We were looking inland, anxious about the coming Cold War hurricane. Meanwhile, behind us, the dark wall of water was gathering height and speed.

What might it mean, after the great wave (and before the next one), to trust the God of the Exodus? Simply this: that the pillar of cloud and fire, the presence of the world's mysterious Lord, goes before us, carving a path of freedom, away from the slavery of ethnic conflict, territorial claim and counter-claim, and blood-feud, and on towards a new promised land. In Christ, trilingually condemned at the place where the world's cultures and angers chafe and grind like tectonic plates, a wind has blown which has held back the waters so that humankind can leave Egypt for ever and find the way home.

That is the message of Romans 14. Paul faces a familiar challenge: how can different cultures, with their innate taboos, prejudices, suspicions, memories and wounds, live together as family? I write this in the international lounge at Vancouver Airport, surrounded by swirling throngs from every nation and tribe and tongue. They mix happily, but they don't live here. When they go home – to the North West frontier, say, or Jerusalem or Belfast – things may not be so easy. The Roman church, numbering perhaps somewhere between 40 and 200, meeting in small house-groups according to ethnic origin in Rome's poorer suburbs, needed to be challenged to model an entirely new way of being human, in which blood and turf, and their concomitant taboos, would cease to be the ruling powers. The waters of cultural prejudice would be a wall to their right and left, and they would pass through, with Jesus as their pillar of cloud and fire, ahead of angry pursuing slave-masters.

Paul's technique is striking. He will not name the ethnic origins of the taboos. He does not say 'some of you are Jews, some Gentiles'. He simply says 'some of us eat anything, some only vegetables'; 'some of us keep special days, some don't'. Heady stuff, relativizing major symbols like that. It's only possible because of who the Lord is who leads the way through the dark waters. Try it any other way – as the liberal West has done – and barbarism will lurk beneath the surface of the waters, ready to rise and swell, as it has done so often in this sad old century, into another Sunami.

And now can we understand why the last words of Matthew 18 are not a bizarre picture of an arbitrary, vengeful and angry God but simply a statement of fact?

Proper 20

— ☙ —

Exodus 16.2–15
Philippians 1.21–30
Matthew 20.1–16

The wilderness wanderings of Israel are a regular New Testament metaphor for the life of the Christian family between Easter and God's final victory. The grumbling of the people, redeemed and sustained but not yet home in the land of milk and honey, is sadly characteristic of Christians as well; or why would so many passages, in Philippians and elsewhere, warn against it? There is a constant tension between believing in what has already been achieved and appreciating the scale of what has yet to be achieved. Stress one and people think you're ignoring the other. The 'now' and 'not yet' are the regular left–right of the long march through the desert. Those who don't appreciate this end up wondering why they are limping.

The grumblers of the parable (a vineyard owner and his hired labourers is fairly obvious code for God and Israel) appear to be those who thought they had it made, a first-class seat on the advanced flight (yes, I'm still in the airport). Why should they, who had paid so much for their tickets, share their status with the rabble who ought at best to be in the small, hard seats further back? The context of Matthew 20 is provided by Matthew 19: just as the rich young man couldn't earn his way into the Age to Come, so the disciples cannot assume that their giving up everything to follow Jesus automatically entitles them to the best seats in the Kingdom. From first to last, first and last are ambiguous categories, easily exchanged, each with its own Achilles heel. If the first temptation is to use worldly symbols and status to elbow the way to the front, the last is to use, as a subtle second-order status symbol, the faith by which all status and symbol (land, family, taboos) have been renounced. God's generosity cannot be blackmailed.

Recognition of this will sustain the little Philippian church, socially at risk from their allegiance to Jesus as Lord. Their civic behaviour (v. 27 has overtones of this, not just of privatized ethics) is to reflect the gospel which announces this Jesus; their primary loyalty is to Jesus, and to one another in costly unity. They are to regard their resultant suffering, not as an annoyance, something their faith ought to have ruled out, but as part of the gift of living at the overlap between God's Kingdom and the world's, part of being citizens of Israel currently on their way through the wilderness.

Paul's own story, as usual, is invoked as a model. There is much that would make him prefer to cross the Jordan at once, to be with the Messiah in a new intimacy while waiting for the eventual resurrection (3.21). But there is much that assures him that he has a task still to perform in the wilderness. That task has to do with feasting in the desert: celebrating the Messiah's rule while all around are hailing Caesar as Lord.

Proper 21

— ∼ —

Exodus 17.1–7
Philippians 2.1–13
Matthew 21.23–32

It sounded like a trick, but for those with ears to hear it
answered the authorities' challenge head on. Jesus' Temple
action was an affront to the power of the chief priests, a
thinly veiled claim to kingship. A reference to John the
Baptist, the more powerful for being oblique, underlined
the point.

Many readers of the Gospels forget John after the opening
scenes, but neither Jesus nor the evangelists made that
mistake. Jesus' right to challenge the whole Temple
system, and for that matter the current royal and priestly
claims, stemmed directly from John's baptism, a counter-
Temple movement with a counter-Herodian edge. John had
dug the field, Jesus had sown the seed, and now it was harvest
time. It was at John's baptism of Jesus that the voice from
heaven had named Jesus as Messiah, God's beloved son.

The parable of the two sons has at least two layers of
meaning. Of course, it is better to do what the father wants
than to say you will and then change your mind; but, as
usual, the shallow moralistic surface meaning invites us to go
beneath for the real thrust. Those who seemed to be flouting
God's will ended up being baptized by John; those who
seemed to be following God's instructions to the letter
refused to do so. This suggests a further reason for Jesus'

Temple action: he was following through John's warnings, verbal and symbolic. His authority came from the God in whose name and power John had prophesied. But the parable has a further twist as well. Now that the chief priests were in a rebellious state, they too, like the ne'er-do-wells, could have changed their minds and obeyed after all. Even at this stage the challenge contains a coded final appeal.

Philippians 2.5–11, one of the noblest early Christian statements of Jesus' person and accomplishment, retells compactly several of the great biblical stories in order to mount a statement of Jesus' humble yet triumphant authority. Jesus succeeds where Adam failed, refusing to take advantage of his equality with God (not, as some translations suggest, giving it up; rather, rejecting the chance to exploit it). He thereby accomplishes the task of Israel, God's servant-people, dying under the weight of the world's sin. He is thus revealed not only as the truly human one, the true Israel, but as the embodiment of the God who is Israel's only saviour and Lord (compare Isaiah 45.23). And so, most importantly for the Philippian Christians to grasp, he is the Lord, the reality of which Caesar is the parody.

Only when the Church is grasped by this vision of Jesus, rooted in the Scriptures and confronting the might of pagan empire, will it achieve the seemingly over-idealistic unity and obedience of which the surrounding verses speak. Those who are thirsty for these great blessings will find Philippians 2 a staff with which water can be produced from what might have appeared impenetrable rock.

Proper 22

— ∼ —

Exodus 20.1–4, 7–9, 12–20
Philippians 3.4b–14
Matthew 21.33–46

The parable of the wicked tenants tells the story of Israel in such a way as to highlight Jesus' own work and fate as the plot's denouement. But, as with many parables, and many great non-biblical stories, the plot is never simple. It contains a twist at its heart, corresponding to the fatal twist in the human heart, not least the religious human heart.

Landowner and vineyard: obvious first-century Jewish code for God and Israel. The fence is presumably Torah, the law given to Moses, designed to make Israel God's special people, the fruit-bearing nation, the light of the world. Some rabbis of Jesus' day spoke of putting a fence around Torah itself, adding new commands for extra security, but the idea of Torah itself as a fence would be natural as well. The other details echo Isaiah 5, the song of the vineyard, which like this parable ends in tragedy. There the fault is with the vine, here with the tenants; but the result is the same. Rebellion leads to fruitlessness, fruitlessness to inevitable judgement.

But Jesus' story is stranger than Isaiah's. The prophets themselves are now characters in the narrative, and they are violently abused. At last there comes one in the line of the prophets, yet much more than a prophet. He is the son, the Messiah. What will they do with him? The answer is all too obvious. The present tenants – the spotlight falls on the Jerusalem regime of the chief priests – know that the Messiah will take from them their present shaky primacy. They must kill him, to gain the inheritance for themselves.

The parable explains Jesus' Temple action and points to its result. On its surface it contains no saving interpretation of the son's death. But look at the riddle that follows. In Hebrew 'son' is 'ben', and 'stone' is 'eben'. The stone of Psalm 118.22 is linked to the (messianic) stone of Daniel 2.31–45; both are linked to the son in the story. Jesus is challenging his hearers to search the Scriptures and understand what was going on before their eyes.

Paul (unlike some of his interpreters) does not challenge the God-givenness of the law. He has grasped that, precisely because the vineyard tenants (himself included) exhibit the same fatal flaw as the rest of humankind, their national charter cannot now be the badge of the true, redeemed people of God. He must therefore cling to the Messiah, and him alone. In a passage rich with theology and devotion, he states his aim: to know the Messiah, to be found in him, to gain him, to trust him, to share his sufferings and his resurrection, to respond in love to the one who has loved him, to follow his call to the life of the age to come. Christianty wasn't a religion for Paul. It was a person, the one through whose shameful rejection the fatal twist in human nature was to be cured at last.

Proper 23

— ❧ —

Exodus 32.1–14
Philippians 4.1–9
Matthew 22.1–14

The party was ready, the guests were on the way, but somehow they got distracted. Today's gospel fits Exodus 32 like a glove, forming a combined warning.

Readers of Exodus perceive the golden calf incident in black and white. It was a wicked blasphemy. But at the time it must have appeared in shades of grey. The key question is: who brought Israel out of Egypt? Moses, say the people, growing restless while Moses is away getting the instructions for the tabernacle (the physical object, symbolizing both the presence and the untameability of Yahweh, upon which golden earrings were to have been lavished). Treat the leader as God, and you'll have a vacuum when the leader goes off doing business with God. So Aaron gives another answer: the calf brought them out (imagine Isaiah's mockery).

God's reaction is interesting. He scornfully agrees with the people: *Your* people, he says to Moses, whom *you* brought out of Egypt. Moses knows that this means trouble, but in his prayer he goes straight to the point: No, he replies to God, they are *your* people. You brought them out. You were fulfilling promises made long ago and establishing a worldwide reputation. You can't go back on it.

It is a defining moment in the relationship between

Yahweh, Moses and Israel. From now on nothing will be the same again. There is still hard bargaining ahead; Moses spends the next two chapters persuading God to accompany the people in person, rather than just sending an angel. But the people have effectively shown themselves to be that strange hybrid, the people of God who yet bear the mark of Cain. They carry God's light for the world, but remain capable of darkness. The rabble of slaves now invited to feast in God's Kingdom still need to put on the wedding garment.

The best way to stop the weeds of idolatry growing is to plant flowers. Paul, after his word of reconciling encouragement to two otherwise unknown women, offers two basic plants which will leave no room for thorns and thistles: celebration and thinking.

Both require a positive decision. You can't just drift into rejoicing in the Lord, or the prayerful renunciation of anxiety which follows. In the pagan world of Paul's day, anxiety was a major factor in daily life, to be kept at bay by ceaselessly appeasing the malevolent deities. Since the true God is revealed in Jesus, this anxiety can and should be replaced by celebration, but you've got to work at it if you want the peace, undreamed of in a place like Philippi, which follows.

Likewise, you have to work at putting into your mind all the positive things in God's good world. The media bombard us every day with the negatives; go with the flow and that's what you'll get. Remember, instead, who it was that brought you out of Egypt, and ponder the thousands of things that are good in creation. It's a great party; don't get distracted.

Proper 24

— ⁓ —

Exodus 33.12–23
1 Thessalonians 1.1–10
Matthew 22.15–22

The multiple echoes of Exodus 33 bounce around the New Testament. The first letter to the Thessalonians, held by many to be the first surviving Christian writing, offers another reminder that the gospel's basic call is to worship the true God rather than idols.

To pagan ears Paul's message would have sounded profoundly Jewish. There is one God, the creator; man-made idols are lies and delusions. The true God is alive and life-giving; idols, lifeless themselves, cannot give life. But Paul's message went further. Ever since Exodus, Jews had believed that no one could see God face to face and live. Paul believed that the true God had been made known personally in and as Jesus of Nazareth, the summation of Israel's destiny, the Messiah.

The Thessalonians had themselves become God-imitators, Christ-imitators, Paul-imitators (1.6–8). It boggles our minds that until Paul arrived nobody had thought of living out the Christian ethic. They wouldn't have believed it possible. Paul had modelled it before them (1.5); now, to his delight, they were themselves modelling it before the world. Eager as we are to affirm God's presence within the whole world, we shouldn't forget the call to distinctive and sometimes shocking behaviour.

The Thessalonians' new lifestyle was the result of the Spirit's work through the proclamation of Jesus as the risen one, the coming judge and deliverer (1.10; compare Acts 17.31). This was so unexpected and crazy-sounding (attempts to show that the pagan world was bored with its own religions and just waiting for something like Christianity to show up are doomed to failure) that, as Paul well knew, their new-found faith, hope and love (1.3) could only be the result of God's work through the gospel announcement. They had been marked out as people who worshipped and waited for the true son of the true God, in the world where Caesar demanded both worship, as the son of his divine predecessor, and political and economic fidelity.

The clash between Caesar and the true God resurfaces in the cryptic gospel passage. The first great messianic movement of Jesus' day, that of Judas the Galilean, had been a tax revolt; was Jesus' movement to be like that too? The Maccabean heroes had been exhorted, ambiguously, to 'pay back the Gentiles what they deserve – and keep God's commandments!' (1 Maccabees 2.68). Roman coins added theological insult to political injury: they bore a human image, offensive in itself, doubly so when the inscription declared him to be the son of a god.

Jesus, however, is leading more than a mere tax revolt. Give the dirty stuff back to Caesar who deserves it, he said. Caesar's absolute claims are as nothing before the all-embracing claim of the one true God. Jesus, himself the divine Image, was on his way to symbolize and embody, as only the unique Son could, the God whose face is unveiled at last, not in financial demands but in self-giving love.

115

The Last Sunday After Trinity

— ∾ —

Deuteronomy 34.1–12
1 Thessalonians 2.1–8
Matthew 22.34–46

Like a bored videotape-watcher, the lectionary suddenly presses the fast-forward button, skipping three-fifths of the Pentateuch and stopping only just in time for the death of the hero.

Moses' lack of known burial place is spoken of with awe, almost shock. There is nowhere for family to gather, nowhere to serve as a memorial. In some traditions he is not buried at all, but, like Elijah, ascends straight to heaven. But however we read it, he remains among the greatest of Israelites, his story all the more powerful for its poignant end, so near and yet so far. He symbolizes the importance and yet the limitations of the Law which is linked with his name: as Paul might say, it will get you to the brink of the Jordan, but you will need someone else to shepherd you across. And that someone will be called Joshua, *Yeshua*, Jesus.

Jesus' own summary of the Law points the way, the way he himself would tread, through the river and into the promised land. Like all his sayings, 'Love God – love your neighbour' is not first of all demand, but rather gift. It is what Jesus himself was doing, and would do supremely on the cross; it is what, by the Spirit, Jesus' surprised followers found themselves doing, or beginning to do. It is what Paul was determined at all costs to do in his evangelism

116

and pastoral work. Though it represents in one sense the internalization of the Law, it encompasses all the continuing externals as well.

By highlighting this double command, the very premise of the question is challenged. From a Pharisee, the question of the greatest commandment was a matter of defining Israel, now and in the age to come. But if these two commandments are the greatest, love for the creator and love for one's neighbour will mean throwing open the borders to all and sundry. At the heart of Israel's Law is the sign that reminds Israel that she exists for the sake of the world, not vice versa.

All is drawn together onto the person of Jesus himself. Uncharacteristically, he himself asks the last question in the long sequence; unsurprisingly, it remains unanswered. It seems to hinge on the multiple resonances of Psalm 110, which poses one of the central puzzles of the letter to the Hebrews: the Psalm's central figure is both a king and a priest, and one to whom even David looks up as Lord.

The relative status of kings and priests had been a live issue in the Jewish world for two centuries by Jesus' day. Jesus seems to be setting forth, on scriptural premises, a theology of kingship which would upstage both the existing Jerusalem priesthood and the royal house of Herod. Somehow, David's Lord would be David's son. Only when people got their minds round that would they appreciate how the new Joshua would do what the Law could not, and lead God's Israel home at last.

117

Sundays Before Advent

The Fourth Sunday Before Advent

— ∼ —

Micah 3.5–12
1 Thessalonians 2.9–13
Matthew 24.1–14

Those of us who earn our living by speaking and writing about the Bible sometimes feel nervous in the presence of Micah and Paul. There is the apostle, doing his day job making tents, debating with customers about the quality and durability of the product and of the gospel, and then going off to expound the word of God, free, to the tiny group of disciples. They know it is God's word because his lifestyle backs it up. The character of the messenger is a powerful argument for the truth of the message – and a powerful incentive to imitation.

And there is the prophet, contemptuous of those who pipe the tunes of their paymasters. Rulers, priests and prophets are all on the make; they go through the motions, they look and sound genuine, but it's all a sham. The signs are plain: injustice flourishes unchecked, corruption eats away at the heart of society, and those who are supposed to be speaking out are instead reaching out their hands for the next bribe. The result is not only the warning about the great and beautiful city being ploughed as a field; it is the more sinister threat, that prophecy itself will fail. People will look for light from God, and receive darkness instead. I have an uneasy suspicion that if Micah were to show up in the modern

Western world, or church, he would instantly be branded as a wild man, an extremist, a fanatic.

But there, towering over apostle and prophet alike, is the master. Zion is not merely to be ploughed as a field: its beautiful stones will come down until not one is left upon another. Deceit will multiply until people can't tell who is a real prophet, or even a real Messiah, and who isn't. Wars will come and go; nations and kingdoms will rise and fall. A good description of the generation after Jesus, which is what it's intended to be; and a good evocation of so many generations since. And the Church's place within this turbulent world is not to seek the security of compromise, but to announce the good news of God's Kingdom – which is, of course, bad news for those who live by inequity and oppression – and to take the consequences.

Placing Jesus between Micah and Paul helps to see what's going on. His prophecies were specific to the first century (and were dramatically fulfilled), but they resonate out into the world where the Church lives by the apostolic and prophetic word. His warnings to Jerusalem must be translated into warnings against all corruption, violence and injustice. What he said to Israel, the Church must say to the world. Not to follow this path is not merely to court disaster; it is to risk having the prophetic spirit itself withdrawn. Night without visions, darkness without dawn; that is the stark alternative awaiting the church, or society, that decides to co-opt and tame its prophets.

121

The Third Sunday Before Advent

— ⁓ —

Wisdom of Solomon 6.12–16
1 Thessalonians 4.13–18
Matthew 25.1–13

You should only treat yourself to Wisdom of Solomon ch. 6 if you are prepared to live with the rest. The righteous and wise are persecuted and killed by the wicked and foolish; but God knows them, and they will be vindicated. Lady Wisdom has piloted the little ship of God's covenant people throughout its long history, and the raging storms of pagan empire cannot and will not swamp or sink it. No wonder many in the early Church loved this book, seeing it as a prophecy of their own struggle against pagan force in general and Rome in particular.

Still interested in Wisdom? She is not just eager to be known, found by those who get up early, offering release from care. She is the one who strengthens the resolve of God's people to stand in the evil day; she will guide monarchs in their unenviable and often misunderstood tasks. Seek wisdom, and you will get, not the interesting but unthreatening life of the dilettante intellectual, but hard-won practical knowledge about being God's people in a threatening world.

Having sorted that out, 1 Thessalonians 4 should be no problem. On the day I write this, I faced twenty bright students with the problem: what are verses 16 and 17 about? Half of them knew about 'the rapture'; America's bookstores stock fundamentalist fantasy novels about the saints being snatched up to heaven (leaving suddenly empty cars piled up on freeways, and other Hollywood-style horrors) while the rest of the world either goes to hell or manages as best it can. The other half – sheltered liberals, I suppose – were innocent of all this, but equally uninformed as to Paul's possible meaning.

Paul, never one to use a single image if three will do, brings together the Sinai-picture (Israel's leaders going up the mountain to meet Moses coming down with the law), Daniel 7 (God's people vindicated, exalted 'on the clouds'), and the Emperor-picture (Caesar coming to a city, the nobles going out to meet him and escort him in). Colour this three-dimensional picture of God's future in gaudy apocalyptic language, cook it in the urgent heat of a difficult pastoral problem, and you have an exegetical puzzle to last a millennium.

Compare it, though, with Paul's very similar statements in 1 Corinthians 15.50–57 and Philippians 3.19–21, and you will see what he is affirming, in and through it all. When God makes all things new (as opposed to abolishing the world of space, time and matter), the Christian dead are to be re-embodied, i.e. resurrected, and the Christian living are to be transformed and vindicated. A message not too far, in fact, from that of Wisdom, despite initial appearances.

Wisdom and apocalyptic meet in the parable of the girls with (or without) their oil: Lady Wisdom and Lady Folly, fresh from the Jewish wisdom tradition and multiplied five times each. Wisdom consists precisely in knowing what time it is.

The Second Sunday Before Advent

— ∾ —

Zephaniah 1.7, 12–18
1 Thessalonians 5.1–11
Matthew 25.14–30

This parable gave 'talent' a new meaning, so common that we don't realize how far we have domesticated a warning about more serious matters than developing one's personal potential and skill. In Jesus' day a talent was a measure of weight, particularly of (a large sum of) money. Countless moralizing sermons have applied the parable to what we now mean by 'talents'; the word, and the interpretation, have stuck.

Nor is it a bad lesson to learn at that level (though the normal reading comes unglued at the climax of the story, where the person with ten talents is given one more). But let us not trivialize Jesus' teaching. Here we are in the middle of Matthew 25, itself located within the climactic section 23—25, immediately preceding the huge and dark events of the next two chapters. What is at stake is rather more serious than whether Jack and Jill get Bs instead of Cs in their Physics GCSEs.

The original setting is Jesus' warning, not of a far-off event at his 'return', but of YHWH's coming at last to Israel to seek the fruit from the vineyard planted so long ago. 'YHWH will not do good, neither will he do harm,' they said in Zephaniah's day; the third servant, despite having a rather more pessimistic view of his master, proved equally, and culpably, ineffectual. The God who promised to search Jerusalem with lamps will penetrate to the heart of the matter. The slave's commission has gone unfulfilled.

Jesus' warning is clear: unless Israel makes good and swift use of her privilege and responsibility as God's people, chosen for the sake of the world, the privilege will at last be withdrawn. Jesus stands in the line of the great prophets, looking for justice and discovering corruption, looking for virtue and discovering vice – and warning God's people that, though they will plant vineyards and not share the crop, in the moral sense they will most certainly reap what they sow.

If we are to apply these terrible warnings authentically to subsequent generations, we must begin with the gospel warning to the human race as a whole. Called to be God's wise stewards over creation, what has the human race to show for its commission? Works of beauty and truth, yes. Works of creativity and justice, to be sure. But also plenty of talents buried in the ground, including (alas) by Christians. Called to be human, we prefer other, less demanding, destinies. We may just get them.

Paul, looking towards the same future, issues a bracing challenge in terms of night and day: you must live as day people, even though others think it's still night. 'Peace and security' mumbles the dozy world, turning over in bed; it was a slogan in the early Roman Empire, celebrating Augustus's great but deeply ambiguous achievement. Slogans, though, will not prevent sudden convulsions. Wake up, then, and be ready! Another Pauline mixed metaphor: off with the night-shirt, on with the armour.

125

Christic the King

— ∼ —

Ezekiel 34.11–16, 20–24
Ephesians 1.15–23
Matthew 25.31–46

'I will be their shepherd,' declares God to exiled Israel. 'I will be their God,' he says a bit later, 'and David my servant shall be their shepherd.' All right, we reply to Ezekiel; is God the true king, coming to rescue and judge the sheep, or is it David, the coming king, the Messiah?

The prophet has no answer. The logic of his vision demands that it be both. God will perform the unique messianic task; or, if you prefer, the Messiah will accomplish that which, when all merely human kings have failed, only Israel's God can achieve.

Because a royal vision it was. Shepherding is not a vocation we today associate with royalty, but once they had crowned Jesse's shepherd son the metaphor stuck in Jewish imagination. There, however, lies the problem. The people had refused Samuel's advice. Rejecting their one God as the true king, they had chosen Saul instead. The deep resulting ambiguity of the monarchy lurked thereafter as a dark monster beneath the glossy surface of Israel's royal institutions. God's choice of the shepherd boy as a man after his own heart is only redeemed from that often crushing ambiguity when the sheep finally reject the shepherd and leave him to the wolves, with the contemptuous sign, 'God's

126

shepherd', nailed above his head. Only Calvary can bring into focus the double vision of Ezekiel.

Within that royal vision there must lie judgement. Fat sheep and lean, rams and goats: images of the great divide that runs, unexpected and unwanted, through Israel, the world and (alas) the Church. Close up, this behaviour and that may not look too dissimilar; extend them into infinity, and the small act of mercy and the small act of cruelty are seen for what they are, and judged accordingly. It is noticeable how, in Jewish and early Christian visions of the future, the stronger the emphasis on resurrection, on God's definite act within history both in Jesus and for the human race, the stronger the emphasis on judgement. That, perhaps, rather than simple rationalism, is one reason why the resurrection is so often rejected.

But if we refuse to accept the rising of the king we turn our back on the glory of Christian hope, which is what Paul prays that the church in western Turkey will grasp beyond all else. Exalted over the whole cosmos, fulfilling God's purpose for the human race as well as for Israel, King Jesus holds out the hope that comes, not as an added extra, but as the very substance of the Christian's vocation. This hope is articulated in terms of goal and power. The 'inheritance' evokes images of the milk-and-honey promised land, now transposed into the cosmic sphere. It is guaranteed by the same power that raised the king from the dead and exalted him as chief shepherd for the world. In the background, for those with eyes to see, there is a smile on the face of the exiled prophet.

YEAR B

Advent

The First Sunday of Advent

—— ⮾ ——

Isaiah 64.1–9
1 Corinthians 1.3–9
Mark 13.24–37

Advent has stolen the old Christmas mystique. The symbolism of darkness awaiting dawn makes sense in a postmodern world where Christmas razzmatazz has been debunked, demythologized and deconstructed. Hope in the night, not glitzy commercialism, is what we want and need.

This is a deeply biblical move. Cut Christmas out of the Bible, and you lose three chapters (the doctrine of the incarnation hardly hinges on it, as the evidence of Paul makes clear). Try cutting Advent, and you lose half the Old Testament and most of the New. Jews and Christians have always, though in a wide variety of ways, lived within and by the story of God's order appearing within the world's confusion, God's fiery light burning away the shadows. The New Testament re-uses the Old Testament language and imagery of God's breaking into world history, not least 'the day of the Lord', to speak of what will happen on 'the day of our Lord Jesus Christ'. Get Advent right, and you will find Christology comes along with it.

But why? And what are we to hope *for*? Advent has its equivalents of shepherds and wise men, and perhaps also of Father Christmas – the walk-on parts that can all too easily get in the way of deeper understanding. Clouds, trumpets, angels, cosmic catastrophe – a Christian version of *Star Wars* and *Apocalypse Now*, easily beguiling us into thinking that it's all make-believe.

It isn't. It speaks of the time when the thin but opaque curtain that hangs in the midst of reality, the bright veil between heaven and earth, will be ripped aside. Our present reality, existing – did we but know it – a hair's breadth away from the terror and splendour of God, would be confronted with that other Reality, setting the cosmos burning and bubbling, calling forth the deepest shame ('we are all unclean') and the most intimate hope ('yet, Lord, you are our Father'). Afraid of shame, we are often ready to trade in hope if only we can be left without such an Advent.

We can't. It's already happened. What we ought to celebrate at Christmas, instead of wrapping it tightly in trivia to prevent the glory bursting out, is the story of heaven opened, glory unveiled, God's shame and intimacy meeting ours. Advent, rather than the recently introduced pre-Advent 'Kingdom season', is the end of the church year, as well as the beginning. Those who await the final unveiling of God's majesty and love are to be sustained by meditating on its first mysterious appearing.

Yes, and by waiting in readiness. Jesus' warnings about the imminent fall of Jerusalem resonate into subsequent history. The shame which befell the unbelieving city points ahead to a yet greater shame. The watchful hope of Jesus' loyal followers calls us to further vigilance. To believe in God's future is to see why it is vital to stay alert and take action in the present. Christmas has become cosy. Advent calls us to stay awake.

3

The Second Sunday of Advent

—— ≈ ——

Isaiah 40.1–11
2 Peter 3.8–15a
Mark 1.1–8

If John the Baptist was going to raise up the valleys and flatten out the mountains, he started in the right place. Jericho lies a long way below the road-sign that says 'sea level'; Jerusalem, a long way above. Topography won't matter when YHWH returns.

Nor will the transience of the rest of the natural order, including not only grass but human beings. What matters is God's Word. The later Christian inclination to take all references to God's Word to refer to the Bible itself is understandable but limiting. God's self-disclosing, self-expressing being goes forth powerfully, emerging in prophetic oracles old and new, creating new worlds and new people to match and inhabit the new day that God's return to Zion will bring about.

All this can of course be said of scripture, when rightly handled. It remains living and active. But the image here is not of a book, safe and domesticated (as we so easily suppose) on a shelf, but of the authoritative word which called into being the first creation and now brings forth the new one, the 'new heavens and new earth' that still form the stuff of Christian hope. This is why Isaiah's herald has something to shout about.

Isaiah combines what we find it so hard to: majesty and

4

comfort. The more authoritative our God-picture, the more we find it difficult to speak at the same time of tender comfort for the long-term prisoner (v. 2) or of gentle leading of lambs and mother sheep (v. 11). The message of the Baptist, too, seems more at home with the other pole of Isaianic language, the imperious command to clear a path for the Mighty One, whose arm rules for him, who brings rewards and recompense. Yet part of the point of Mark's picture of John, and part of the paradox of John's whole career, is precisely that when he spoke of the Mightier One (perhaps evoking Isaiah 40.10) we look around and see Jesus. It is like that moment in Revelation 5 when, looking for a lion, we discover a lamb.

And in that Lamb God's glory has been revealed, for all flesh to see together. We easily think of 'glory' as meaning 'luminosity', but this, though often implied as well, is not its primary denotation. 'Glory' is what you see when the inner truth of God is revealed, when God's own very self is known, not misunderstood or distorted but recognized as what it is, and so loved and adored.

Mark is telling us, by the very framing of his story (even if, as some suppose, his own opening has been lost, leaving us with a rather abrupt editorial introduction), that this is what we will see in Jesus of Nazareth. 2 Peter reminds us that, within the tumultuous and world-shaking events of which prophecy and Gospel speak, we are to remember the loving patience of the Lord, and to see in that our salvation.

The Third Sunday of Advent

—— ❧ ——

Isaiah 61.1–4, 8–11
1 Thessalonians 5.16–24
John 1.6–8, 19–28

Restrain the impulse towards Isaiah's rolling cadences and John's pregnant simplicity, and ponder what Paul has packed into such a small space. Apart from verse 23 (a benediction for those awaiting the Lord's presence), the rest of this nine-verse passage is very clipped. No argument; no discourse; only one explanatory phrase; eight commands; a concluding promise. Forty-one words in the Greek, just over five per verse. Blessed is the one who ponders each, and the way in which they bring the Advent hope into present reality.

First, celebration. 'Rejoice always'; easy to caricature, but easy too to miss the point. Present celebration is rooted in what has already been achieved in Christ, and what is thereby guaranteed.

Second, ceaseless prayer. Easier said than done, we think, and settle for less than one hour in 24; yet Paul was busy too, had much to be anxious about, and could still speak of anticipating here and now the life of heaven.

Gratitude in all circumstances: Paul's were more trying than most, yet one hint of trouble and we back off, despite his interesting explanation. Gratitude, it seems, is at the heart of the genuine humanness not only modelled but given to us in Christ; it is, again, a key sign of living in the present in the light of the promised future. These first three commands, like

6

the opening clauses in the Lord's Prayer, are all about looking to God and God's future.

We then have two commands to be open to fresh winds of the Spirit: don't quench the Spirit, don't despise prophesying. New wine is inconvenient in church, embarrassing even; but unless God is doing new things how can we be living as future-oriented people?

Finally, three commands to serious moral decisions. Test everything; cling tight to what is good (if you don't, it'll slip out of your fingers); back off from everything that even looks evil. God's future judgement is to work forwards into appropriate moral seriousness. Again, there are echoes of the Lord's Prayer. Was this, perhaps, the kind of quick teaching Paul would give his converts at a very basic stage? Have we improved on it?

Finally, the promise: he who calls you is faithful, and will accomplish it. A beloved aunt wrote the first three Greek words, *pistos ho kalon*, on a card for my confirmation, and I have it still, all these years later. The future assured action of the Lord undergirds the future-oriented behaviour of the disciple. Like John the Baptist, so preoccupied with what (and who) was coming that all he could do was to point away from himself and towards God's future, we are to pray, dance, and be holy, for tomorrow we live.

Now place this brief picture of Christian behaviour within the majestic promises and flights of imagery of Isaiah 61. Sit back and enjoy the ride. But remember: in an aeroplane, the nuts and bolts are just as important as the wings.

The Fourth Sunday of Advent

—— ❧ ——

2 Samuel 7.1–11, 16
Romans 16.25–7
Luke 1.26–38

It always was a mystery. Not just a puzzle – there are enough of those as well, God knows – but a genuine mystery, a truth whose parallel lines disappear behind God's dark curtain, to meet in that infinity of truth where all is literal and all is metaphorical. Did God intend Israel to have a king? Read 1 Samuel 8 and ponder. Did God intend Israel to have a temple? Read 2 Samuel 7 again and ponder.

At one level they seem simply concessions to Israel's desire to be like everyone else. A king, like all the nations; a temple, like the ones up the road. There's the problem: borrowing light from the world, instead of being the light *of* the world. Kings become corrupt, and are exiled (beginning with David himself, whose immorality, copied among his children, leads to Absalom's rebellion). Temples become first idols, then ruins.

And yet. God desires justice and mercy for his people, not unredeemed anarchy. God desires to dwell among his people, not to remain distant. A king after God's own heart? A temple that is simultaneously movable and appropriate to God's majesty?

The ambiguities of this double dream converge on the apparently jokey pun in 2 Samuel 7.11 (do read verses 12–15 as well; I know the lectionary is trying to stimulate us to fresh thought, but we have enough puzzles without home-made ones). David wants to build God a house; God promises that he will build David a 'house' – a son who will be God's own son, whose Davidic throne will be established for ever.

Why did God change the subject? Had he forgotten David's suggestion about a temple? No. There was an appropriate way for the living, loving God to dwell in the midst of his people: the stone temple would point the way towards it, but would remain an ambiguous signpost. The reality would be a human being, reflecting God's image; a king, embodying God's wise ordering of the people; a man after God's own heart, whose heart would be broken by the pain of the world but who would in that moment render all man-made temples redundant.

No wonder, as Paul says, that this is a mystery hidden long ago and only disclosed in Jesus. (Paul's language tumbles over itself in getting to the end of his great letter, but the confusion – is the glory going to God, or to Jesus, or both? – is thoroughly appropriate.) Mary becomes the temporary dwelling-place of the living God: the presence of the Holy Spirit, and the 'overshadowing' of the Most High, both evoke the temple-idea. This passage struggles to say something for which words hardly exist: that in Mary's womb temple and king came together once and for all, that the scriptures came true in ways never imagined, and that God found at last the house, neither tent nor temple but flesh and blood, that would most truly and fully express his royal, self-giving love.

Christmas

The First Sunday of Christmas

—— ∾ ——

Isaiah 61.10—62.3
Galatians 4.4–7
Luke 2.15–21

God sent the Son ... and God sent the Spirit of the Son. St Paul brings together Christmas and Pentecost – as unlikely a pair, to our culture-conditioned minds, as plum pudding and a May Bank Holiday. Son and Spirit remain inseparable. Ask Mary.

Paul is describing how slaves become God's adopted children and heirs. Telling, as so often, a fresh variation on the story of the Exodus, he sees the law itself as the instrument of slavery. It locked up the Jews in condemnation; it locked out the Gentiles from membership. Is God then powerless to keep his promise to Abraham, the promise of a worldwide family?

No. The birth of the child, as with Abraham himself, signals God's faithfulness, God's grace breaking through human impossibility. Born of a woman, born under the law, the Messiah has come to the slave-market, and has purchased his people's freedom. Christmas people are to think of themselves as Passover people, and then also as Pentecost people: what God did in the birth of the one child, God now does in the birth of dozens, thousands, tens of millions in whose hearts the Spirit is poured out, and on whose lips is the newborn cry, 'Abba, Father'. ('Abba' isn't just a child's word, but here it is treated as the sure sign of new life.) Father, Son and Spirit: God's inner life, shared with us all.

Come back to Bethlehem, therefore, and see what has come to pass. Only come now, with the angels singing, and see not one babe in the manger, but more than anyone could count: children and heirs of the free love of God, Passover people, Pentecost people. Christmas is the time of celebration because this new birth heralds all new birth. In this young son all God's Exodus people are called to be sons and daughters, free heirs of God's lavish grace, clothed (as Isaiah says) with the garments of salvation. If we are in danger of becoming blasé about Christmas, we may run the risk of becoming complacent also about the miracle of the Spirit's work, perhaps for similar reasons. We know the story too well, and have stopped pondering it in our hearts.

'Pondering' is a powerful word in the original. It isn't just puzzled musing or focused daydreaming. It speaks of bringing together, or even throwing together, a collection of people, ideas or objects, and seeing what happens. Like the sages and visionaries of old, Mary guarded great and terrible secrets in her heart, turning them this way and that, letting them knock sparks off each other. God and the farmhands. Angels and straw. Grace and blood. Journeys and lodgings and babies and prayers. In and through them all, for her and for us, there weaves the story of God's unexpected love and power, setting the whole to a music at once strange, wild and redemptive, a Magnificat that now heralds each new birth, each Spirit-led baby-cry, each new personal Christmas.

The Second Sunday of Christmas

—— ≈ ——

Jeremiah 31.7–14
Ephesians 1.3–14
John 1.[1–9] 10–18

'He gave them the right to become children of God,' says John. 'I have become a father to Israel,' says God to Jeremiah, 'and Ephraim is my firstborn.' 'He destined us for adoption as his children,' says Paul. Exodus-imagery, of course: Israel's status as God's firstborn, announced to Pharaoh as the reason for freeing Israel from slavery, will be reaffirmed through covenant renewal (Jeremiah), and has been so reaffirmed in Jesus (John and Paul).

These writers are not primarily concerned about status. They are celebrating actual knowledge of God: first-hand, intimate, astonishing knowledge that swept them off their feet and left them unable to keep silent. Jeremiah had witnessed the depth of self-caused suffering of those who turned from the living God to idols; now, in a sustained two-chapter poem, he invites us to gaze at fresh-minted promises springing from sheer grace. Israel has no merit or innate worth to cause the covenant God to replace the judgement of exile with the assurance of new delight. These lavish promises, worth pondering every new day, let alone every new year, let alone every new century, spring from love, and love alone: not from the will of the flesh, nor from the will of man, but from God.

Jeremiah's words are flesh-words: words of singing, of

exiles returning home, of shepherds with flocks, of grain and wine and oil. Eden will come again; young and old will celebrate together. Nor should we write the flesh-dimension out of the celebration when we turn to Ephesians. The 'inheritance' has been transformed from a single country to the whole world (compare Romans 8). But the entire paean of praise (verses 3–14 are a single sentence in the Greek) remains earthed – the metaphor is appropriate – in the Jewish tradition, with its unreserved celebration of God's goodness in creation.

The blessings are called 'spiritual', and we already have them 'in the heavenly places', but that is simply their present mode and location. Everything in heaven and earth is being summed up in the Messiah (v. 10), himself the truly human one, to whom, as in creation's original intention, all is now subject (vv. 20–23). God's eventual design is for a single heaven/earth reality; Jeremiah will recognize in it the things he was talking about. And in Christ, once more, all is given as a gift of grace, not accomplished by the will of the flesh, nor by the will of man, but by God.

The kaleidoscope of grace thus reveals ever-new glimpses of a glory in which the delights of creation are caught up within the larger purposes of God. This God, known and experienced now as the Father-God, the Exodus-God, is discovered – and if we aren't regularly surprised by this something has gone wrong – in his perfect image, the flesh-word, God the Only Son. Grace upon grace. Re-set the calendar by that basic principle, and who knows what might follow?

Epiphany

The First Sunday of Epiphany

—— ❧ ——

Genesis 1.1–5
Acts 19.1–7
Mark 1.4–11

Wind and water. Light and dark. Heaven and earth. The beginning.

There is a quiet joy about the opening of Genesis. Quiet, not because it's only slightly exciting, but because we know at once that these are the soft opening notes of a theme that will grow and swell, rise and develop, until the whole orchestra has joined in with wild, exuberant harmony and counterpoint. Even that will only be the completion of the beginning. God saw that it was good. But there is more.

The wind of God sweeps over the waters. Difficult to know how much to hear in that phrase. 'Wind' is the same Hebrew word as 'spirit', or even 'Spirit'; there is a good deal to be said for thinking that the writer, editor(s) and transmitters of Genesis 1 would not have made the finicky post-Enlightenment distinctions that we do. A full range of meaning is available, from 'a mighty wind' through to 'God's Spirit'. The wind blows where it wills, and we don't know its origin or destination; so it often is with meaning. Best to spread sail and be carried along.

Not for nothing do we find John the Baptist in the Johannine prologue, up there along with light and life, part of the new Genesis. As Mark makes clear, John's baptism is a signal of new creation: he appears as a prophet, a sign of renewal and restoration, both in his garb, his diet, his location, his message and his very person. Forgiveness of sins was not just what everyone knew they needed personally; it was what Israel needed, because unforgiven sin was directly correlated in the corporate consciousness with the present parlous state of Israel's national fortunes. The meaning of a royal pardon is not simply that the prisoner enjoys a good feeling of innocence restored, but that he gets out of jail.

Scarcely surprising that we find disciples of John in Turkey 25 years later. His message had spread far and wide. But you can't stop with John. Just as Genesis moves forward, so does the story of which John knows himself to be a part. He prepares the water and invokes the Spirit, through which will come the judgement which is also mercy, the new Day which will show up the Night as 'darkness'. (Notice how God saw that the light was good, and separated it from the darkness; think what that might have meant to a first-century Jew.) Then it happens. A figure emerges from the water. Heaven and earth are suddenly present to each other. Wind becomes Spirit, Spirit becomes dove; every section of the orchestra takes up the theme, and over it all is heard a solo voice. My son. My beloved. My delight.

God saw that it was good. What does he see now, at the start of a new year? Where are the signs of new creation? Where are the dark, formless voids that still await the rushing mighty wind?

The Second Sunday of Epiphany

—— ⁓ ——

1 Samuel 3.1–10 [11–20]
Revelation 5.1–10
John 1.43–51

The word of the Lord was rare in Eli's day. The scroll remained sealed until the Lamb appeared. Nathanael sat under his fig tree, unknown, undisturbed. Not because God couldn't speak or didn't care, but because his foolishness is wiser, as always, than human wisdom. A voice in the night at Shiloh. A man from Nazareth, the town from which no good comes. A Lamb that had been slain. The strange stamp of authenticity.

Eli, old, blind and no longer in control, still recognizes the source and the method, even though the new word brings judgement on his family. 'It is YHWH; let him do what seems good to him.' The previous chapter chronicles the disobedience of his sons, the growth of Samuel, and the earlier warnings. Now the scene is set for the new thing Israel's God will do, and it will begin with the word, initially misunderstood but finally unmistakable: a gentle repeated call, demanding that Samuel first listen and then speak. That rhythm of costly obedience, learnt in a night and sustained through a lifetime, sets a pattern for prophetic ministry then and now. Where are today's Samuels? Have they the courage to tell Eli what they have heard?

From the shrine at Shiloh to the heavenly court. John the Seer, like a Hebrew prophet of old, stands as an onlooker in

20

the divine council. He is called to report back to his fellow-mortals what he has seen. Within that, he is called to long for God's purposes to come to pass and to grieve if they appear thwarted. But then the Lamb is given the right, because of his redeeming death, to open the seven-sealed scroll. He has created a new people, destined to be priest-kings in God's coming kingdom. God's will shall be done, on earth as in heaven.

This vision of 'heaven' is not a forward glance to a final non-earthly destiny. It is a glimpse of the *present* time in God's dimension of reality; and in that present time God's plans for the future are stored up, waiting to be unrolled. God's kingdom will come, through the victory of the Lamb, 'on earth' (v. 10), not just in heaven. The rest of the book, not least its climax in chapters 21—2, will confirm this.

Fresh revelation, for which the Church should pray and wait and pore over scripture, is a matter of a window opening, a bridge being created, between the heavenly and earthly dimensions. Jesus' banter with Nathanael, each seeming to test the other out but with Jesus retaining the initiative, suddenly gives way to a promise of just such prophetic vision. Jacob's ladder, joining heaven and earth, is replaced by the Son of Man himself, not only a Messianic figure (v. 51 confirming vv. 45 and 49) but the one through whom the heavenly throne-room is glimpsed, the divine purpose is accomplished. The Word of God comes again, calling the world to fresh allegiance.

The Third Sunday of Epiphany

—— ∼ ——

Genesis 14.17–20
Revelation 19.6–10
John 2.1–11

Considering how many symbolic themes John has woven together here, it is remarkable that the story remains clear and powerful. Like a great Shakespearean speech, it simultaneously drives us forward and urges us to pause and ponder.

Strike each of these bells, and see what echoes are set off. The third day. A wedding. More wine needed. Purification-pots. Glory revealed.

Weddings spoke of God's coming kingdom, as they still do in Jesus' parables and in the closing chapters of Revelation. Wine recalls the salvation-feast in Isaiah 25, as well as the strange refreshment Melchizedek offered Abram. Jesus' 'hour' has not yet come, but with this action the clock moves forward another minute. Water tells of life, the Spirit, new birth. Within the Jewish purification-rites, and without Messianic intervention, water is available but not lifegiving; salvation is of the Jews, but for the world. The last-minute new wine speaks of new creation, coming at last through the Word made flesh. And so on. In this story at least, when the reader discovers allegorical significance the chances are the author intended it.

John's summary points on to the final disclosure of glory. This is the first sign; more will follow, in a sequential crescendo. As a good writer, John reminds us of this only once (4.54). When we reach 12.37 we realize we should have been counting; with 13.1 the hour has struck; and by 20.30 we understand that the last signs, the final unveiling of glory, have occurred in Calvary and Easter. Only then do we fully grasp what was going on at Cana in Galilee.

Only then, for instance, do we see the full picture of Jesus and his mother. She longs for him to be the Messiah she had imagined; as here, he both is and isn't. He fulfils Israel's hopes, but in a new way. Think of her in this story (as the beloved disciple must have thought of her) as the woman who will stand, still uncomprehending, at the foot of the cross: Lady, what have you to do with me? Why put me on the spot? What did you expect? She has both understood and misunderstood. She must travel the long road, and wait in darkness for the hour to strike.

Like the wedding itself, she becomes a symbol, rushing to Jesus wanting instant solutions. The answer may be given, and will point on to more yet to come; but Jesus is not there at our beck and call to smooth over social embarrassments, to make water into wine as required, or to square inconvenient circles. He is there to reveal God's glory. Like Mary, we must learn where, and how, that will take place.

And, like the servants, we must obey even when the order seems bizarre or even plain daft. Fancy risking your job, and the steward's anger, by serving purification-water on the say-so of a stranger. Fancy disobeying and missing the glory.

The Fourth Sunday of Epiphany

—— ≈ ——

Deuteronomy 18.15–20
Revelation 12.1–5a
Mark 1.21–28

Authority, so problematic for us, is central to the biblical message. The Kingdom of God is not a democracy, as a character in *Chariots of Fire* pointed out. When the Israelites banded together to decide things their own way, they voted either to go back to Egypt or to make a golden calf. Almost the only time the apostles acted unanimously was when 'they all forsook him and fled'. God's redemptive word of authority, calling us to order, breaks through the noise of humans stampeding in the wrong direction. Admitting this means swallowing pride. Refusing to recognize it means conniving at self-destruction. Lemmings all go together when they go.

And yet. We learnt long ago that power corrupts; we learnt more recently that all authority is to be distrusted. Humanly speaking these are important lessons. Yet one can no more live on suspicion than one can eat a Marxist tract. Without trust breaking through afresh we condemn ourselves to bleak, cynical lives. Trustworthy authority appears, as a strange gift from God, so that we may find the way forward out of our self-imposed prison.

Of course, the costs of freedom sometimes make us shrink back. Notice how the destructive, dehumanizing 'unclean spirit' shrieks out its accusation that it is the one being destroyed. Truth is an early victim in spiritual warfare, as

24

in other kinds. The new teaching, 'with authority' (as Jesus' onlookers remark with surprise), comes to cut through the shroud of lies, to announce the presence of the living, life-giving God, the only one in whose name a true prophet will speak, and to declare the victory of this God over the ancient dragon.

Turn this scenario into lurid apocalyptic dream-language, and you have Revelation 12 in a nutshell (though why one should break the paragraph before verse 6 is a mystery). Many cultures told tales of a young prince, born to destroy the old tyrant, spirited away until the final battle lest the tyrant strike first. First-century Rome told a story (not least through images on coins, the main mass medium of that society) of the resplendent goddess Roma giving birth to the young emperor who would rule the whole world, defeating all rivals. The early Christians adapted the first of these, and showed up the second as a ghastly parody of the truth.

In the Christian story, replete with biblical echoes (e.g. of Psalm 2.9), the old tyrant is the satan, the accuser. Rome becomes the agent of evil, not the redeemer. And Jesus, born from within the messianic community, is destined to overthrow not only all arrogant human authority but all destructive spiritual forces as well.

True authority is thus the liberating rule of the woman's child. The idea that all authority is suspect turns out to be the last great lie of the jailer. But if valid authority is revealed in Jesus, its shape and goal are very different from what we have come to expect.

Ordinary Time

Proper 1

— ∾ —

Isaiah 40.21–31
1 Corinthians 9.16–23
Mark 1.29–39

Nobody in Corinth had seen it before. Nobody had *thought* of it. It wasn't on their mental map, any more than it is in our world. So when Paul wanted to tell them that as Christians, working out how to live in a pagan environment, they might face times when they should voluntarily forgo something to which they had a complete right – an intricate but vital principle – the only example he could give of what this might look like was his own.

Hence this bit of autobiography, providing a fascinating glimpse of both Paul's practice and his theory. The underlying point (chapters 8, 10) concerns food offered to idols. Christians, believing in the creator God, are free to eat whatever is sold in the market. But because they believe in this God through the crucified Jesus, their freedom is further defined by the gospel's confrontation with evil, and by the conscience of fellow-believers. They must not give offence.

The equivalent point in Paul's regular practice is poignant in context: he has refrained from charging the Corinthians financially for his services as an apostle. He claims the right to such support, but voluntarily does without it, in order to spread the gospel as widely as possible. The same rule has governed his behaviour when faced with different groups in society: he will voluntarily submit to their social customs while among them, not because his own salvation depends upon it but because theirs may. Those who today take the gospel into fresh territory, geographical or social, will need to work out the equivalent in each case.

They may also need to think out answers to the inevitable charge of inconsistency. Being loyal to the gospel seems to mean being prepared to appear disloyal from time to time to what seem to others like principles. Distinguishing this position in turn from currently fashionable relativism may be one of the great moral challenges of our time.

The flurry of activity on a single busy Sabbath in Capernaum no doubt raised similar questions both for the townspeople and for Jesus' initial disciples. What was going on? Where would it lead? Was Capernaum now to be the centre of a new movement of healing and teaching? Everybody was looking for Jesus; a few more days, and the whole town would have been on his side. But he had to move on. Other places needed to hear. The gospel took precedence over human success and even human stability. Another hard lesson, now as then.

Underneath the hard lessons we find the unshakeable trust of both Jesus and Paul in the purposes of the one true God. Human traditions and structures were as nothing compared to the sovereignty and supremacy of this God. Isaiah's majestic vision of God, dwarfing both the stars of the heavens and the princes of the earth, remains an excellent starting-point for living in God's presence, and for pondering what the gospel demands of, and assures to, those who announce it.

Proper 2

—— ∿ ——

2 Kings 5.1–14
1 Corinthians 9.24–27
Mark 1.40–45

Naaman's wife's maid knew more about Elisha's healing powers than the king of Israel. All the king could do was tear his clothes and rage against his Syrian counterpart, suspecting that a request for healing was a disguised excuse for renewed hostility in their already long-running, and still continuing, border disputes. In such a setting, a concession or a friendly request or gesture is instantly regarded with suspicion. As we know, three thousand years of tussling over territory is not easily forgotten.

Could Naaman's own story – including the verses after our passage ends – indicate ways forward? He, too, one of the great ones in that little world, has to learn from his servants what he could not see for himself: that the humiliation which leads to health is better than the pride which leaves you a leper. The rivers of Damascus were indeed greater than the muddy stream of Jordan, but they had never parted to let God's people through to the promised land. They could not serve as symbols of new life.

Naaman's conclusion is striking, now as then: there is no God in all the earth except in Israel (v. 15). No other god does this sort of thing. But if the outsider Naaman can be welcomed and healed, the insider Gehazi, who behaves like a shameless pagan, is thrust out. Humiliation and pride

30

know no boundaries; judgement, like mercy, is applied even-handedly by the one true God. Those who grasp all they can will find that it chokes them. Those who humble themselves will find healing. The self-control of which Paul speaks is required in full measure at this point, both in personal and communal life.

Mark's description of Jesus' confrontation with a leper is puzzling, particularly v. 43. Some translations soften it, but it looks as though Jesus is overcome with fierce emotion. Has the leper taunted him, challenging him with a harder act of healing than his previous ones (perhaps ruled out by v. 41)? Is it that Jesus suspects the leper is deliberately approaching him as if he were a king (he kneels to him, v. 40)? Is it because such a healing will now let the cat out of the bag, inviting attention on a scale Jesus had not wanted, or not this soon? Or is Jesus, perhaps, anxious that his followers, Gehazi-like, will try to turn his strange powers into a get-rich-quick stunt?

In any case, Jesus is determined to provide multi-dimensional healing. A leper could only be reintegrated into the community if given a clean bill of health by the local priest, not if he simply claimed to have been cured by a wandering preacher. But the ex-leper has no inhibitions: he tells people everywhere what has happened to him. Mark's strange story moves on, with the Galilean villagers discovering more of God's healing and grace than Herod, up the road in his palace, had ever dreamed of. Some things don't change.

Proper 3

—— ❦ ——

Isaiah 43.18–25
2 Corinthians 1.18–22
Mark 2.1–12

Forgiveness is always shocking, even when it's God who's doing it. Indeed, that's often the worst: in a paradox whose only solution is the depth of human pride, we shrink from the undeserved, and hence humbling, grace and love of God. We remain paralysed, locked within the cycles of our own folly.

Watch how it works. 'Look at my new creation!' says God, 'Look at the oases appearing in the desert!' 'How boring', say God's people, not even troubling to pray, let alone offer sacrifice; 'how pointless it all is.' We sometimes think of people battering heaven with cries for forgiveness, pleading with God to hear and be gracious. Isaiah's picture is of God battering earth with offers of forgiveness, pleading with his people to accept what is lavishly offered.

This gives extra depth to the story of Jesus' ruined roof. I assume, by the way, that the house whose roof was torn up for the paralysed man to be let down was Jesus' own: Mark says 'it was reported that he was at home', and it looks as though he had no chance to move anywhere else before the crowds pressed in. Thus, at the first level, Jesus' offer of forgiveness may have carried a wryly humorous meaning: 'Don't worry about the roof; your sins are forgiven!' But something in the tone of voice, perhaps, alerted hearers to the second level of meaning, the one regularly noticed. Jesus was

32

aware that the man's problem was more than physical, and that to address the deeper level, of unresolved guilt and the crippling self-hatred that accrues from it, would be the way to address the obvious symptoms too.

What Isaiah's passage adds to the picture is the possibility that the bystanders' anger at Jesus' offer of forgiveness, though expressed in terms of theological orthodoxy, may itself have been an outward symptom of a deeper problem. Granted that humans in general, and even God's own people, find divine forgiveness so shocking, is it any wonder that it comes as an affront to find forgiveness standing there in human form, reaching out a hand, speaking words that functioned at several levels simultaneously? Is it not actually offensive that all God's promises find their 'Yes' in Jesus? Would we not find it easier to cope if things were more oblique?

The Corinthians were ready with their accusations, too. Paul, they say, is just muddling along, can't make up his mind whether he's coming or going. But (as the succeeding passage makes clear) Paul has had one consistent motive throughout: the love of the apostle for a wayward community, and the constant desire to let that love work appropriately in relation to a changing situation. It is the Corinthians that have vacillated in their allegiance to him, not he in his care for them. Jesus Christ, himself misunderstood precisely when freely offering love, stands at the heart of the unscrambling of the tangled relationship, facilitating God's work of establishing, anointing, sealing and promising.

The Second Sunday Before Lent

—— ⟨∼⟩ ——

Proverbs 8.1, 22–31
Colossians 1.15–20
John 1.1–14

Eyebrows will be raised at the reappearance of John's prologue so soon after Christmas. But our surprise at the lectionary's turns and twists is nothing to that launched upon
the world by John's famous first 14 verses (better, his first 17
verses). Put them alongside Colossians 1, and you have some
of the most explosive new thinking the Jewish traditions ever
produced.

Let's be clear: this apparent novelty emerged within
Judaism. It was not an alien import. Speaking of Jesus as
the unique personal revelation of the one true God, as the one
through whom the Creator made all things, was at one level a
shock. Yet, both Colossians and John insist, it might have
been guessed all along.

They both go back to Genesis: 'In the beginning, God
created ... and made humans in his own image'. Jesus is the
truly human one because he is himself the Image. But they
also have Proverbs 8 in mind. Wisdom was YHWH's handmaid, his personal agent, in the creation of the world, the one
through whom all things were made. YHWH 'possessed' or
'begat' Wisdom before all things; YHWH was never without
Wisdom. Thus, if humans want to reflect God's image in
their daily life, Wisdom is what they need; the down-to-earth
character of Proverbs corresponds precisely to the down-to-

earthness of the incarnation. The attentive reader of Proverbs is one in whom God's word becomes flesh on a daily basis.

Colossians, in particular, exploits the multiple possibilities of Proverbs 8.22 ('YHWH possessed me, the beginning') and Genesis 1.1 ('In the beginning, God created'). The Hebrew word for 'beginning' also means 'sum total', 'head', and 'firstfruits'; the word for 'in' can also mean 'through' and 'for'. The poem exploits these meanings within a simple structure. Christ is the one in, through and for whom creation (vv. 15–16) and redemption (vv. 18b–20) are accomplished; he is the start, the sum total, the head (vv. 17–18a). At one level this is a way of exulting in the wild glory of the incarnation and the hidden depths of God's word. At another, it prepares the ground for the practical teaching to come. Colossians is a true heir of the Jewish Wisdom tradition: celebrating the limitless splendour of God's creative and redemptive character and person, and living with both feet firmly on the ground. If God is precisely the *creator*, what else should we expect?

John has the same picture but within a simple and breathtaking storyline. New creation appears as God's gift within the first creation. The Word becomes flesh to reveal God's redemptive glory where it is desperately needed. The twist in the tale for us must always be: how are these words to become flesh, how is this God to be known at ground level, in today's world and Church? Unless we address that, Lady Wisdom has made her appeal in vain. And if the answer raises a few eyebrows, so be it.

The Sunday Next Before Lent

— ∾ —

2 Kings 2.1–12
2 Corinthians 4.3–6
Mark 9.2–9

Mark sees the Transfiguration as an anticipated fulfilment of the promise in the previous verse ('Some here will not die until they see the kingdom of God come with power'). The thin curtain separating God's dimension from ordinary life is pulled back, and mortals gaze on abiding heavenly realities. The coming of God's kingdom will involve earthly events; but those events will be precisely moments of revelation, unveiling God's power and presence.

Past and future telescope together into a dazzling present. Elijah and Moses (that way round, oddly, in Mark's account, highlighting Elijah as the forerunner and thus Jesus as the Coming One) stand for Prophets and Law, the context within which Jesus' work makes sense. Both had met God on the mountain, Moses in earthquake, wind and fire, Elijah in a still small voice. Which was this more like?

Peter blurts out a garbled suggestion designed to freeze the frame, to stop the moment in its tracks – the same futile instinct that makes us photograph a sunset. Then come the cloud and the voice, a Presence above and beyond that of the great heroes of old. The words confirm what was said at Jesus' baptism, assuring the terrified watchers that Jesus is indeed Messiah, and that his summons to follow must be obeyed.

36

These are the foothills of the event itself, which historians of Jesus often skirt round with embarrassment. It isn't a misplaced resurrection story, as used to be said: in the Easter narratives themselves, Jesus does not shine. It isn't the kind of story that first-century Jews would make up to express, 'mythologically', some aspect of their faith. It belongs, rather, with many accounts ancient and modern of the physical transformation that sometimes accompanies the sudden special and overpowering presence of the always-present God. When that happens, bodies may quiver and faces shine.

Such moments, unbidden and unpredictable, come not for their own sake but in relation to particular tasks. One day, after we had trudged for hours through freezing cloud in the Cairngorms, the clouds rolled back and we saw, for a few seconds, the path we had trodden and the crags that lay ahead. That spine-tingling combination of revelation and vocation was what the early Christians spoke of when, like Paul, they looked into the face of Jesus and there discovered not only the glory of God but also their own calling.

There has never been an easy time to be a Christian. It isn't only our own world that screams at us how futile and silly it is to believe in Jesus, let alone to follow him. Those who walk around in the fog, never glimpsing the sky or the path, claim that both are just wishful thinking, that nobody sees these things clearly anyway. But those who have seen the glory can never be the same again. Like Elisha with Elijah, we will not now leave this man until we have been assured of a share in his spirit.

37

Lent

The First Sunday of Lent

———— ❧ ————

Genesis 9.8–17
1 Peter 3.18–22
Mark 1.9–15

Noah is conspicuously absent from much of the New Testament. When he does appear, as in 1 Peter 3, it isn't immediately obvious why. Who were those 'spirits in prison' from Noah's day? In what sense did Jesus preach to them? How can Noah's ark help us understand baptism (apart from the obvious sense of coming through water to salvation)? And how does all this relate to what Peter is saying?

He is explaining why it is better to suffer for doing right than for doing wrong. Jesus' innocent suffering, as elsewhere in the letter, is the model for that of Christians. And those who, through Jesus' death and resurrection, belong to the one true God are assured that, since Jesus is already sovereign over all spiritual and temporal powers, they must not be afraid of what those powers can do to them. Standing before God with a clear conscience (vv. 16, 21), they know that whatever 'flesh' can do to them God's Spirit is stronger. (In v. 18 '*in* the flesh' and '*in* the Spirit' are better rendered 'by': Jesus was killed *by* mere mortals, and raised *by* God's Spirit.) Verses 18 and 22 set the parameters for the dense passage in between.

Christians stand before God on the basis of the fact and meaning of baptism. Coming through the water, with its echoes of the creation narrative, the Noah story, and above all the Exodus, now receives yet more colouring from Jesus' representative dying and rising. Baptism symbolizes passing through tribulations, of which death is the greatest, to stand in the presence of the true sovereign one – as opposed to the petty tyrants who rant and rage against the subversive gospel.

Why Noah, then? Partly because he symbolizes God's grace, saving his people through terrible catastrophe. But also because that catastrophe came about, in the story, not least because of the wicked angels of Genesis 6.2. To them, and their equivalents in the first century, Jesus has already made the decisive proclamation: their rule, based on the power of sin and death, is broken. (This announcement is not, then, the same as that in 4.6, which seems to be to pre-Christian members of God's people.) Victory is won; the temporal and even spiritual powers ranged against the Church are a beaten rabble. The story of Noah is a vivid reminder, through the symbol of baptism, of who the Christian really is, and before whom he or she stands.

If this lesson, and this way of putting it, seem remote to comfortable Western Christians, whose fault is that? We do well to ponder the anguish of fellow Christians for whom tribunals, injustice and innocent suffering are daily realities. As we hear the Gospel story of Jesus' baptism, wilderness testing, and kingdom-announcement, we may ask ourselves, as a conscience-clearing exercise, not only which contemporary Christians are closest to the dominical pattern, but also which principalities and powers have tricked us into compromise and collusion.

41

The Second Sunday of Lent

—— ∕≈∕ ——

Genesis 17.1–7, 15–16
Romans 4.13–25
Mark 8.31–38

Abraham and Peter offer a stark and sobering contrast. Abraham looks at his good-as-dead body and believes God's promise of life. Peter looks at his dreams of being the King's right-hand man and refuses to hear the King speaking of the royal vocation to suffer and die. Example and warning keep us on the Lenten path.

Abraham's faith is the badge, Paul insists, of his whole world-wide family. People still sometimes think that Paul left the Old Testament behind; nothing could be further from the truth. His gospel is all about the way in which Abraham's God has at last kept his promises. He has done so, however, in a startling fashion. Some translations bracket the end of verse 16 and the start of verse 17, but Abraham's being 'the father of many nations' and hence the father of all who believe, from whatever ethnic background, is part of the chapter's main theme and thrust. Part of Paul's point about faith is that it is open to all, not just those who possess the Jewish law as their ancestral code or circumcision as their covenant sign.

Behind this point, as so often in Romans, stands Paul's picture of God, the creator, the covenant-keeper: God gives life to the dead and calls non-existent things into being (v. 17). Even so, Paul seems to be saying, God can revive

42

that Jewish covenant membership that was under sentence of death for its failure to keep the law (v. 15), and can also call as covenant members those who were outside the covenant by birth and inclination – in other words, Gentiles. The covenantal faithfulness of the creator God: that is what is unveiled in the gospel of Jesus.

But how does that gospel relate specifically to Abraham's faith? Here is Paul's master-stroke. Abraham looked at God's promises, recognized that they meant that God would give life where there was none, and believed. The Christian listens to the gospel message that the creator God raised the Messiah from the dead, recognizes that this means God doing what is normally impossible, and believes. Faith here is not so much 'in' this or that event (still less is it 'a general religious attitude to life'), but active and personal trust in the God who characteristically acts in this way.

It was this faith that Peter sadly lacked, looking at things from a human point of view, not God's. He could not see that the way to life was the way of the cross. He was, like the rest of them, looking for Israel's redemption. But he had not yet penetrated to the secret at the heart of Israel's vocation: that Israel's God, the world's creator, took delight in acting in this topsy-turvy fashion, precisely to redeem a topsy-turvy world – and called his followers to do the same. To be ashamed of this God, to refuse this path, is not just cowardice. It is to miss the point altogether.

The Third Sunday of Lent

―― ᘓ ――

Exodus 20.1–17
1 Corinthians 1.18–25
John 2.13–22

Jewish jokes testify to the terror of the Ten Words from Sinai.
Headache? Do what Moses did: take two tablets. Moses to
the people: we've got them down from twenty to ten, but
adultery is still in. Moses to God: How much do these tablets
cost? God: They're free. Moses: Fine, I'll have two.

Irreverent? No; rather the reflex of reverence, the nervous
need for safe space between us and God. The Commandments are spoken, not intimately to Moses, but in thunder
and trumpet, audible for miles around. People who advocate
getting back to the Commandments (not that they normally
want a prohibition of all images, or a seventh-day sabbath)
don't usually envisage the earthquake, wind and fire of Sinai.

The Ten Words were God's way of life for God's redeemed people, the covenant charter between YHWH and
Israel. The two tablets most likely each contained all the
commandments: one complete document for each party. So
why did Moses retain both? Because, as Exodus continues,
God also commanded appropriate provision for his own
presence to accompany the people. Only when we grasp
Israel's dread before the mountain will we understand
why the tabernacle, too, was threatening. And why, when
Moses delayed on the mountain, a darker perversion of
reverence came into play: the creation of safer, less demand-

ing gods, cheap parodies of the God whose only appropriate image is loving, breathing human life.

Law and tabernacle were not themselves images of God. They were signposts, pointing to the God who speaks, who is mysteriously present, who has redeemed and will now guide. This utter demand, and dread presence, are the hallmarks, too, of the gospel Paul preached: the message of the crucified Messiah, the redeeming yet all-demanding message of the God who had come as a living, loving, self-giving human being and had embodied that strange presence to the uttermost.

Human fear invents jokes, human wisdom invents systems, to keep this God at bay. The message of Calvary pierces through, working its healing yet wounding way from the heart of the living God to the heart of human need. The Lenten journey to the foot of that other terrible mountain must renounce the signs, the wisdom, the idolatry and perhaps even the humour that domesticate what we find there. Otherwise (God forgive us) we will first trivialize the truth and then denounce it for its triviality.

If Jesus embodies yet transcends the deepest meaning of the law – God's truly human way of life – he also embodies and transcends the tabernacle and its successor, the Temple. His outburst against its abuse, and his coded message about destruction and rebuilding, are the reactions of truth to parody. They form for us a final challenge: whatever downgrades or domesticates the full revelation of the living God must be set aside. Nothing and no one but the crucified and risen Jesus, terrible as Sinai, mysterious as the tabernacle, must be both our goal and our guide through the wilderness.

The Fourth Sunday of Lent

— ⁀ —

Numbers 21.4–9
Ephesians 2.1–10
John 3.14–21

The serpent slithers its way through myth and legend, poetry and art. Too potent a symbol to be ignored, some cultures have worshipped it, while others have feared and loathed it. Freud said predictable things about it, echoed in D. H. Lawrence's famous poem and in numerous pop-psychology theories about getting in touch with our darker sides.

To the surprise of some brought up on Numbers 21 and John 3, where the bronze serpent on the pole foreshadows Jesus on the cross, the image of a snake twined around a staff had long been a symbol of healing, perhaps of the healing god himself, in (for instance) the cult of Asclepius. And the serpent who makes his first entrance in the third chapter of the Bible remains at least a background figure until he receives his final doom in the third chapter from the end. The serpent embodies or reflects human beliefs about our deep disease and its ultimate cure.

Jewish and Christian traditions frame this symbol within their historical stories of creation and redemption. Mark's extra ending envisages Christians handling snakes. In Acts, Paul survives a deadly snakebite. Mary, in some icons, tramples on the serpent; in some paintings she teaches the boy Jesus to do so. Here Moses' bronze serpent shines a startling light on the cross.

The serpent is hardly an image of Jesus, despite the surface parallel. That which was poisoning the people is displayed as a beaten foe, just as for John evil itself is judged, condemned and defeated on the cross. The Lenten gaze on the ugly gallows at the crossroads of history is the look that brings life.

Redemption is, after all, not a matter of taming or befriending the serpent, but of defeating it and of creation thereby emerging into light out of old darkness. The strange divine love, of which the too-famous John 3.16 speaks, is not the laissez-faire tolerance that accepts everything and everybody the way they are. It is the potent and tenacious transforming energy that deals with the darkness, that defeats the rulers of the world, that banishes the serpent at last, and creates – not a new garden, with a reptile house to keep the serpent alive but harmless! – but the city of God where all is light, and where, as on certain islands that pride themselves on the fact, serpents are banished for good.

The Christian gospel, classically stated in Ephesians 2, speaks not of Yin and Yang, but of sin and forgiveness, of evil power and victorious divine mercy, of the passions of the flesh and the new bodily life in Christ. This is not dualistic. There is such a thing as Evil, and it is not the necessary other side of Good. There is such a thing as mercy, and mercy does not relabel or redescribe 'evil' as 'good'. I do not know, and I do not think anybody knows, why there was a serpent in the garden; but that there will be none in the city I have no doubt.

The Fifth Sunday of Lent
(Passiontide begins)

—— ∼ ——

Jeremiah 31.31–34
Hebrews 5.5–10
John 12.20–33

Imagine the simple request echoing along the corridors of church bureaucracy. It is passed from office to office, from secretary to secretary. It is left on voice-mails and e-mails, faxed through to headquarters, scribbled in shorthand for later typed memos. They phone the biblical studies departments, but they are busy with the Christology of Q and the pseudonymity of Ephesians. They call the history departments, but they have stopped talking about people and events and now explore the social construction of fictive narratival worlds. And the Greeks at the feast, then and now, wait patiently with their request: Sir, we wish to see Jesus.

Is there anyone else to see, anything else to ask for? So simple a question as to be touchingly naive (like the Salvation Army lassie asking the bishop if he's saved), or possibly cloyingly manipulative: in synods, when somebody says people should stop listening to each other and start listening to Jesus, it usually turns out that on this question Jesus and the speaker happen to agree. But that doesn't mean we shouldn't be stopped in our tracks, in the middle of Lent of all times, and confronted with the question: what about

Jesus? Can we please get to see him? Here's a bracing pre-Holy Week question, for individuals and church structures: to what extent does what we do contribute to an answer?

Having said all that, we note that John does not have Jesus hurrying off to meet these enquiring foreigners. Instead, he regards their question as a further sign that the hour is coming at which, through his apparently tragic death, he will bear much fruit. Through his 'lifting up' he will draw all people to himself. The rulers of the world, human and super-human, are to be put down. People of all sorts are to come and worship the true king.

The request to see Jesus may of course be expressed in-articulately or obliquely. We have to learn to hear it within the symbols of a culture as well as in face-to-face questions. But only when we are answering the request, paradoxically, can we see the relevance of Hebrews's exploration of Jesus as the great High Priest, which initially seems hardly the place to start a simple answer. By bringing together Psalms 2 and 110 (both common early christological texts) the author portrays Jesus as that strange double combination, a king who is also a priest, the unique Son of God who suffered, wept and died as a fully human being.

Find ways of saying that without technical language: explore ways of talking about politics and religion which converge on Jesus, discover language about divinity and humanity which, instead of competing, complement each other at the point of Jesus; and you will be well on the way to showing Jesus to the Greeks at today's feast. 'They shall all know me,' says God through Jeremiah, promising covenant renewal. If that's true, why can't we answer the question?

Palm Sunday
(Liturgy of the Passion)

—— ❦ ——

Isaiah 50.4–9a
Philippians 2.5–11
Mark 14.1—15.47

'In spite of that, we call this Friday good.' They didn't at the time, but Jesus' surprised friends, and some very surprised enemies, quickly found themselves telling the horrid and brutal tale as the story of God's unthinkable salvation.

Within three decades Paul condensed into 36 Greek words what it would take Mark 119 verses to narrate. 'In God's form, but not thinking to exploit equality with God, he emptied himself, taking a servant's form, born in human likeness; found in human form, humble and obedient unto death, the death of the cross.' Hidden there are five lenses through which to view the story, and Paul puts two more at the head. One for each day of Holy Week, perhaps.

First, Jesus' own human story. The leader weeping alone in the garden. The truth-teller mocked as a false prophet. The peace-bringer arraigned as a rebel. The God-forsaken man of God. Saving meaning is not superimposed upon this human story, but discovered within it.

Second, the story of Adam, primal humanity, all-of-us in mythic perspective. Humans in God's image, snatching at equality with God, becoming servants of sin and death. The human story of arrogance, greed and tragic consequences.

50

Inside Mark's story, listen to the cry of crippled human-kind.

Third, the story of Israel, the Lord's servant. Israel enslaved in Egypt, burdened and groaning. Israel exiled, songless in a strange land. Israel persecuted, mocked by the nations, polluted, overrun, ruled by traitors and oppressors, clinging to God's promise of vindication even as the back is beaten and the beard pulled out. The redeeming people themselves in need of servant-redemption. Read Mark as the story of Israel's vocation uniquely fulfilled.

Fourth, the Emperor. Caesar (so said Roman flattery) was equal to God, had been a servant of the state, and was now exalted. Paul and Mark alike point to the strange enthronement of the world's true monarch – and, thereby, to the redefinition of monarchy itself.

Fifth, God's own story. Consider at every step along this verbal Via Dolorosa: this figure is the incarnate one. Forget the shallow idea that he stopped being God in order to become human, to suffer and die. The gospel message is precisely that this beaten, broken and bedraggled creature ('some of you', as the newsreaders say, 'may find this picture distressing' – and there's something wrong if we don't) was indeed God's Son, the living presence of the God we thought we knew but perhaps didn't, or not well enough.

Enough there already, you may think. But Paul adds: this is the way you should think among yourselves. Identify by all means with the minor characters in the story, but identify, corporately, with Christ himself. The suffering Church follows in the steps of the Master.

And finally, of course, we are each to walk this way alone. Mark 14 and 15 stand under the rubric of Mark 8.34, where the subject is singular: to follow, take up the cross.

Easter

Easter Day

—— ❧ ——

Isaiah 25.6–9
1 Corinthians 15.1–11
John 20.1–18

This Gospel reading is not, as one writer has suggested, 'a sanitized story about a trip to a garden and a lovely surprise'. If Easter is in any sense the happy ending after a sad story, that is the least important thing about it. It is not primarily an ending, but a beginning. It is the start of God's new creation.

Line up John 20 alongside John's prologue (1.1–18). The themes come full circle: light and darkness, new life 'in' the Word, the right of Jesus' followers to become children of God (in v. 17, for the first time, Jesus calls God '*your* Father ... and *your* God'). The later scene with Thomas echoes 1.18: the Son has unveiled the invisible God. John 1 echoes Genesis 1; in John 20, God's new day has dawned. Twice John reminds us that it is the first day of the week.

Of all the passages which strike me as eyewitness testimony from the shadowy figure we call 'the beloved disciple', verse 8 is among the strongest. This 'other disciple', who had reached the tomb first but had paused and allowed Peter to go in ahead, went in, 'and he saw – *and believed*'. Simple words with limitless depth.

This is a moment of great intimacy and power. As many find when they hear this story, the previously unthinkable dawns, not as the logical conclusion of an argument, nor as a scientific proof, but as a sudden but lasting warmth of heart and mind, an assurance in whose light the rest of the world makes a different and more powerful sort of sense. Don't be fooled by the way people talk of 'belief' as a lesser kind of 'knowledge' ('Is it raining?' 'I believe so' – in other words, I don't know for sure); when John says 'he saw and believed' he is talking at the level of world-view, speaking of rock-bottom convictions that create the context within which knowledge itself can spring to new life.

This new sort of believing is hardly, then, the recognition that Jesus had simply 'gone to heaven' – as one frequently hears people say, both outside the Church and inside. As Paul emphasized, quoting the earliest known confession of Christian faith, this was an event that happened at a specific time after the crucifixion (if Jesus had 'gone to heaven when he died', why would anyone suppose it had taken place 'on the third day'?).

Jews like John and Paul believed firmly that the souls of God's people were in God's hand against the day when, in the future, God would raise them all to new life. If all Easter had done was to reaffirm that belief, there would have been no news, no new creation, no reason to break into a trot, let alone a breathless chase (people hardly ever run in the Gospels; on Easter morning they do little else). Isaiah spoke of death being abolished. Beware of speaking, instead, of its being merely redescribed.

The Second Sunday of Easter

—— ∽ ——

Acts 4.32–35
1 John 1.1—2.2
John 20.19–31

'Peace be with you', said Jesus. And again, two verses later, 'Peace be with you.' Like a great bell, a single note with multiple overtones, the promise of peace tolls out across the world. Not just an inner peace of heart for every individual who hears and believes. Not just an agenda for peace for a warring world. The old Hebrew word *Shalom* speaks of a quality of life which includes but transcends both: rich and fruitful human living, God's new creation bursting into many-coloured flower.

The peace declaration is flanked with simple but profound actions. Jesus shows the disciples his hands and his side, the marks of the love which had loved them to the uttermost, the signs that the bill had been paid (compare 19.30, where 'It is finished' means, among other things, 'the price is paid'). Easter means, amidst much else, that peace, never other than costly, has truly been purchased on the cross.

As often in John, we move quickly from love's evidence to love's commission. New creation again: Jesus breathes on the disciples, as God breathed on the first human pair, to make them living beings of a new sort, peace-bringers, sin-forgivers. 'As the Father sent me, so I send you': the highest possible ecclesiology, grounded in the highest possible Christ-ology, made effective by the gift of the Spirit. Peace is not so

56

much a state of being, more a power let loose upon the world.

For Thomas, peace comes in person to confront the warring spirits of doubt. Scepticism was not born in the eighteenth century; believing in Jesus' resurrection is not a matter of the ancient world struggling to convince the modern one, but of the creator's power confronting the age-old assumption of all humankind – the potter, you might say, confronting the clay. But if Easter peace brings order to the world's confusion, it also brings glorious confusion to the world's order, opening up undreamed-of possibilities, not so much of random miracles but of new creation in place of decay, new peace in place of war.

The Church perceived very quickly what this might mean. To sell ancestral property and share the proceeds was not a matter of primitive communism. It was a renunciation of one of the central Jewish symbols. It went alongside the rejection of the Temple as the centre, the Torah as the defining charter, and Jewish ethnicity as the necessary qualification, of God's people. Jesus and the Spirit took the place of all, in a new symbolic universe appropriate for the new covenant and the new creation.

Barnabas's sale of a field was as important, symbolically, as Jeremiah's buying of one (Jeremiah 32). It was a sign of that fellowship, that partnership (*koinonia*, another great bell-like word), of which John's first letter speaks, again with disarming and deceptive simplicity. Life, light, fellowship, forgiveness: these, among many others, make up the overtones that give the great bell of *Shalom* its particular note.

The Third Sunday of Easter

—— ≈ ——

Acts 3.12–19
1 John 3.1–7
Luke 24.36–48

The ancient world knew all about ghosts, visions, apparitions, and spooks. Ancient literature has plenty of people being found alive after being supposed dead, plenty of spirits of the dead returning to haunt, spy on, or chat with the living. Jesus' disciples could easily have used such categories to explain their extraordinary experiences of the presence of the risen Jesus.

That they did not is powerful testimony to what actually happened. People sometimes suggest that Luke and John, writing late in the first century (so it is supposed; the evidence for this is not as strong as sometimes imagined), were at pains to make Jesus' resurrection appearances more 'physical' than they had actually been, to combat the view that Jesus wasn't truly human, but only 'seemed' to be (the heresy known as 'Docetism'). Frankly, if that was what Luke was trying to do he made a very botched job of it. For Jesus to be touched, and to eat broiled fish, is one thing. Appearing through locked doors, disappearing after breaking bread at Emmaus, and finally withdrawing into God's heavenly dimension – none of this strikes one as immediately useful in a fight against Docetism.

The real explanation is stranger, and is backed up by evidence of various kinds. The disciples were confronted

58

with a new form of reality, for which they were unprepared, but for which the language of resurrection (not of ghosts, or of mere resuscitations) was available. Jesus, they believed, had gone through death and out the other side into a new mode of life. This was, naturally enough, difficult to describe, but it seems to have involved his physical body being transformed so that it was now inhabiting both our space and God's space.

This new mode of being is regarded, in the New Testament, as both the model for the future of Christians and the source of power for life in the present. There aren't words to describe what we shall be, says John, but when Jesus is revealed we shall be like him. We shall see him as he is; since you become like what you worship, we shall thus be changed into his likeness, into the Easter mode of being. Mind-boggling, of course, but that's the point. Good theology requires good imagination.

Easter humanity, in fact, is genuine humanity, as opposed to humanity distorted and defaced by sin, decay and death. One of the great lies of our time is that abstaining from sin means failure to live a fully human life. Resurrection power comes to us, as it were, from our future, so that we can anticipate the truly human life in the here and now. When John says 'no one who abides in him sins' the tense of the latter verb is continuous: sin, though still a possibility, is not now our continual, habitual situation and state. The power that healed the physical cripple, glorifying the God of Israel in the process, is available to heal moral cripples as well.

The Fourth Sunday of Easter

—— ∼ ——

Acts 4.5–12
1 John 3.16–24
John 10.11–18

The text about the rejected stone has itself become something of a stumbling stone. The point of the quotation from Psalm 118.22 is that, though Jesus appeared to the 'builders' of Judaism (the Chief Priests in particular) to be unusable, God had other ideas. The unique shape that made the stone useless for their building qualified it exactly to be the cornerstone, or keystone, of God's building. One stone and only one of that shape was needed: Jesus is it.

Thus, as the next verse explains, 'there is salvation in no one else'. No other name will do; if it's salvation you want, it's Jesus or nothing. What arrogance, shrieks the relativist. This is Christian imperialism, sniffs the secularist. Many paths up the same mountain, murmurs the sophisticate. This is now becoming a fashionable argument against the bodily resurrection of Jesus: it commits us, people say, to a politically incorrect view of 'other religions'. It means that Christianity possesses a truth that the others do not. Back comes the answer from the early Christians: only one resurrection; only one Jesus.

Now of course 'Christianity' covers not just the opening affirmation but two thousand years of faith and folly, wisdom and wickedness. However, just because the Inquisition happened, just because the Constantinian settlement was ambiguous, that doesn't mean the resurrection wasn't unique, or that there are lots of different paths to salvation. There is such a thing as Christian imperialism, and may God save us from it; but the abuse of truth shouldn't impugn the truth itself.

The entire New Testament speaks of a saving act which stands out from all others. No other name speaks of innocent life laid down for others, generating spontaneous love for the outsider and the needy. One of the reasons Christianity spread in the Roman world was that nobody had ever looked after the sick and friendless with the self-sacrificial love that the Christians showed. This name speaks of love with skin on, then and now.

It speaks, too, not of an abstract religious experience, of a general sense of 'the divine', but of the personal mutual knowing of shepherd and sheep. There are such persons as hired hands who don't care for the sheep; there are such creatures as wolves. When it comes to religion, we do not live in a vacuum, where all explorations are equally safe and successful, and where there are no dangers and pitfalls. It's a jungle out there, and the sheep need a shepherd. No other shepherd lays down his life on behalf of the sheep, and then takes it again.

It was of course politically incorrect – indeed, disastrously foolish – for Peter and the others to say all this before the Jewish authorities. But the healing miracle on a lifelong cripple was undeniable, and they claimed it had come about through the powerful name of the risen Jesus. Healing power and powerful love are the signs which enable the Church to speak the truth about Jesus.

61

The Fifth Sunday of Easter

—— ❧ ——

Acts 8.26–40
1 John 4.7–21
John 15.1–8

If you like evangelism, you'll love Philip's story. A spirit-led meeting with a court official, who happens to be reading Isaiah 53 and asking the right questions. There is time to converse at leisure; there is water for baptism when required and requested.

The Ethiopian eunuch was a gentile God-fearer. He couldn't have been a proselyte; as a eunuch he was disqualified anyway, and since many eunuchs were partially dismembered as well as castrated he couldn't be circumcised. You probably didn't want to know that; some people might read this piece straight after breakfast. But you won't understand the story without it.

This black man (there was, by the way, remarkably little colour prejudice in the ancient world) had been to Jerusalem to worship Israel's God, *and he wouldn't have been allowed to celebrate the festival.* Physically unfit, ritually excluded; all that way and no entrance ticket when he arrived. He could have prayed at a distance, but that was it. And yet Israel's God still so captivates him that he's reading Isaiah on the way home. Was there something in chapter 53 that caught his eye? 'In his humiliation, justice was denied him.' I wonder.

There were two traditions of reading Isaiah 53 at the time.

62

One saw the servant as the Messiah, but the sufferings were what he inflicted on the pagans. The other saw the servant as the righteous martyrs, but they weren't Messiahs. Philip puts them together, and embodies the result, announcing to this black eunuch that in Jesus Israel's God has revealed his universal welcome, and showing him by his own welcome what that servant-love looks like. Suddenly the Ethiopian's physical, social and cultic exclusion is overturned. He is embraced by the God who is revealed in the crucified Jesus, and welcomed gladly by the evangelist who represents his master. And (of course) he goes on his way rejoicing.

Result: a new branch is added to the vine, 'made clean', as Jesus says, 'by the word that has been spoken to you'. The vine was a symbol of Israel, pruned and kept pure by the God-given cult and its symbolic world. But if the crucified and risen Jesus is now the true vine, the new symbols – the empty cross, the empty tomb – speak of a different sort of cleansing, a dealing with sin and death (two of the main pollutants in the Temple system) once and for all, a free welcome of overflowing love for all who hear and receive. New branch, new life, new responsibilities, new power. If the Ethiopian Church is to be believed, the eunuch went home and bore fruit that lasts to this day.

John's letter weaves a Trinitarian pattern in honour of this overflowing divine love. That's how much God loves, he says; and that's how much we should love one another. In the New Testament, 'love' regularly describes not so much how people feel as what they do. What might that look like? Step forward, Philip.

The Sixth Sunday of Easter

—— ❦ ——

Acts 10.44–48
1 John 5.1–6
John 15.9–17

'His commandments are not burdensome.' Hard to take, that, in a world where *all* commandments are burdensome, where anybody telling anyone else what to do – even God telling his creatures what to do – is felt as an imposition, a belittling or patronizing attempt to keep people down.

But John, let alone Jesus, won't let us get away with that. Loving God means keeping his commandments; and the greatest commandment is love. Circular? Maybe, but not viciously so. The upward widening spiral of Christian commitment uproots us from the swampy ground of the romantic movement, where everything that is not generated by our own 'feelings' is somehow 'inauthentic', and replants us in the firm soil of God's conquest of 'the world'. This is where the vine can grow best, and where its branches can bear fruit that will last. This is where prayer to the Father in the name of the Son will surely be answered.

But what does it mean to pray in the name of the Son? Jesus Christ came 'not with water only, but with water and blood'. He was not, that is, simply a human being who had become 'divine' at his baptism, but was the full Son of God, supremely in his death. Even so, those who believe this complete gospel are to be marked not by a super-spirituality which will take them out of the real world, but by a Jesus-spirituality in which moral effort and world-conquest go hand in hand. 'His yoke is easy and his burden light'; yes, but that doesn't mean that yokes and burdens are themselves a bad thing. In that context (read on a little in John 15 and you'll see how relevant it is) specific prayer is neither selfish nor whimsical, but rather the expression of the life of God already flowing through the branches of the vine.

What matters, then, is the Spirit. Not a general religious feeling, or a sense of 'the spiritual' as opposed to 'the material', but the Spirit of Jesus, known by bearing witness to Jesus, recognized, as was the risen Jesus himself, through the marks of world-conquering suffering. The Spirit brings people into a partnership with Jesus, a friendship where commandments are neither arbitrarily imposed nor obeyed without comprehension, but are part of a shared strategy to which all are gladly signed up.

Conquest of the world is not a negative thing, like the Vietnam soldiers who claimed they had 'to destroy the village in order to save it'. It is a conquest of the present structures and power-systems of the world, through which humans are enslaved. In the early Church the most obvious of these was the sky-high wall that separated Jews from Gentiles. But when Peter preached at Cornelius's house, the Gentiles heard the gospel message, and found that, believing it, new languages of praise came naturally. The wall came tumbling down. Water and Spirit testified that the commandment of love was not burdensome.

The Seventh Sunday of Easter
(Sunday after Ascension Day)

— ∾ —

Acts 1.15–17, 21–26
1 John 5.9–13
John 17.6–19

The interesting thing about the choice of Matthias has nothing to do with Matthias himself. Nor is it the striking method of his selection, which if applied today would simplify clergy appointments no end. It is the fact that it was deemed necessary. The Twelve were one short.

Instead of regarding Judas's demise as the beginning of a process of natural wastage – the Twelve did not appoint further successors when, quite soon after this, they began to be killed off – they saw it, on biblical grounds inconveniently omitted by the squeamish lectionary, as constituting a hole needing to be plugged. The symbolism of the twelve tribes had to be maintained for the initial witness to make its point. The prophets had foretold that Israel would be regathered; most of the tribes, after all, had long since disappeared when the northern kingdom was devastated seven hundred years earlier. Even before the covenant-renewing wind and fire of Pentecost, the young Church found its identity in the belief that in Jesus these prophecies had come true.

Much of the New Testament's language about the Church can be seen as filling in this belief. In the Johannine writings this regularly means the combination of two things: the

Church's witness to, but separation from, the world, and the Church's inner or spiritual life, through which the startling claims it makes become true at every level of the person and the community.

The first of these involves a tough balancing act. 'In the world', we say, 'but not of the world', summing up John 17; and yet the smooth little steps by which 'in' turns into 'of' are the dance that comes naturally to our wayward feet. Conversely, when we see the danger, the strides by which 'not of' becomes 'not in' march us towards a dualism which makes nonsense of the incarnation itself, not to mention the ascension of the still-human Jesus. Israel, of course, wrestled with the same problem, oscillating between compromise and hostility. Both sides in today's Church can tell horror stories about the other, reinforcing either position by rejection of its polar opposite.

One might then say that the inner life of the Christian and the Church should steer us along a broad middle way between the two; but the reality is on a different plane, in which the strengths of both extremes are combined. The first letter of John speaks of having God's testimony deep within ourselves, evidenced by the core belief in the fully human Jesus as fully God's son. The high-priestly prayer of Jesus in John 17, whose texture is so rich that we may choke on it unless we chew it slowly, speaks of God's word spoken in Jesus, God's name revealed in Jesus, and God's glory given through Jesus. Together these constitute the disciples in their inner selves, despite their own muddles and mistakes, as God's holy people for God's needy world. Unless they are holy, they will do the world no good.

Day of Pentecost

— ∼ —

Acts 2.1–21
Romans 8.22–27
John 15.26–27; 16.4b–15

It is one of the striking features of the New Testament that Luke, Paul and John, so very different as writers and theologians, sing in rich harmony when it comes to the Spirit.

At the heart of the music is the sense of uncontainable newness. The sneering reaction on the day of Pentecost wasn't too silly: in a sense the disciples *were* filled with new wine, and the old wineskins were showing signs of splitting. Or, in Pauline language, the groaning of all creation was now located within the believers themselves, so that the tension between the old world and the new had become an inner tension within the Christian, longing for the resurrection body which would give appropriate physical expression to the astonishing new energy welling up within.

Or, in Johannine language, the Spirit demonstrates, in a quasi-judicial fashion (it isn't only Paul who uses legal metaphors), that the world is in the wrong. It's in the wrong in its modes of morality (the cardinal sin is not believing in Jesus); in its notion of justice (the world's justice sent Jesus to the cross, but God's justice uses that as the means of Jesus' glorification); and in its eager judgement (it condemned Jesus, but actually his death was the condemnation of 'the ruler of this world'). The Spirit makes God's people sing out of tune with the rebellious and decaying world. Pentecost is, after all, the festival of the giving of the Law on Sinai, 50 days after the Exodus, marking out Israel as God's peculiar people.

But just when we might think that the Spirit was taking us out of the world altogether, making us a cult of flaky fanatics, the same writers make it clear that the Spirit is the agent of creation's renewal and redemption. This is the same Spirit that brooded over creation, that spoke through the prophets. John has Jesus breathe the Spirit into the disciples precisely at the resurrection, the moment when the old world is brought to new life after death. Paul envisages the whole created order as a woman going into the pains of labour, longing for the child to be born in which her destiny as a mother will be fulfilled. Luke, through Peter's fresh reading of Joel, indicates that this new experience will bring about the reconciliation of young and old, slave and free, male and female, heaven and earth.

Too idealistic? Don't settle for less than the ideal vision. But expect, in embracing it, to be called to groan in prayer. It isn't only the individual Christian, but the whole community, that needs the Spirit's help in our weakness. Precisely when we are confronted again, in our communities as well as in our selves, with the pains and problems of our continued un-redeemed existence – that is the time when the Christ-shaped dialogue of Spirit and Father, which is what Christian prayer is all about, can flourish. The harmony of Pentecost depends on precisely this paradox.

Ordinary Time

Trinity Sunday

—— ❧ ——

Isaiah 6.1–8
Romans 8.12–17
John 3.1–17

God's love, Jesus' death, new life in the Spirit. The irreducible minimum Christian story; yet, like Julian of Norwich's small nut, this well rounded little truth contains all that there is.

Trinity Sunday, of course, celebrates not a new truth, something else beyond Pentecost, but rather what you see when the excitement and drama of Pentecost has made its mark and you pause to reflect on it all. Or, if you prefer, Trinity Sunday is where you find yourself when, having been swept off your feet by the rushing mighty wind, you get up, dust yourself down, and survey your new surroundings.

The room where you are now standing is filled with light and warmth. Sunlight streams in from open windows and skylights, bathing every corner in its glow. The room is large but curiously shaped, being long and quite thin, but with lateral extensions either side about two-thirds of the way along. Exploring, you discover that within this shape there is everything you need for a rich and fulfilling human life. And, as you make your way around, you realize something else. The air you are breathing has a different taste – like exchanging the city for the mountains, only more so. It's clearer and fresher, and you feel as though with that stuff in your lungs you could do things you'd only dreamed of up to now.

In the New Testament the Trinity isn't an abstract theory, it's where you live. And, hence, *how* you live; 'fulfilling' means also 'challenging'. Breathing this air, you find yourself not only discovering the otherwise distant or unknowable God as a loving, wise and very present father, but also being called to do something that might otherwise look suicidal. 'Putting to death the deeds of the body' seems a strange way of *avoiding* death, but that's the logic of the new Christ-shaped life: the layout of this room means that certain otherwise apparently desirable activities are ruled out. This, and nowhere else, is where true humanness (otherwise known as 'holiness') flourishes, and the delicious air helps us believe (which we otherwise mightn't) that this is so.

We wish it always felt like this. The layout of the room, though, prevents anyone seeing more than part of it at any one moment. We never have it in our power. 'Born of water and the Spirit': ah, says someone in one corner, then I share this room with all the baptized. No, says another, I share it with those who experience the Spirit the same way I do. Nicodemus would like to have explained the new room in terms of the old, but he couldn't. Isaiah was overcome with guilt, individual and corporate, at seeing the unseeable thrice-holy God. (Repeating an adjective three times is a Hebrew form of superlative; as George MacLeod used to say, 'if you think that's a coincidence, I wish you a very dull life'.) Holiness goes with humility. It is, after all, God's room, not ours.

Proper 4

— ≈ —

1 Samuel 3.1–10
2 Corinthians 4.5–12
Mark 2.23—3.6

Like a cathedral chorister, Samuel has been brought to live and work in the atmosphere of prayer, worship and pilgrimage. Considering the lively human interest, it's surprising this story didn't entice the great classical artists; there is one painting of it, by the seventeenth-century Gerbrand van den Eekhout, in the Ashmolean Museum in Oxford.

As so often in biblical 'call' narratives (Ezekiel 1, Isaiah 6, Revelation 1), there is a darker side; again as usual, the lectionary misses it out. The previous chapter introduced Hophni and Phinehas, the sons of the ageing priest Eli. Eli has been warned about their cynical corruption, but he seems incapable of putting things right. Now God chooses young Samuel, wide-eyed and eager, to declare the word of judgement. When he says 'Speak, your servant is listening,' what follows is enough to make him wish his parents had never brought him in the first place. Samuel has the unenviable task of telling his guardian the news of imminent judgement. His fearless later ministry was rooted in his earliest experiences of hearing, and then speaking, God's word.

You can omit the confrontational material in 1 Samuel if you try hard enough; but you can't do that with Mark, which from the start pits Jesus against powers and authorities, human and spiritual, actual and self-appointed. Mark's framing of these two sabbath-controversies shows what he thinks they're about. They aren't merely instances of 'legalism', with Jesus as the great teacher of a non-legal, or non-ritual, kind of religion. They are all about the new thing that is bursting into the world through his presence and authority, a new thing for which the best precedent was God's new action in and through King David (2.25–6; see 1 Samuel 21.1–9). At the time referred to, David had been already anointed by Samuel. Saul was still king, and David was on the run from him; but he still claimed the right to eat the holy bread, a sign perhaps of his coming kingdom. Jesus now claims the right to put into action his own kingdom-path which would make redundant the customs by which Israel guarded its national life. And, just as one of Saul's servants went and told his master (1 Samuel 21.7; 22.9–10), so the Pharisees got together with the Herodians – hardly their natural allies! – to conspire against Jesus. This incident is one of many in which the shadow of the cross falls across Mark's whole narrative.

Paul's apostolic vocation, like Samuel's prophetic one, was not meant to be comfortable. In fact, he saw his sufferings as part of the point: they were a sign of the message he had to speak. But those in whose hearts God has shone the light of his glory will, like both prophet and apostle, have no hesitation in saying what has to be said. It is not themselves that they speak of, after all, but the King, the Lord.

Proper 5

—— ∼ ——

1 Samuel 8.4–11[12–15]16–20[11.14–15]
2 Corinthians 4.13—5.1
Mark 3.20–35

So: did God want Israel to have a king, or didn't he? The question haunts not only this passage in 1 Samuel but much of the rest of the account of the monarchy, from the ill-fated Saul right down to the exile. Of course, David himself, and then Solomon, are fêted and celebrated (albeit with devastating criticisms). Hezekiah and Josiah are seen, later, as models. But most of the kings lived up to Samuel's warnings, and more so. Verse 18 says it all: *your* king, whom *you* have chosen for yourself. It sounds like God's contemptuous words to Moses in Exodus 32.7.

This story sets up a tension which is only resolved in the person of Jesus, and then only in his royal, messianic death. The people wanted a king because they didn't want God himself to be their king; they wanted someone on to whom they could project their own idolatries and have him legitimate them (8.8). Nevertheless, God gave them a king; and, when he removed him, he raised up a man to whom he would make extraordinary promises, seen in the New Testament as fulfilled in Jesus himself (2 Samuel 7, Psalm 2, etc.; see e.g. Romans 1.3–4; 15.12). The early Christians believed that in Jesus the riddle of 1 Samuel 8.7–9 had been solved. Here at last was a human king who was owed the allegiance proper to the one true God. And he, though the true king, took upon himself the folly and shame of all those who went before, bearing in his own body the pains of a thousand years of misguided monarchy.

The same tension crackles through Mark 3 as Jesus' family think he's mad, his enemies think he's demon-possessed, and Jesus himself responds by redefining his family around himself. Mark 3.31–35 is stark to the point of rudeness. Jesus does not 'belong' to his own human family any more. He will not be seen in terms of them. He is pioneering God's new work, God's restored Israel, and its nucleus is not defined in terms of parentage, brothers and sisters by blood. It is defined in terms of God's will; and Jesus sweepingly assumes that doing God's will means sitting around him and hearing his teaching. This king won't steal people from Israel in order to lord it over them, as Samuel warned. This king will teach them the truth and so set them free.

The tension between the kingdom you can see and the one you can't echoes on in the promise of the resurrection body. Like Samuel's challenge to the Israelites, Paul's challenge to the Corinthians is to trust God for his kingdom, for the 'house' kept ready in heaven against the day when it will be brought on to the stage of history, not to snatch at visible status or power here and now. It might have been clearer if the passage had included verses 2–5 as well.

Proper 6

—— ≈ ——

1 Samuel 15.34—16.13
2 Corinthians 5.6–10[11–13]14–17
Mark 4.26–34

Once again the lectionary cuts Paul off just when he's getting interesting. Next week's passage starts at 6.1; what happened to 5.18–21, one of Paul's greatest summaries of his life and thought? However, the foothills that lead to this stunning mountain-top are themselves full of beauty and interest. Walking by faith, not by sight; appearing before the judgement-seat of Christ; the love of Christ constrains us; if anyone is in Christ, there is a new creation! As the old lady said of *Hamlet*, this passage is 'full of quotations'.

The theme is Paul's vindication of his own ministry, which the Corinthians had challenged, suggesting he was not as smooth or smart an operator as the teachers they now had. Paul doesn't care what they think; he and they must all be judged before the Messiah himself. He is who he is because he has been formed by the Messiah's love (v. 14), a love shown in death, evoking a response of self-giving love coupled with a re-evaluation of oneself and everybody else. Like someone feeling their way around a darkened room and finally, discovering the light, able to see everything clearly at last, so the estimates of other people that humans form in the darkness of prejudice are shown up when the light of the Messiah shines on them (v. 16). Paul had originally regarded even the Messiah in the old, prejudiced way.

Now he was challenging the Corinthians to see everyone, himself included, not by the standards of their prevailing culture but in the light of the Messiah in whom all things had become new.

This up-ending of worldly ways of making judgements finds classic expression in David. Fresh-faced, energetic, ready for anything, he was so much the young shepherd that nobody had thought of summoning him home sooner. Mortals, the Lord reminded Samuel, look at outward appearances, but the Lord himself looks at the heart (16.7). David was good-looking as well, but that wasn't the point. God was searching for 'a man after his own heart' (1 Samuel 13.14). No early Christian could miss the overtones of what happened next. When he was anointed, YHWH's Spirit came upon him in power.

The contrast of outward appearances and God's strange hidden design is of course the subject of several parables, not least those in Mark 4. The seed grows secretly; the man who planted it doesn't know what's happening to it, which is ironic since he does every day what the seed is doing, going to bed and getting up (Mark 4.27). So too with the tiny mustard seed, which one might be tempted to scorn, like the Corinthians with Paul, not realizing what it would do next. Training the eye to look at things with faith and hope is not just a matter of Christian obedience. It is the way to overthrow prejudice and to see God's kingdom in unexpected places and people.

Proper 7

—— ～ ——

1 Samuel 17.[1a, 4–11, 19–23] 32–49
2 Corinthians 6.1–13
Mark 4.35–41

Right from the start in Mark, Jesus is up against it. Tempted by Satan in the wilderness; shrieked at by benighted souls in the synagogue; criticized by the self-appointed religious experts. Now the sea itself, with all its dark and evil mytho-logical overtones, rises up against him. And he is ... asleep. There is as much mystery here as when the Word, through whom all things were created, lay asleep in his mother's arms.

The pattern, though, is familiar. David is anointed by Samuel and empowered by the Spirit, and here in the next chapter he is asking what Saul will give to the man who kills Goliath, and then enlisting to do exactly that. This launches him on a long career of opposition to the present regime, until at last the time comes for which, in the people's eyes, his victory over Goliath had prepared him, and he is anointed again as Israel's true and representative leader.

The evangelists, for whom Jesus' baptism was full of Davidic overtones, saw his subsequent career through that lens. What Mark conveys, in addition, is the sovereign freedom of Jesus in and through it all, sleeping through the storm and, when aroused, rebuking not only the wind and sea but also, because of their lack of faith, the disciples.

The poetical overtones of the storm on the lake (sea-

80

monsters and so on, looking back at least to the crossing of the Red Sea) indicate what's going on, and point forwards to Mark's last scenes. The monsters conspire to send Jesus to sleep once and for all, only to find him waking on the third day and sending them packing. Like most Gospel stories, this one has a double effect: first, the sovereign and unrepeatable action of Jesus himself, like a boulder thrown into water from a great height, and, second, the waves and currents that splash outwards into the life of the Church.

The early Christians, reading Mark, would undoubtedly have thought of the Goliaths that lay in wait for them, challenging them and their God in the name of various kinds of paganism, forcing those anointed with the Spirit into a series of struggles that must often have felt as though they would be fatal. To them this story will have brought home once more the challenge to be faithful despite everything.

Thus, too, Paul's apostolic pilgrimage. Invoking Isaiah's servant-passages, he stands in the line of servant-messengers of God, battered yet still going forwards. The smooth stones he takes from the wadi are his sufferings and the fruits of the Spirit (look at the overlap between 2 Corinthians 6.6 and Galatians 5.22). With these to hand, he has no need of the heavy armour the Corinthians wanted him to wear, the sophisticated skills and tricks of the popular philosophers. The battle has now shifted to the hearts and lives of Christians themselves, and will be won by the weapons of the gospel and nothing else.

Proper 8

—— ❧ ——

2 Samuel 1.1, 17–27
2 Corinthians 8.7–15
Mark 5.21–43

Mark folds one story inside another, like someone tucking a second letter inside a first. (A Markan sandwich, some say; but food is important within the story itself, so let's not confuse the issue.) As in 2 Samuel, a double lament forms the backdrop for the new king to reveal his power.

The main, outer story is well known, but worth pondering. What did it cost Jairus, as a synagogue ruler, to seek Jesus' help? Why are Jesus' Aramaic words, *Talitha cum*, recorded, when almost all his other native speech is not? Why did Jesus tell them not to tell anyone? Is there any other story where the sovereignty and gentleness of Jesus are both on such equal, and integrated, display? When Jesus tells the parents to give their daughter some food, is Mark preparing us for 'You give them something to eat' in the next chapter? If so, so what? And, behind all these, more mysteriously: granted that many children must have died in Jesus' vicinity during his public career, why did he only do anything about it when, here and in Nain (Luke 7), it was brought to his attention?

Inside this story Mark has enfolded the intimate and surprising account of the woman with the 12-year haemorrhages (the years tally, of course, with the girl's age in the outer story). Nowhere else is Jesus' power described in such a physical way, so that when he is touched he can sense the release of healing energy. Nowhere else, perhaps, is it so clear that for him 'faith' could mean simply 'belief that I have the power to heal'. When Peter in Acts tells Cornelius the story of Jesus, this power forms a central part of the tale. It is a sign of God's anointing.

The story holds out comfort to those who cannot, as it were, march up and address Jesus. Enough to creep up behind and touch ... though don't be surprised if you're then gently but firmly brought out into the open. The whole passage invites slow meditation, identifying with one character after another, watching the unfolding scene through their eyes (including Jesus' – if you dare), and folding our stories in turn inside Mark's. Prepare for surprises.

A memory of Jesus' gentle sovereignty lingers in Paul's appeal to Corinth – which, incidentally, ought to be a comfort, and a lesson, to all ecclesiastical fund-raisers, not least unwilling ones. Paul takes two chapters in the middle of a deeply personal and theological letter to say that the church needs to have the cash ready when he comes, and preferably plenty of it; but he manages to say it without once mentioning 'money' as such. The motivation, he says, should be reflection on Jesus himself: he was rich, yet for your sakes became poor, so that you by his poverty might become rich. It's the same power-in-weakness theme which dominates 2 Corinthians, and it still takes us by surprise as it did Jairus and the rest.

Proper 9

——— ❧ ———

2 Samuel 5.1–5, 9–10
2 Corinthians 12.2–10
Mark 6.1–13

The paradoxes of power. David bided his time, refused to lift up his hand against God's anointed (though he knew himself to be anointed also), and then at last became king in a further anointing. The move to Jerusalem was politically shrewd (though obscured by the omission of verses 6–8): one of the last unconquered strongholds, it gave David a new capital independent of earlier tribal memories, as well as a victory which, completing Joshua's work, sealed David's royal vocation in the public eye.

And yet. When Jesus came to his home town he could do almost nothing. This strange inability, related to the faith, or lack of it, that he found, belongs with the whole theme of the Gospel. After all, when Jesus went to David's capital it was with different weapons, and to a different throne, from those of his ancestor. Yet it is in Jesus that God's spectacular promises to David, of perpetual world-wide dominion, have come true.

So different are their styles of kingship that many have doubted, what the New Testament is at pains to affirm, that Jesus' Davidic Messiahship remained of crucial significance. Power, like Messiahship itself, is redefined, but not abandoned, in the Gospel. It is not an exaggeration to say that the Church, oscillating (in Henry Chadwick's phrase) between the desire to rule the world and the desire to renounce it, has always struggled to work out what in practice this redefined Messiahship ought to mean.

It is a measure of Paul's theological insight that he was already grappling with this within thirty years of Jesus' death. He in turn has been woefully misunderstood here, and accused of subtle manipulation and cynical power-games.

The truth is very different. He is refusing to go along with the Corinthians' desire that he should be the kind of powerful apostle they had in mind. A more robustly Davidic leader would have suited them nicely. He will not play to the gallery that wants tales of spectacular spiritual triumphs. His greatest moment, he says, was a long time ago, and he's not allowed to say anything about it – except that he ended up limping, like Jacob after his encounter with God.

Paul had discovered that real power was hidden precisely in weakness. He learnt this with his head, we may suppose, when he encountered the crucified and risen Jesus on the road to Damascus; he learnt it with his body and his heart as he was thrown into jail, beaten up, abused and mocked. He discovered that when the Christ-pattern was thus stamped on him the power of the risen Christ came through as well, and he was able not only to work healings (he doesn't say much about that, but it seems to be presupposed) but also to exercise an effective servant-authority in the communities founded through his preaching.

If all this seems a long way removed from current questions about power structures in the Church, whose fault is that?

Proper 10

—— ⁓ ——

2 Samuel 6.1–5, 12b–19
Ephesians 1.3–14
Mark 6.14–29

Two kings, a thousand years apart, and both in trouble at home. David brings God's ark into Jerusalem, and is so carried away with dancing and leaping before the Lord that his wife despises him, remembering no doubt the dignity of the former king, her father. Perhaps the narrator is already preparing us for the sad moment five chapters later, where David, successful and prosperous, sows the seeds of later disaster by seducing someone else's wife.

Plus ça change. Herod Antipas had taken his brother Philip's wife; a shrewd political move, most likely, as well as a passionate romance. Did Antipas still hope for recognition as the true Messiah? We can predict the reaction from the wild prophet by the river: how can this be the Lord's anointed?

Herod knows he's in trouble; John is a righteous and holy man, and many revere him as a prophet. He likes listening to him (an interesting comment from Mark, making Herod more than a one-dimensional villain) but is worried by what he hears. Then the birthday party: the wine, the guests, the girl, the disaster.

Now observe Great David's Greater Son (an ambiguous description if ever there was one), the Lord of the Dance, the one whom Herod considered a resurrected John the Baptist.

Nobody is yet saying he was the Messiah – they all think he's a prophet – yet Mark's readers know enough to see the way things are going. This is real kingship: Herod is a ghastly parody, even David only an oblique forerunner. And Mark's readers also realize that if the herald has come to a bad end at the hands of wicked people, the monarch may go the same way. If this is what happens to prophets, think what will happen to the king himself. This king, too, has been despised by his own family (3.31–5; 6.3–5), and will end up rejected by all. Paradoxical maybe, but this is the royal leadership for which Israel had waited a millennium.

But David really did bring the ark to Jerusalem, and throughout that millennium, with much joy and much sorrow, the people of Israel had gone there to worship the one true God, to tell the story of his mighty acts in the past and to pray for their completion in the future. Jerusalem was God's city, and David's city, and it was to Jerusalem that the new king would shortly be making his way to recapitulate those mighty acts, and to bring them to a new and unforeseen completion.

That completion gives Paul his vantage point. He tells the story, in the form of a great Jewish-style thanksgiving-prayer: 'Blessed be the God and Father of our Lord Jesus, the Messiah, who ...' has now accomplished the long-awaited purpose. It is the story of creation and exodus, of redemption and inheritance: the great Jewish story, now seen from a new angle, the redefined royal angle, the Messianic angle that never entered Herod's head.

Proper 11

— ≈ —

2 Samuel 7.1–14a
Ephesians 2.11–22
Mark 6.30–34, 53–56

Read 2 Samuel 7 through the eyes of a second-Temple Jew, and watch New Testament theology come into focus. This passage, read messianically at Qumran and elsewhere, fuses together four things. God promises David a perpetual royal line; a son who will build the Temple; a son who will be counted as God's son; and a son who will be 'raised up' (the Hebrew and Greek words in v. 12 could be read as 'I will resurrect'). This entire train of thought, reshaped around Jesus himself, was present in the mind of the early Church; see, for instance, Romans 1.3–4.

The passage turns on a pun. David, living in luxury while God's ark stays in a tent, proposes a house for God. 'House' can mean a building or a family, a 'royal house' either a palace or a lineage. God hears David's offer of a more permanent dwelling, but a true temple cannot start with human initiative. Nor, actually, can a building be the ultimate solution to the problem. God will raise up David's family; the son to be born will build the Temple; but the final response to David's underlying question is not bricks and mortar but a living human being, God's very self in human form. 'The glory of God', wrote Irenaeus, 'is the living man; and the life of man is the vision of God.'

The Temple, then, became the home of God's glory. But

the early Christians believed that, as always intended, this glory had now taken up permanent residence in Jesus. This early, high, deeply Jewish Christology was rooted, via passages like this, in the belief that the Temple-promises of the Old Testament had come true not in a building but in a human being.

With similar speed, they concluded that those who were 'in the Messiah' were likewise the temple of God's glory, through the Spirit of Jesus which lived in them. This, particularly in 1 Corinthians and, as here, in Ephesians, became a source of early ecumenical theology: the single temple, built of different bricks, has no dividing wall, as did the Jerusalem Temple, to separate Jews from Gentiles (or, for that matter, one to separate women from men, but that isn't the point here). Precisely because the Messiah took the hostility of the two groups upon himself, caught as he was in the crossfire of Roman intransigence, Jewish popular revolution, and Jewish aristocratic power-games, he has abolished the symbolic universe, represented by the Torah as well as the Temple, in which Jew and Gentile were locked into irrevocable hostility, and has achieved what the God of Israel always intended: a new humanity. Notice how even within the temple-metaphor the underlying thought remains human; the structure 'grows into a holy Temple in the Lord' (v. 21).

Like an art thief taking the canvas but leaving the wood-work, today's Gospel omits the story, replacing it next week with someone else's version, and leaves the framework. No comment.

Proper 12

—— ∽ ——

2 Samuel 11.1–15
Ephesians 3.14–21
John 6.1–21

Think of the Lord's Prayer while reading Ephesians 3. Paul prays to the Father, from whom all fatherhood 'in heaven and on earth' is named, that he will give us ... all things in Christ, because to him belong the power and the glory for ever, Amen. Perhaps this, along with John 17, is one of the earliest expanded meditations on the great prayer.

If so, the bit we're missing in the middle nicely corresponds to the story in John 6 (replacing Mark's version in our sequence of readings). Give us this day ... but what they wanted was not food, but a king and a kingdom. The sign, not only the bread and the fish but also the twelve baskets left over, did not appear out of the blue to people watching to see what a conjuror would do next for their entertainment. It was given to people hungry for Israel's restoration, eager for a king to give them Passover-food, freedom, power and glory. That was the context within which they saw the sign, and it was almost too much.

In the evening, Jesus and his followers enacted the remaining part of the prayer. Evil, in the form of wind and wave, threatened to engulf them, but Jesus came to them on the water. (When will someone have the courage to translate *ego eimi* in this passage as 'It's me!'?) If the kingdom really is invading hostile territory with God's power, we should expect to be tested, to need to pray for deliverance. Paul prays not for bread, forgiveness and safety but for strength, for the indwelling of the Messiah, and for God's powerful love to sweep us off our feet.

All this makes the story of David and Bathsheba, and the sorry stories of our own day inside the Church as well as outside, the more shocking. Is Paul's vision of the moral power of God, living within Christians through the Spirit, simply unrealistic?

Many would say No. As every spiritual director knows, for every Christian who has followed David down the easy road to short-term pleasure and long-term disaster there are many with the same opportunities and temptations but who have found the way of escape, often to their own surprise. Moral courage and God's power are strange and sometimes apparently unpredictable, but they are realities none the less.

Within the wider narrative of 2 Samuel, David's double sin (adultery plus murder) is the point from which his other failures begin to emerge, resulting in Absalom's rebellion, public humiliation (not that the palace would be ignorant of what had happened that spring afternoon), civil war, the decimation of his family, and squabbles over succession. As often in scripture, the wider fate of the people of God is nicely balanced with their private lives. The Church has often found it difficult to address both simultaneously, but both Testaments, not least in the Lord's Prayer itself, hold them together as two necessary parts of the same reality.

Proper 13

—— ≈ ——

2 Samuel 11.26—12.13a
Ephesians 4.1–16
John 6.24–35

Hands up those who took one look at this week's Old Testament lesson and gave it a wide berth. All right; now hands up those who seized upon it as a chance to preach on How Not To Commit Immorality. Full marks to the lectionary for including one of the Bible's shockers – though not for losing its nerve and stopping, like Britten's *Rape of Lucretia*, just before the deed itself.

The point, of course, is neither to draw a veil over such incidents, nor to wallow in wickedness, but to reflect with sober sorrow on the larger story that here turns a fateful corner. David's own immorality and violence have set a tone; he can't now stop his sons going the same route. Absalom, Tamar's full brother, takes murderous vengeance on Amnon, starting the rebellion which tears the heart out of David's kingship. David's sins find him out, by a long and shamefully public process of feuding in the family – from which, according to the promises made so soon before, God would raise up the coming great king. Private lives and public events cannot be separated. You cannot partition integrity any more than you can fence off part of the sea.

It is that wholeness of genuinely human life, in both personal and corporate aspects, that Paul describes in the majestic exhortation of Ephesians 4. Each is given a gift, but the gifts together make up the single body of Christ. Selfish impurity breeds corporate disintegration (4.17–24, omitted from the sequence of readings, might be a comment on Amnon and his successors ever since); personal holiness (which includes gentleness and humility) leads to mutual upbuilding and unity.

It doesn't take much reflection to see where our own society is in all of this, not least in the way that sin and selfishness deceive, darken understanding, and twist logic so that people start to believe good is evil and evil good. Inside the Church as well as outside, there are such things as trickery, cunning, and pseudo-doctrines which carry off those who lack the maturity to spot the flaw. Teaching and leadership are what's needed, and what's given in Christ; they are the marks, and the means, of the community which reflects the renewing and transforming love of God.

All this, of course, needs faith. Jesus challenges the puzzled crowd to see through the physical loaves to the true bread beyond. How easy for us to over-spiritualize, to suppose that Jesus is unconcerned with earthly bread (feeding a crowd would be an odd way to make that point). The God-given earthly world functions as an icon or sacrament of the heavenly, which intermingles with the earthly and gives it its full meaning. Greedy abuse of the physical world makes dualists out of the morally sensitive. Jesus invites his hearers to trust him, the Word made flesh, to taste in him the bread of life, and to find heaven and earth united in the promised kingdom.

Proper 14

— ∿ —

2 Samuel 18.5–9, 15, 31–33
Ephesians 4.25—5.2
John 6.35, 41–51

Come, believe, and eat. Simple yet profound, carrying us with characteristic Johannine effortlessness from bread by the lake to the bread of life. The bridge between them is Jesus himself, who will give his flesh, that which the Word had become (1.14), for the life of the world.

The physical and spiritual, the bread Moses gave and the true bread that Jesus gives, must be held together around the person of Jesus himself. We cannot collapse it into the idea that the physical is irrelevant and the spiritual all-important. To 'come' to Jesus means to approach Jesus himself, not some Jesus-fantasy that could be pulled into new shapes at will. The hope is not disembodied eternity but bodily resurrection (6.44). To 'believe' in Jesus means to grasp, with heart, intellect and will, that in this human being the true and living God is fully and personally present.

'Justification by faith', though the phrase is Paul's, summarizes John's message too. Those who believe – and 'believe' isn't a general religious attitude to life, but the specific faith that embraces Jesus himself as the bread of life – are marked as God's people in the present, and assured of the (newly embodied) life of the age to come. This Johannine emphasis is controversial (verses 41–3) for the same reason as Paul's: if this faith is the key to it all, it is open to everyone, irrespective of ethnic origin. The cost of this breathtaking inclusivity is, as always, the humiliating exclusivity of the focus on Jesus and his death. Otherwise 'Jesus' becomes a cipher for whatever makes us feel good at the time.

Take all this theology, turn it into a story and a symbol, and you have John 6 in a nutshell, or perhaps a breadbasket. The eucharist cannot have been far from John's mind, and that of his readers, and its meaning is given by Jesus himself, and the faith which comes to him. Jesus' forthcoming death (6.51) is the clue to it all. They had wanted to make him king (6.15), but Jesus' royal claim would be that he had done what his ancestor had wanted to do: 'Would I had died instead of you, O Absalom, my son, my son'.

To live within this story, to make it one's own in prayer and eucharist, in devotion to Jesus himself, is to find the key to that way of life, startling and subversive in the world of Graeco-Roman paganism, that Paul describes in Ephesians 5. Just as radical as giving up immorality (the previous and following paragraphs) is the challenge to abandon lying and bitterness. This isn't simply a call to 'be nice to people' as a matter of ethical effort (though, to paraphrase Charlie Brown, being nice to people ain't everything, but being nasty to people ain't anything). It's a call to copy God – the God whose startling love has been fully unveiled in the cross of the true King.

Proper 15

— ~ —

1 Kings 2.10–12; 3.3–14
Ephesians 5.15–20
John 6.51–58

A glance at the bits of 1 Kings 1—3 which are not read in this sequence will explain why Solomon so desperately needed wisdom. His father's victories, though remarkable, could not be relied on for long-term security. His own family, whose struggles over the succession had soured his rise to power, could certainly be relied on for long-term squabbles. The coalition of Israelite tribes, held together around the non-tribal capital of Jerusalem, was under strain even in David's day. If ever a young leader needed wisdom, it was Solomon.

The fact that he met these challenges, postponing the break-up of the fragile kingdom through a long reign, is itself a sign that his perennial reputation for wisdom is justified. And of course the main achievement of that wisdom was the building of the Temple. Here we find several elements of later Jewish thinking: wisdom as God's handmaid, given to enable humans to be co-creators of God's intended projects; the Temple itself as the place of God's dwelling, of worship, prayer and sacrifice; David's son and heir bringing the two together, as long as he fulfils the law. Half of New Testament Christology is stored away in this narrative, laid up like a fine wine for a thousand years.

Solomon's humility and wisdom contrast sharply with the

arrogance and bumbling short-termism we find in much ancient and modern history. What might it take to get us back on track?

Paul's recipe for wisdom is bracing. Avoid the folly of comfortable, and fashionable, immorality (Ephesians 5.3–14, which forms the backdrop to this exhortation to wisdom). Make the most of the time (literally, 'buy it back'; assume it's being snatched from you, and get it back under your control). Understand God's will: think it through and see where it conflicts with the easy option. Glad and grateful worship takes priority over booze and sleaze. Think of the pagan rulers, and their imitators, of Paul's day, and perhaps our own as well, and you'll see what a contrast he is recommending.

But it can only be attempted by those who, through that thankful worship, are being fed on the bread and wine which is Jesus himself. Wisdom, Temple and Torah point forward to the one who offers his own flesh and blood as food and drink.

This shocking affront to Jewish sensibilities (cannibalism? drinking blood? No wonder they found it hard to take) is meant to jolt us into recognizing what is in fact being said. Solomon's prayer for God's wisdom was a prayer for God's own life, God's own second self, to live within him, clothing itself with his thinking, his decisions, his leadership. Our feeding on Jesus, in the eucharist of course but in so many other ways too, is our prayer for God's own life, made flesh in Jesus, to clothe itself afresh with us, to get (as we say) into our bones and our bloodstreams, our thinking, our decisions, our leadership.

Proper 16

——— ❧ ———

1 Kings 8.[1, 6, 10–11]22–30, 41–43
Ephesians 6.10–20
John 6.56–69

Jesus returns, at the end of the long 'bread of life' discourse, to the central thrust. Don't look for more loaves and fishes; look for the different dimension of life which the Son of Man offers, the dimension which will be signalled by his eventual exaltation to be with the Father.

All very well, but today's hearers are almost bound to misunderstand. 'The spirit gives life; the flesh is useless'; fine, we think, and off we go with Plato into radical dualism. Don't worry, we think, about the world of space, time and matter; concern yourself with the world of pure spirit.

The problem is that 'spirit', here and elsewhere, is not the opposite of 'matter', morally or ontologically. The Jewish way of life – Temple, food laws and all – was commanded and blessed by the same creator God who made the physical world and called it good, the same God whose Word has now become flesh, flesh that will rise from the dead and go to the Father. This is the God whose Spirit fills the word 'spiritual' with its true meaning. In Jesus, as in the Temple, flesh and spirit, heaven and earth, have been brought together once and for all.

Of course, if you try to live on the material level alone it will become 'flesh' in the negative sense, corruptible and corrupting. But in John, as in Paul (despite repeated assertions to the contrary), and as indeed throughout Genesis to Revelation, the two spheres of God's created and glorious world, the earthly and the heavenly, are made to interlock, to work in intricate harmony.

That's why Paul's warning about the battle Christians face is not about escaping from the (evil) physical sphere into the (good) spiritual sphere. The spiritual sphere is precisely where you meet the worst foes, the foes of which even Caesar and his brutal henchmen are just pale copies. 'Spiritual warfare' conjures up bizarre images today: Superman-like characters flying around the sky blitzing pterodactyl-like demons with supernatural ray-guns. But just because *Jaws* was over the top, that doesn't mean sharks don't eat people. Just because some people cherish ludicrous and caricatured fantasies about spiritual warfare, that doesn't mean Paul is talking nonsense. Anyone who genuinely tries to take two steps forward for the kingdom of God will know that there are unseen forces which try to drag you back at least one step, possibly three.

The weapons for the battle are not showy, flashy, or Hollywood-friendly. They are sober, almost boring, mostly defensive. The belt of truth. The breastplate of justice. The shoes of the gospel of peace. The shield of faith. The helmet of salvation. And – the only attacking weapon – the Spirit's sword, God's word. All to be surrounded with prayer.

Think back to Ephesians' earlier statement about the Church as God's renewed Temple. Now read 1 Kings 8 again, and ask yourself what it would mean to be builders, dedicators, guardians and worshippers in this Temple today.

Proper 17

— ∾ —

Song of Solomon 2.8–13
James 1.17–27
Mark 7.1–8, 14–15, 21–23

The main bit missing from Mark 7 is about nullifying God's word through human tradition. Hmmm.

Granted, there are two different issues at stake here: cleanness and uncleanness (with a further subdivision: clean hands and clean food), and tradition versus Scripture. But even supposing we highlight the first, omitting verses 9–13, we cannot understand Mark's point without the transition in verse 17, and his own comment in verse 19. Let's put this right before we too end up making a tradition of misreading Scripture.

The point of the passage, for Mark, is that Jesus couldn't say in public what he says here in private. Think of the Maccabaean martyrs, dying rather than defile themselves with unclean food. Think of Daniel 1, where the heroes don't die, but will shortly face pagan persecution. Remember how such stories function in a beleaguered community (think of Belfast or Bosnia, where tales of atrocity and heroism, like a blaze in a forest, can leap across the fire-break of centuries and spark fresh fury and enthusiasm). Think of first-century Jews in 'Galilee of the Gentiles', fiercely maintaining their loyalty to God and the Torah. And now imagine Jesus saying casually to all and sundry (as the lectionary makes him do) that unclean food cannot defile a person. He's asking to be lynched.

Mark is emphatic: this sort of thing could only be said in private. And even then Jesus is cryptic with his explanation, so that Mark himself has to rub home the point. This means that all foods are clean.

Only now can we face the real problem: the food-laws are not 'tradition', they're Scripture. Does that mean that Jesus is doing the very thing he is rebuking them for?

The answer cannot be simply that Jesus has the right to set aside even Scripture. That isn't incarnate sovereignty, it's cavalier casualness. What we find, instead, is Jesus' strong sense of *what time it is*. It's time for the kingdom of God to break in. And when that happens, laws which had a strong point as part of God's preparation are no longer needed.

God was now calling all people, not just Jews, to belong to his people; because God was now dealing with the root disease of humanity, the problem resident in every human heart. The time had come to blow out the candles and watch the sun rise. Scripture would be truly fulfilled when that to which the purity laws pointed – God's longing that his people be holy through and through – was achieved. James speaks of the perfect law being that which makes people doers as well as hearers. However accurate the signposts are, you don't need them once you've arrived at your destination.

Remember this subversive Jesus when you think of the traditional interpretation of the Song of Songs, in which he is the Bridegroom. His message? The time has come. Everything is now going to be different. If this is romance, it's based on realism.

Proper 18

—— ∽ ——

Proverbs 22.1–2, 8–9, 22–23
James 2.1–10[11–13], 14–17
Mark 7.24–37

James' comments about faith and works, part of his wide-ranging application of 'the law of liberty' (1.25, 2.12), have become famous because of their apparent contradiction of Paul's insistence on justification by faith alone. Perhaps that's why his strong emphasis on the 'no favourites in church' rule (2.1–7) has so often been ignored; if Luther said James was an epistle of straw, who are we to take him seriously? Thus the entire Wisdom tradition in both Testaments (consider James' closeness to Proverbs, in both style and content) is often set aside.

Here, though, it is Luther, not James, who is made of straw. When James says 'faith' he means a verbal formula, intellectual consent to Jewish monotheism (2.15, 19); for Paul 'faith' is the response of 'faith*fulness*' which God sought from Israel, found in Jesus, and evokes through the gospel. When James speaks of 'works' he means neither the attempt to earn one's own salvation by moral effort, nor the attempt to confine God's grace to those who can perform 'works of Torah', i.e. Jews. Rather, he means the outward effects that faith must have if it is to be genuine – what Paul himself calls 'faith working through love' (Galatians 5.6). James and Paul, in different ways, are opposing Jewish attempts to seek security in ethnic identity without the need for the life-changing grace unveiled in Jesus.

What's more, James' main concern is salvation (2.14), that is, *final* justification, which Paul also aligns with good works (Romans 2.6–11, also interestingly in a context where 'no partiality' is a major theme). When Paul speaks of 'justification by faith' in Romans and Galatians, he is speaking of the *present* justification which anticipates that final verdict. Paul and James are singing different parts within the wider harmony of the gospel.

That harmony includes Mark 7 as well. Jesus has placed a time-bomb beside those Jewish institutions that stressed ethnic separateness; he is now confronted with the need to explode it, sooner than expected. 'You can't give the children's bread to the dogs'; a harsh saying, hardly one the early Christians would have invented, but turning quickly into warm acceptance of Gentile faith. Though Jesus (like many Jews of the day) clearly envisaged a future time when Gentiles would come to share the blessings of the kingdom (think of the centurion's servant, and Jesus' comments on that incident in Matthew 8.10–12), he seems to be surprised that it is all happening this quickly. No more privilege for the 'children'; all can be healed, all must hear, and soon.

The kingdom is rushing forwards, and it is imperative that he teach the disciples its meaning as soon as possible. Mark, here as elsewhere, uses the story of the deaf-mute as part of his build-up to the time when the disciples, in the next chapter, will hear plainly, and be able to speak the truth about Jesus.

Proper 19

—— ≈ ——

Proverbs 1.20–33
James 3.1–12
Mark 8.27–38

The first nine chapters of Proverbs introduce two personified figures: Lady Wisdom and Mistress Folly. Both appeal to 'the sons of men'; we had better not try, in the interests of inclusivity, to flatten out the genders, since they are part of the point. The discourse winds to and fro between the Lady and the Mistress, both as metaphors for the appeal of Wisdom and Folly in every area of life, and as a metonymy in which sexual morality is a key illustrative aspect of human decision-making.

The underlying counsel (1.7) is that the fear of YHWH is the beginning of wisdom ('fear' here, of course, means awe and reverence before God's greatness, sovereignty and holiness, not cowering away from an unpredictable bully). The premise, and promise, is that YHWH is the creator God in whose image humans are made. To worship him is to become more truly human, more fully what one was meant and made to be.

If humans are made to reflect God's image into his world, then wisdom, the one through whom that world was created (8.22–31), is precisely what they need. Wisdom will be given to those who fear YHWH so that they can understand how his world works and act appropriately, and indeed joyfully, within it. This is the fountainhead from which flow the later, often apparently random, streams of advice, collected from many sources but now made available through the fear of YHWH.

James, the New Testament's nearest approach to Proverbs in style and content, picks up in this chapter the regular theme of human speech, with its huge potential for good and ill. Jesus had warned of judgement on the basis of one's words (Matthew 12.36–7); James warns of the danger of inconsistent speech to one's neighbour, and even to God. The untameable tongue can set things ablaze. Those who use words for a living are in special danger.

The underlying theology concerns speech as a key part of the image-bearing capacity of humans, reflecting the God who is not silent but reveals himself in words, and ultimately in the Word. We are so aware of the dangers and limitations of our own words that we sometimes try to rescue God from the same problem. The fault, however, is not with God's habit of speech, but with our inability to reflect him truly and appropriately.

Peter's words, blurted out finally after a long and slow process of education (see Mark 8.14–26, a careful setting of the scene for this climax), illustrate the point nicely. He is right to declare that Jesus is Messiah, but wrong to project on to him his own distorted (though conventional) ideas about what Messiahship might mean. Jesus' vocation will stand conventional wisdom on its head. The way of the cross is the true, though shocking, reflection of God's thoughts. Peter must learn to renounce conventional, skin-saving folly and to walk the steep path of subversive wisdom.

Proper 20

— ≈ —

Proverbs 31.10–31
James 3.13—4.3, 7–8a
Mark 9.30–37

Fortunately, Jesus stopped the disciples in their tracks before they acted out James 4 as well as James 3. Envy and selfish ambition, yes; but covetousness had not yet led to murder. The internecine strife in Jerusalem 40 years later (just after James was writing?) shows how easily it could have happened. Do, please, read the missing verses from James (4.4–6, 8b–10), and allow them to colour your hearing of the gospel. Who is God's friend, and who God's enemy, and where is this drama worked out today?

Classic Markan irony: Jesus telling the disciples about his approaching death, the disciples arguing over who was the greatest. Mark insists that they couldn't understand him; what might they have thought he meant? Jesus so often spoke figuratively that it's not surprising his literal sense (betrayed, killed, rising again) was too much for them to swallow. Was he perhaps talking about the suffering that would herald the arrival of the kingdom? Well, yes, but not the way they thought.

Jesus' response, using the child as both example and promise, comes across as oblique. We expect teaching about humility, as in the similar incident in 10.13–16. But this is different. Why does Jesus speak of 'receiving' a child in his name? How does that address their wrong attitude, or encourage them to the right one?

They were each hoping, it seems, to become Jesus' official spokesman. Jesus would be king; the question was, who would be Chief of Staff, head of the royal household? Who would speak for Jesus? Who would be his ambassador, welcomed with the honour due to Jesus himself? Answer: anyone at all, and the humbler the better. An insignificant, unnamed child can become Jesus' official representative, so that receiving him or her means receiving Jesus. Furthermore (a claim heavy with Johannine-style christological implications) by receiving Jesus, not least in the person of an insignificant child, people will receive 'the one who sent him'. Friendship with God is on offer, as in James, but it will mean turning one's back on friendship with the world and its expectations.

James is the New Testament's chief 'wisdom' book, and in Proverbs 31 we have one of the genre's crowning moments. The earlier chapters contrast Lady Wisdom and Mistress Folly, and here at last personified wisdom becomes a real person: a cheerful, independent-minded, multi-skilled wife, whose life is by no means restricted to managing her own household, though of course she does that, but who runs a business (v. 18) and cares for the poor (v. 20). Of course, as the cynics point out, this is a man's view of what a good woman does; but let's give credit where credit is due. If more Christian teaching about the role of women had started from Proverbs, fewer mistakes would have been made. And if the disciples had had an ounce of the wisdom Proverbs offers, their conversation with Jesus might have gone somewhat differently.

Proper 21

— ∿ —

Esther 7.1–6, 9–10
James 5.13–20
Mark 9.38–50

The ancient world was full of stories in which the threatened hero or heroine is rescued at last, and the people who had almost overcome them are condemned instead. David kills Goliath. Homer's heroes – some of them, anyway – defeat their rivals after tense battles. The Son of Man is exalted, the Beast destroyed. Plenty of plays and novels follow the same line. We tell the story of the twentieth century in similar terms: think of Hitler, or Mussolini.

So why do we find Esther chapter 7 hard to take? The vengeance is stark and shocking, particularly when two verses are removed (typical: they refer to Haman's supposed attack on Esther's virtue). Haman is hanged on the gallows he had prepared for Mordecai, Esther's uncle. Rough justice at best, we think; at worst a bad-tempered lynching. This impression isn't helped if you go, as I once did in Jerusalem at the height of the intifada, to a Purim celebration, where the whole book is read, and discover that at this point in the story crowds of children with toy trumpets and drums raise the roof in celebration. My host on that occasion, a learned Jewish scholar, leant over to me and muttered 'I never like this bit'. Neither did I.

Haman had of course asked for it. He had plotted a major pogrom against a large and widespread Jewish community.

108

Not for nothing have twentieth-century Jews felt history repeating itself, with Hitler partially succeeding where Haman failed. But what does the Gospel say?

Well, not exactly what we might think. The worm is turning in our sensibilities, and some of the finest theologians are now reminding us that being nice to everybody, seeking reconciliation at any price, has to be balanced by naming, and dealing with, evil. Even in the last chapter of James, where forgiveness, healing and the restoration of sinners are the order of the day, the great example of fervent prayer is Elijah; and a glance at his story will reveal that the decisive moment in the coming of the rain was the slaughter of the prophets of Baal. And in Mark 9, with its tender care for 'the little ones who believe in me', there are ominous words about millstones around necks and unquenchable fire.

The problem seems to be that, when people give themselves to the practice of genuine wickedness, a good God must hate, and deal with, not only the sin but the sinner; but that those who follow the crucified Christ (upon whom the Haman-like, contemptuous wrath of Rome had fallen) are forbidden to seek or practise revenge on their own account. Omit the first, and the cry for justice will rise higher than our squeamish sentiment. Omit the second, and you sprinkle holy water on the lynch mobs. Leaving vengeance to God, as Paul instructs (Romans 12.19–21), was revolutionary then and remains so today. It doesn't mean denying that evil is real and that God hates it.

Proper 22

—— ≈ ——

Job 1.1; 2.1–10
Hebrews 1.1–4; 2.5–12
Mark 10.2–16

Angels are one thing; angels as God's heavenly council, discussing policy, are another; 'the Accuser' (the word 'Satan' is a title before it is a proper name) as himself an angel, a celestial Director of Public Prosecutions, is harder still; God giving this DPP carte blanche to see if he can find a charge against an unsuspecting human – well, this is beyond the pale. Yet this is what we see, as the prologue to Job takes us round to the back of the stage. Behind the drama and debate of Job and his friends, this is what is 'really' going on.

One might, of course, say that if you don't like what Job says about the problem of evil you're at liberty to offer an alternative. Answers on a postcard, please. But part of the answer is that there isn't an 'answer' in any sense that would 'solve' the problem; the book is, rather, a fuller way of stating the problem itself. Until we have all the dimensions before us we don't know what we're talking about – if indeed talking is the most appropriate thing to do.

Jesus, after all, didn't talk about 'the problem of evil' in that sense. He lived, breathed, taught and eventually died for the Kingdom of God, God's saving sovereignty over evil on earth and in heaven. Juxtaposing Job and Hebrews, as we now begin to do, produces some interesting reflected light: Jesus wasn't an angel, not least because, for the task he had to accomplish, it was necessary as well as appropriate for him to be fully human. (Appropriate, because the one who was from all eternity the true reflection of God (1.3) became the truly human one, that is, the one who reflects God's image.)

It isn't, then, that Jesus offers an abstract or intellectual answer to Job's problem. Jesus, we might say, had to *become* Job, suffering unjustly at the hands of the powers, 'in order that by God's grace he might taste death for everyone' (2.9). A 'solution', it seems, doesn't mean 'a theoretical framework within which it all makes rational sense'. In God's many-sided world, solutions take the form of a living embodiment of God's healing love and power.

That living embodiment challenges today's world, as it did Jesus', with his words about divorce (and about children). The Pharisees' question was political, not just about abstract ethics: remember why John was imprisoned and beheaded, look where Mark locates this story (10.1), and reflect on the trap set for John's cousin. Again, 'the solution' isn't a the-oretical framework, but a life reflecting God's image. God's will in creation, for man and woman to become one flesh, is not set aside by a Mosaic permission 'given because of your hardheartedness'. The implication, shocking and difficult then and now, is that Jesus, restoring God's creation to its original intention, is offering a cure for hardness of heart. Once the word becomes flesh, solutions must be more than words.

Proper 23

—— ∿ ——

Job 23.1–9, 16–17
Hebrews 4.12–16
Mark 10.17–31

Two moments jump out at us from this intense little drama. Jesus looks at the man and loves him; not, perhaps, our natural reaction to someone claiming to keep six out of ten commandments perfectly. (A pity Job 23.11–12 is omitted, since there Job says much the same thing.) The disciples are flabbergasted at Jesus' comment about camels and needles; not, surely, our natural reaction to being warned about the danger of riches (we've heard all that before, but they clearly hadn't).

These flashes warn us that the story isn't saying what we expect. We assume the man will be asking 'how to go to heaven when he dies'. He isn't, and Jesus doesn't tell him that. The journey he wants is horizontal, not vertical. God will bring in his kingdom, the Age to Come; heaven will arrive on earth; some will be adjudged worthy to inherit this new world. This isn't 'eternal life' as in 'timeless existence', but 'the full life of the Coming Age' ('eternal' is from the same root as 'age'). 'Treasure in heaven' isn't something you go to heaven to enjoy, any more than having money in the bank means you have to spend it in the bank. It's waiting for you against the day when heaven and earth become one.

Jesus' response, too, is hardly what you'd expect. 'Keep the commandments?' Hadn't Jesus read Luther? Why not 'believe the gospel'? Answer: because part of the question is, what does it mean to be a true Jew, who will be vindicated when God finally acts? The definition of Jewishness focused on keeping Torah; Jesus has come, not to abolish it, but to fulfil it. The gospel is new, but it's not merely novel.

But notice which commandments Jesus *doesn't* quote (there is an extra problem, as to whether 'don't defraud' is meant to cover the last commandment; we can leave that to one side). What's happened to the first four? The sabbath is not mentioned; no surprises there for Mark's readers. But what about the first three: No gods before YHWH? No graven images? No taking YHWH's name in vain?

The answer is world-shaking. Jesus substitutes three things for the opening words of the Sinaitic covenant: sell up, give it away, follow me. The commandments have become devastatingly simple and personal. The implication, as with the divorce discussion earlier in the chapter, is that Jesus is moving beyond the Mosaic covenant into a new area, as indeed you'd expect if the Age to Come is being born. And behind that again there looms up the suggestion, like a great cathedral suddenly emerging out of a thick mist ahead of you: loyalty to Jesus now functions as the loyalty which Israel's God demands to him and him alone.

This is one of those stories that, as Hebrews says, divides between joints and marrow. Happily, the same Jesus who demands this complete allegiance is there also as the one who sympathizes with our weaknesses.

Proper 24

—— ≈ ——

Job 38.1–7 [34–41]
Hebrews 5.1–10
Mark 10.35–45

'Were you there,' asks the old song, 'when they crucified my Lord?' 'Were you there,' the Lord enquires of Job, 'when I laid the foundation of the earth?' Both questions receive the answer 'No', but for different reasons; born too late in one case, born as a human creature in the other. Yet both questions are invitations, not simply put-downs. You need to ponder what you missed.

Of course, in Job's case it is a put-down as well. The majestic stride through the glories of creation – stars, sea, snow, animals, birds, and finally Leviathan itself (chapter 41) – compels Job into appropriate humility. It isn't so much an answer to his nagging question as a statement of why the question cannot be answered, or not yet. It's a way of saying that God's ways are not our ways, and that the right path lies in submission to the strange wisdom by which the world was made.

From this point of view it isn't so much a matter, as some have said, of Jesus providing the answer to the questions Job was asking, though in some ways that's true too. It is rather, we might say, that Jesus *became* Job, 'learning obedience through the things he suffered', as Hebrews starkly puts it. God was able to save him from death. But Jesus, shouting and weeping in prayer (an important and often ignored

114

historical memory, presumably of Gethsemane), fought his way to costly submission to the divine purpose which was taking him *through* death and into the world of new creation. God was laying the foundations of the new earth, giving the morning stars a new song to sing, taming Leviathan at last.

James and John, like Job, come with the wrong question. They weren't there when God determined on the plan of salvation, and they won't be there when their Lord is crucified. They'll be hiding like rats in a hole, unable (for the moment at least) to drink the cup or share the baptism. Their squabble with the other disciples, like Job's with his comforters, simply keeps the misunderstandings in circulation. They need to be silent before the unimagined, unlooked-for fresh revelation of upside-down divine wisdom. The world goes about things in one way; God does it differently.

When Jesus explains the necessity of the cross he starts with a *political* point. Leviathan, whether the sea-monster or the political 'absolute state', must be tamed, but can only be tamed by the God revealed in the suffering Son of Man. Hobbes, not for the last time, needs to be corrected by Calvin. Isaiah's vision of the Servant will indeed be fulfilled in Jesus; but this was never simply about sinful souls being saved by an arbitrary substitute. It was always about YHWH, the sovereign one, defeating the gods that have enslaved his people and, redeeming them, renewing not only the covenant but creation itself. Were you there? No, but follow this path and you will be.

The Last Sunday After Trinity

—— ≈ ——

Job 42.1–6, 10–17
Hebrews 7.23–28
Mark 10.46b–52

Three very different prayers.

Whatever we think of the ending of the book of Job (some scholars, inevitably, suppose it a later addition; some in our gloomy culture think it spoils the story to have Job so splendidly restored), the turning-point in his story should not be missed. He repents of his own presuming to question God – though God himself declares that he has in fact spoken the truth, that is, that he has maintained God's justice against superficial caricatures – and he prays for his friends, guilty of those same untrue caricatures. The prayer, for the people who had been torturing him with their spurious 'comfort', is itself an act born of the humility that accepts God's justice even when it doesn't understand it. Swift restoration now follows.

Somehow, God's justice is at work not as a blind force out beyond Job and his friends, but as a strange presence, inviting them in their own relationships to taste the humility, but also the new power, it brings to those who cast themselves upon it. Prayer, indeed, depends upon God's reliability and justice; if God were capricious or unjust, it would be better to remain silent. Job's prayer embodies not only his own forgiveness of his friends, but also his new, humble trust in God's reliability.

Intercession for his people is the central task of the Christ of Hebrews. The long passage about Jesus' fulfilment of the Melchizedek promise in Psalm 110 focuses finally on this point: the priest is there to plead to God on behalf of his people, and Jesus fulfils this role perfectly because, as the psalm says, he holds his royal priesthood in perpetuity. Unlike the levitical priests – and unlike Job – he has no sins of his own to deal with first. His central task, acted out physically on Calvary and embodied thereafter in his representative role in the heavenly realms, is to come before the Father with his sinful people on his heart. Nor is this, as in some iconography, a matter of his plaintively presenting his own suffering before an otherwise stern and unyielding Father. The Father himself appointed him for this purpose, so that we should have complete assurance of salvation, being in no doubt of his eternal and all-powerful saving love for us.

That same saving love, embodied in the Jesus who has set his face towards the cross, stands by the gate of Jericho as blind Bartimaeus shouts for mercy and refuses to be silenced. This time the intercession is for himself, simple, direct, and full of faith: 'Teacher, I want to see again.' (Jesus had asked him what he wanted; 'Have mercy on me', from a roadside beggar, would normally mean cash, but this request was altogether different.) From the complexities of Job, through the ministry of Jesus Christ himself, to the simplicity of Bartimaeus: coming before God in prayer is the central God-given human task, the one by which, whether spectacularly or quietly, everything is transformed.

Sundays Before Advent

The Fourth Sunday
Before Advent

—— ∽ ——

Deuteronomy 6.1–9
Hebrews 9.11–14
Mark 12.28–34

For once the lectionary hits the jackpot. These readings dovetail perfectly, revealing powerfully the continuity and discontinuity between Christianity and the Old Testament.

The key is the bit we might miss if we weren't alerted to it. Only Mark records the little exchange between Jesus and the scribe, which shows how the question about the great commandment fits into the whole sequence of thought. Mark 11—13 is framed by Jesus' action in the Temple (a symbolic warning of its destruction), and by the prophetic discourse on the Mount of Olives. The intervening material, including this passage, is not simply a string of miscellaneous controversies. It all explains the same point: what Jesus is doing will take the place of the Temple. From here there is a straight line to Jesus' hearing before the High Priest, at which the question of the Temple is central, and thence to his death, through which (Mark implies) all is accomplished.

Jesus' initial answer is apparently conventional. The *Shema* prayer, starting with Deuteronomy 6, was already central to Jewish devotion. Wholehearted love of God, and of one's neighbour as oneself, is basic to what God had in mind in giving the Torah. (We note, against frequent assumptions, that these are good Old Testament ideals, not Christian innovations. We also note the difference between the unreserved love of God and the measured love of neighbour – no more, but no less, than one loves one's own sinful self.)

The scribe, musing on this apparently obvious answer, draws the devastating conclusion: this is more than all sacrifices and offerings. Exactly so, replies Jesus; and you are therefore not far from the kingdom of God. Not because you're climbing a ladder of spiritual advancement, but because you've grasped the truth at the heart of Jesus' ministry: Jesus has come to offer, and accomplish, the reality to which the Temple points but which it cannot ultimately deliver. Draw another straight line from here to Hebrews: the blood of bulls and goats can never take away sin. All they can do is to point to that deeper taking away which is accomplished through the death of Jesus.

Why then the Temple? This puzzle, very close to Paul's frequent question as to why God gave the Law, is often answered in terms of religious development: people in earlier days thought they needed animal sacrifices, but we've grown out of such things. That's not the New Testament answer. The Temple was given as a true signpost; there was nothing wrong with it. But the signpost isn't the reality, and if people are mistaking the one for the other the time may come to chop the signpost down.

The question, though, bounces back at today's Church. We don't go in for killing bulls and goats, but do we show evidence of the reality to which their blood was supposed to point? Or have we substituted a new regime of 'dead works' which impede, rather than facilitate, our worship of the living God?

The Third Sunday
Before Advent

— ❧ —

Jonah 3.1–5, 10
Hebrews 9.24–28
Mark 1.14–20

'Once, only once, and once for all.' The hymn that starts thus withdraws with the left hand some of what it gives with the right, hinting that Christ's unique sacrifice is still somehow present in the eucharist. This is understandable: every time we stress the uniqueness of Jesus, we risk making him distant, or even irrelevant. All Christian systems of thought have to cope with this question.

But we shouldn't tone down Hebrews' insistence on the one-offness of the sacrifice of Jesus Christ. Hebrews isn't about the eucharist, but about that upon which the eucharist (and everything else) is based. The letter, like the whole New Testament, assumes a Jewish world-view: the story of Israel, in both its sequence and its smaller elements, is the story of how the one true God is dealing with the ruin of humanity, embracing the whole world with forgiveness and hope.

Hebrews 8—10 expounds Jeremiah's prophecy of the new covenant in which sins would be forgiven once for all. That's the point. It draws together earlier themes, focusing on Christ as the high priest who accomplishes, finally, all that the sacrificial system had spoken of. As with birth or marriage, you don't repeat the decisive event; you live by, and within, its consequences. To suggest that Jesus' death needs repeating to be relevant or contemporary is to admit that we haven't understood it.

In the present passage, Christ's death is both like and unlike the Day of Atonement ritual. The high priest disappears into the sanctuary, and reappears to sort out the continuing sin of the people. He'll do it again next year, too. But Christ has gone into the heavenly places, making atonement once for all; his reappearance will not be to deal with sin, but to save those who await his coming. Christian life takes place on the timeline between completed atonement and Jesus' final reappearance.

Theories about atonement are out of fashion at the moment. We prefer straightforward stories like the call of the first disciples: Jesus calls, and Simon, Andrew, James and John obey and follow him. But this isn't as straightforward as it seems. 'The time is fulfilled,' said Jesus, 'and God's kingdom is at hand.' This, too, is a unique moment: history is drawing to its climax. 'Repent, and believe the good news'; the call is not just to work, but to be turned inside out, to reorder priorities, to change direction as well as allegiance. The people of Nineveh repented at Jonah's preaching (perhaps, it is hinted, because they knew of his astonishing rescue from the sea and the fish). Will the people of Israel repent at this seaside prophet, this greater-than-Jonah?

Decisive, one-off challenges are threatening. That's why we turn eschatology into religion, preferring the regular performance of duties to absolute allegiance to the unique Jesus. 'Making the gospel relevant' can sometimes be an excuse for domesticating it, not only in eucharistic theology but in every corner of the Church.

The Second Sunday
Before Advent

—— ✑ ——

Daniel 12.1–3
Hebrews 10.11–14 [15–18] 19–25
Mark 13.1–8

The lady in the icon shop may not have understood my
English, let alone my Greek. Did she have an icon of
Jesus' resurrection? Yes, she said, pointing at the wall
behind her head. There it was, in sequence, preceded by
Palm Sunday, the Last Supper, and Calvary, and followed
by Ascension and Pentecost.

'But it isn't Jesus' resurrection,' I said; 'that's Jesus raising
Adam and Eve at the general resurrection. Haven't you got
one of Jesus' *own* resurrection?'

'That is the resurrection,' she said firmly, smiling at my
theological incompetence. I smiled back, and bought a
smaller one (of Paul).

A typical East/West muddle, and we were of course both
right. For the Orthodox, Easter *was* the general resurrection;
we may use arm-waving phrases like 'in principle', or 'in a
real sense', which mean 'we have to say something like this
but we don't quite know how.' We Westerners prefer to
separate different historical events, not least (or so we tell
ourselves) because the world is still such a sad and wicked
place that it doesn't make sense to speak of the resurrection
having already happened. (Indeed, 2 Timothy 2.18 warns

against such teaching.) But theologically Christ's victory at the first Easter is not different from the victory on the last day. Unless we see Easter like this we diminish it.

The opening verses of Daniel 12, which became the favourite rabbinic text on the resurrection, point in Christian reading *both* to the general resurrection, historically still awaited, *and* to the resurrection of Jesus, following his 'time of anguish' on the cross. New creation began at Easter: Daniel's language about people of dust becoming like the sky and the stars is a way of saying just that. As we move towards the close of the Trinity season (relabelled now as Sundays Before Advent, that is, Sundays Before Sundays Before Christmas), our focus is turned towards the victory of Christ at the cosmic, not only the personal, level.

Within that, of course, the victory is to be seen also as the accomplishment of the new covenant. Hebrews reaches its crowning moment in this passage: Jeremiah's promise is fulfilled (some random electricity seems to have got into the choice of readings, and the selection of verses, at this time of the year). Christian life is designed to take place not in an atmosphere of fear and anxiety about whether God is after all gracious and forgiving, but in the certainty that we have, permanently, that access to God's presence which the Jerusalem Temple both symbolized and restricted.

Jesus and the Temple are thus bound to be set in opposition. If he has spoken and acted truly, there is no room for the signs and symbols which foreshadowed his achievement. But we who still live in a world of wars and rumours of wars may appropriately re-apply his warnings to the time still to come. What are the Temples to be set aside when Easter is finally complete?

Christic the King

— ≈ —

Daniel 7.9–10, 13–14
Revelation 1.4b–8
John 18.33b–37

The 'Feast of Christ the King' was invented by Pius XI in 1925. Only in 1970 was it moved from October to the last Sunday before Advent. It slid into Anglicanism very recently, introducing three muddles.

First, the proper feast of Christ the King is Ascension. Any suggestion that Christ only becomes King at the end of a long post-Ascension process is unwarranted.

Second, the idea that 'the kingdom of God' denotes either a purely future reality, or the reality which the saints presently enjoy in heaven (as some liturgies now say), is likewise way off the mark, radically distorting the Bible's kingdom-language.

Third, Advent itself celebrates Christ's second coming and the consummation of all things, not as the end of a process but as a fresh act of grace. Having 'Christ the King' here effects a subtle but radical change in the Church's year, in its implicit story and theology.

Having said all that, one of the great achievements of the current lectionary is its correct reading of Daniel 7 not as the Son of Man 'coming' from heaven to earth, but as his triumphant vindication and exaltation. The direction of travel is up, not down. The Son of Man represents the saints of the Most High, who have suffered at the hands

126

of the beasts and are now rescued and vindicated. This speaks both of the resurrection, ascension and heavenly kingship of Jesus and of the future vindication of the martyrs.

Thus, in Revelation 1 (though a few verses later the Son of Man looks like the Ancient of Days as well), Christ's public vindication is the foundation of the suffering Church's confidence: 'the firstborn of the dead' is in fact 'the ruler of the kings of the earth'. This is the ground both of hope for the future and of political action (including martyrdom) in the present.

We watch the multiple ironies set up by this claim as Jesus stands before Pilate. 'My kingdom is not from this world' doesn't imply that Jesus' sphere of rule is purely heavenly, leaving earth to stew in its own juice. The saying isn't about the kingdom's *location*, but about its *character*: this kingdom isn't the sort that advances by violence. It will come on earth as in heaven, because it is about truth. Pilate, who doesn't know what truth is (do please read half a verse more, and let the famous question hang in the air for a moment), doesn't know that there can be a kingdom without violence.

But we can't really blame him. Even those who name the name of Jesus have taken two millennia to get to the point of imagining that Jesus might really have meant it. As we learn to tell the story right, let's remember that it ends in the embrace of mercy and truth, justice and peace.

YEAR C

Advent

The First Sunday of Advent

—— ≈ ——

Jeremiah 33.14–16
1 Thessalonians 3.9–13
Luke 21.25–36

It is January, AD 69. You are a Greek-speaking Christian in a Roman town in Turkey. You are deeply anxious about the fierce war in Judaea: the Romans have laid siege to Jerusalem; the city faces starvation, civil strife and military defeat; many Christians are caught in the middle. Official news from Rome has confirmed that the Emperor, Nero, committed suicide a few months ago, to be succeeded by Galba, a general from the provinces. Now you hear a wild rumour that Galba himself has been killed, that other would-be emperors are staking their claims, and that a major civil war is looming. All the fixed points of your ordinary life are suddenly in question. What language can you borrow to do justice to the reality?

'There will be signs in the sun, the moon, and the stars, and on the earth distress among nations confused by the roaring of the sea and the waves. People will faint from fear of what is coming upon the world, for the powers of the heavens will be shaken.' No, you aren't afraid of sea or sky. You use the language of tidal wave and thunderbolt because nothing else will do. And you continue, drawing on traditions going back to the early Christians who, soaked in Scripture, knew well what such words would mean: 'Then they will see "the Son of Man coming in a cloud" with

2

power and great glory'. No, you don't imagine you will see Jesus flying around in the sky. You know that through these tribulations God will vindicate Jesus, and rescue his people. Up till now, the kingdom Jesus announced had been in tension with the continuing existence of the Jerusalem Temple, whose authorities had sent him to his death. Soon it will be clear which of the two God has vindicated. You cling on to these prophecies and promises for dear life. You have nothing else.

Twenty years pass, and with them the immediate crisis. Jerusalem lies in ruins. Rome has another emperor. You and your fellow Christians have had leisure to reflect on what has, and hasn't, happened. The Church is better established, but the world is still full of wickedness. There must still remain a future fulfilment of God's great, world-changing promises. You continue to tell the story of Jesus' warnings and promises, but the symbols now evoke fresh meanings. God's promise of a new world combines with your longing to be in the royal presence, and under the healing rule, of Jesus himself. Other old sayings, mused on over two generations, give this hope specific focus. 'This Jesus, taken from you into heaven, will come in the same way.' Welcome to Advent: a rich mix of politics, prophecy, prayer and perseverance. Oh, and holiness, too: if the Lord, in his royal presence, will 'establish your hearts unblameable in holiness', it would be as well to live in the present in the mode that is to be vindicated in the future.

3

The Second Sunday of Advent

—— ∽ ——

Malachi 3.1–4
Philippians 1.3–11
Luke 3.1–6

I must have sung Handel's *Messiah* dozens of times before I asked myself what its first chorus actually meant. 'And the glory of the Lord shall be revealed, and all flesh shall see it together.' It makes what the late Michael Flanders once called 'a jolly pleasing noise'; but what is it about?

In Luke's day, this passage from Isaiah had a well-established place within the wider Jewish longing for restoration. When Solomon built the Temple, 'the glory of Yahweh filled the house'. The 'glory' departed when the Babylonians destroyed the Temple; but, even when the Temple was rebuilt, the glory did not come back. Post-exilic prophets like Malachi saw the return of Yahweh to Zion as still in the future: 'the Lord whom you seek will suddenly come to his Temple'. When that happened, the whole created order would, of course, roll out the red carpet. Valleys would be filled in, mountains flattened, and Yahweh would return in splendour to Jerusalem.

The earliest Christians had the audacity to claim that this had been fulfilled in Jesus. John the Baptist was the voice preparing the way; Jesus was the coming King, the very embodiment of the returning Yahweh. He made his public appearance, as Luke emphasizes, within the imperial worlds of Tiberius Caesar and Herod Antipas. Tiberius styled

4

himself as 'son of the divine Augustus'; with John's ministry, Jesus is revealed as the Son of the one God, Israel's God. Malachi's prophecy of the coming Lord who would purify the priesthood is strangely fulfilled in Jesus' subsequent actions in the Temple courts.

In none of these cases did the reality correspond to what first-century readers of the prophets might have expected. The priesthood remained corrupt. Tiberius and Herod still ruled, and ruled brutally. The Temple had not been filled with the bright cloud of God's presence. Hills and valleys remained intact. Nevertheless, Jesus' life, and supremely his death and resurrection, forced his followers to read the prophecies with new eyes. This, after all, must have been what they were about.

At the same time, a new sense was born, of a fulfilment still to come, completing what had been begun. Paul speaks of the purity promised to God's people as a future reality already breaking in to the present. Jesus has already purified his people, and will bring that process to completion when the Old Testament 'day of the Lord' is translated into New Testament reality. God's people at present are the new nation of priests, summing up the praises, prayers, and pains of creation and presenting them before the redeeming and re-creating God, anticipating the more literal fulfilment of Isaiah's cosmic prophecy, when the whole created order will be set free.

We should not underestimate the cost of the purification necessary for this role. 'He is like a refiner's fire, and like fuller's soap.' I wish Handel had set that whole phrase. I would like to know what he would have done with the soap.

The Third Sunday of Advent

—— ⟿ ——

Zephaniah 3.14–20
Philippians 4.4–7
Luke 3.7–18

The new lectionary has hardly begun, and I fear I am going to grumble about it as I did about its predecessor. How will people ever learn that the Bible and its message are politically relevant – that the proclamation of God's kingdom challenges the kingdoms of the world – if we omit the verses that say so (in this case Luke 3.19–20)?

Josephus tells us that Herod regarded John as a threat. Well, he would, wouldn't he: a fiery prophet drawing crowds and talking about God's kingdom. Luke tells us that John singled out Herod for direct attack. It wasn't just that Herod's marital arrangements were unethical, out of line with God's ideal. The point was that they disqualified Herod from being God's true king. John pointed to Jesus as the genuine king of the Jews; but this meant confronting the claims of the existing king. How could Jesus be the king? Because Herod was a sham. How could you tell that Herod was a sham? Look at his personal life. The attack on Herod, and John's imprisonment and subsequent death, are part of the inner meaning of his kingdom-announcement.

The pattern of polemical kingdom-proclamation is deeply rooted in the Hebrew Scriptures. Zephaniah's message to Israel, of long-awaited joy and relief, needs to include the reassurance that God will deal with all oppressors outside, and all prejudices within, his people. The enemies that have made Israel's life a misery will do so no more; the destructive honour/shame culture that has kept the physically handicapped as second-class citizens will be swept aside. All God's people will join in the great celebration. No one versed in Scriptures such as these could fail to see that they were coming true in the work of Jesus, as the lame and the outcast found themselves healed, welcomed into the family at last.

We can keep the political implications of the gospel at bay by removing some passages; we can achieve the same result by reading others without noticing their wider context. When Paul told the Philippians to 'rejoice in the Lord', he was writing to a Roman colony where 'Lord' meant Caesar, and where celebration was what happened on Caesar's birthday and many similar imperial festivals. Philippi, along with many other cities in Greece and Turkey under Roman rule, relied heavily on the *pax Romana*, the peace which had come after the civil war a century before, and which was maintained by heavy-handed and often brutal rule. Against this ambiguous blessing, Paul places 'the peace of God, which passes all understanding'. In the true King, Jesus, God has won the victory over enemies more dangerous and subtle than those of the Roman state. The Advent hope that God's peace will one day rule in the world enables it now to rule in our hearts, and gives us the courage to proclaim the gospel of the kingdom, even when this means challenging the kingdoms of the world.

The Fourth Sunday of Advent

— ∾ —

Micah 5.2–5a
Hebrews 10.5–10
Luke 1.39–45

'He shall be the one of peace.' We can feel the sigh of relief rising from prophet and hearers alike. To a world of uncertainty, fear, wars and rumours of wars, there comes the news of a king whose rule will establish peace and security. The portrait combines different elements: the child to be born from the house of David, the shepherd who will feed his flock, the peaceful ruler of the entire world, and, more puzzling, one 'whose origin is from of old, from ancient days'. Somehow the coming king will embody the presence, and saving power, of Israel's God.

The letter to the Hebrews evokes a quite different biblical image for the coming of the Messiah into the world, yet it arrives at the same conclusion. The Messiah's coming, the writer declares, fulfils Psalm 40: God's purpose will be accomplished through his utter obedience, which is the reality towards which animal sacrifice points. All that the Temple stood for is thus taken up, rolled together, and focused on the one for whom God has 'prepared a body'. The Messiah's birth, into a life of obedience and vocation, makes even Israel's central symbol redundant. He will be the true meeting place of heaven and earth, the location, concentration and embodiment of God's promise-keeping

8

grace. All the symbols of Israel's life, history and culture point towards the mystery of the incarnation.

It is hard to know how much of this was in Mary's mind or heart as she made her hurried journey to Elizabeth. She was no doubt taken up with the excitement, the shock, the perplexity of finding herself in the situation of which so many Jewish girls down the years had dreamed but which none before her had actually experienced. 'Until the time when she who is in labour has brought forth': Micah's prophecy had but a few months to go. Would she cope? Was she equal to the challenge of such a wonderful and terrible vocation? The great stories of the Bible, with all their large theological and political significance, enhance and do not eliminate the sense of specific persons being caught up within God's drama, finding their own lives turned upside down or perhaps the right way up, being gripped at the heart with God's mysterious presence, feeling the warm breath of his love, discovering a sense of direction to which they have no choice but be obedient. We must, of course, resist the pressure to turn Christmas into a celebration of private feelings and beliefs. That would be to capitulate to our culture's insistence that religion is set apart from Micah's problems, from the pain and politics of the larger world. But, once we recognize in Mary's womb the one 'whose origin is of old, of ancient days', we may find, like Elizabeth, that something leaps within us. The presence in our midst of the Obedient One may become once more the signal, and the means, of fresh vocation, obedience, hope and joy.

Christmas

The First Sunday of Christmas

—— ∼ ——

1 Samuel 2.18–20, 26
Colossians 3.12–17
Luke 2.41–52

The boyhood stories of Jesus and Samuel jar slightly with one another. Samuel's mother deliberately takes him to the Temple in order to leave him there; Jesus' parents intend to take him home, but leave him behind by mistake. Samuel, designated as assistant to Eli, the priest, is then called to be a prophet. Jesus, whom Luke's reader already knows is the appointed King, appears here as a prodigious student of Israel's traditions. For Luke, after all, the closer parallel to Samuel is John the Baptist, not Jesus: John, born by promise to a childless couple, does what Samuel eventually did and anoints the coming King.

Underneath the surface differences runs the same dark theme. Jesus' twelve-year-old visit to the Temple foreshadows his later visit, in Luke 19, where he weeps over the city, pronounces its doom, and goes alone to confront the chief priests once more. Samuel's apprenticing to Eli takes place in the context of increasing evil within Eli's own house; the verses in which this all-too-contemporary corruption is described are omitted by the squeamish lectionary, producing an apparently cosy scene of a happy and devout family where the text offers one of shocking immorality and forebodings of judgement, of which the boy-prophet is to be the herald. (Notice how the same thing happens when

12

1 Samuel 3 is read out in church, stopping abruptly at verse 10; and, for that matter, Isaiah 6, stopping at verse 8. Clear-cut vocations seem to be associated with unwelcome tasks; hoping for the former without the latter, we muzzle both the text and ourselves.) When Luke, echoing the Samuel story again, says that Jesus increased in wisdom and stature, and in divine and human favour, those with ears to hear will not construe the parallel as indicating a settled, model 'holy family' life, but rather Jesus' strange commissioning and equipping for the task of copying Samuel, bringing God's word of justice to his faithless people.

Luke's story sets up further resonances with his own last chapter. The disciples on the road to Emmaus (husband and wife?) are leaving Jerusalem in sorrow, three days having elapsed after the crashing failure of their dreams. When they rush back to Jerusalem it is with joy, having met the Jesus who had completed his Father's business.

All is not lost, though, for those who still hope that readings about the 'holy family' will offer help for our own somewhat less than holy ones. Paul's bracing injunctions to kindness, gentleness and mutual forgiveness are quite enough to be going on with, simply considered as abstract moral commandments. But they are of course nothing of the kind. They are what happens when the royal life, the Jesus-life, is let loose in persons and communities. The thought of a family, or church, really living out Colossians 3 will puzzle some for whom it appears totally unrealistic. So what? Did they not know that we must be about our Father's business?

The Second Sunday of Christmas

—— ⁓ ——

Jeremiah 31.7–14
Ephesians 1.3–14
John 1.1–18

Take a deep breath, and try reading Ephesians 1.3–14 all in one go. It is, after all, a single sentence in the Greek, a Christian version of the Jewish-style prayer, 'Blessed be the God who...'. Only now, instead of the Jewish affirmations, we have a rethought set of Christian ones. God's choice of his special people; their rescue from slavery; his purpose to bless the whole world through them; his offer, and advance guarantee, of an inheritance. Election, exodus, promised land, and the presence of God himself: this is Israel's story, summed up in the Messiah's story and thus made available to those who are 'in him'. Jeremiah's promise of covenant renewal has come true.

This prayer sums up, in form as much as content, the revolution that has occurred within Judaism with the coming of the Messiah. Just as a house-plant may produce inoffensive leaves for years and then suddenly sprout a spectacular flower, so the steady recital of God's mighty acts, looking back many centuries, now gives birth to something which appears novel but which could only have come from within. This prayer belongs firmly in the Jewish tradition, but its focus on one recent individual, its extension of God's promise to a worldwide people, and its latent trinitarianism all proclaim that something new has come to flower with the birth of the Messiah.

Even Ephesians 1 is overshadowed by the opening of John's Gospel. (How on earth can one hope to read these side by side in a church service in such a way as to let their resonances be heard? Answers on a postcard, please.) John 1 is prayer, theology, history, Scripture and (as the advertisements say) much more: a meditation which penetrates quietly into the mystery of God and the world, drawing eye, mind, heart and will into the life and love of the Creator.

Again we find radical innovation at the very centre of Judaism. How does the one transcendent Creator act within, and for the benefit of, his creation? First-century Judaism answers: by his wisdom, his word, his law, his spirit, and his glory (the last of which dwells in the Temple). John 1 offers an extended meditation on Jesus in precisely these categories. The idea that Jesus is 'God incarnate' is not, as often suggested, a move away from Jewish monotheism into speculative Greek philosophy. It is a means of seeing Jesus and the Spirit precisely within Jewish categories. It is the new flower, bursting unexpectedly from the plant.

If this is the God we worship (and if it isn't, then Christmas has indeed been a waste of time) we would do well to ask: what surprising new flowers has he in store for us today? In January 2000, however misleadingly, we celebrated the Millennium. Inside our regular (and often rather tame) celebrations of God's liberation in Jesus, there might be a new flower waiting to be born. Forget the white elephants: what about the Jubilee?

Epiphany

The First Sunday of Epiphany

—— ≈ ——

Isaiah 43.1–7
Acts 8.14–17
Luke 3.15–17, 21–22

We now have the middle of Luke 3 for the second time in four weeks, and verses 19–20 are still missing. This mightn't matter so much if they didn't relate as closely as they do to the underlying themes of the other readings, chosen in this Epiphany season to emphasize the outward movement of the gospel, beyond the confines of Israel, to embrace the rest of the world.

The problem is that the rest of the world doesn't particularly *want* to be embraced, thank you very much, and often takes vigorous steps to prevent any such thing happening. The crowds were wondering if John was the Messiah, the King of the Jews; no, says John, but he is coming. But there already is a king of the Jews, and he doesn't care for rival kingdom-announcements. John's warning of the fire that will burn up the chaff is partly directed at that supreme piece of chaff, Herod Antipas, a shadow no doubt of his malevolent old father, but still capable of brutal overreaction, not least to disturbing prophets. When you celebrate the three kings, remember that not all kings came bearing gifts.

A more subtle confrontation takes place in Samaria. Like a forest fire leaping across a river, the gospel of Jesus has crossed the most obvious racial and cultural barrier, extending from the early Jewish Christians to the despised

18

Samaritans. As a symbolic gesture, the mission of Peter and John was a vital sign of the Epiphany message: Jesus and his Spirit are for all people, not just for the Jews. (That, rather than any theory about apostolic sacramental 'validity', was certainly what Luke saw as the main point of the incident.) But, like all powerful symbolic gestures, this one provoked a reaction, again conveniently omitted in these readings: the local magician tried to make the apostolic gospel part of his arsenal of lucrative trickery, and Peter's and John's mission to Samaria therefore included sharp and necessary rebuke along with glad affirmation.

Behind all such scenes in the New Testament stands the prophetic awareness that the better the news from the true God, the more likely the angry reaction of the false gods (and those who serve them). Isaiah's wonderful message of comfort is based on the character of Israel's God, the powerful healer; but the reason his people are to be encouraged is that the pagan idols that have held them in their grip have been defeated at last. This knowledge alone will enable the prophet's hearers to pass through fire and water without danger. If, ultimately, we have nothing to fear from the loud and threatening gods that range themselves against God's gospel, we have nothing to gain by pretending that their threats, and their temporary power, do not exist. At Epiphany, we do well to recognize that the kingdoms of the world will not always welcome the kingdom of God. The bracing realism of the Bible is the ground of its true comfort.

The Second Sunday of Epiphany

—— ⁓ ——

Isaiah 62.1–5
1 Corinthians 12.1–11
John 2.1–11

Nuptial imagery rings through the Bible like a peal of wedding bells. The first two chapters of Genesis reach their climax in the creation of man and woman in God's image; the last two chapters of Revelation unveil the New Jerusalem, dressed as a bride adorned for her husband. In between, weddings form significant steps in the story of God and his people (Isaac/Rebecca, Ruth/Boaz, and many others); marriage failure reflects covenant disaster (Hosea); marriage renewal-after-failure follows the work of the Servant (Isaiah 54). In today's reading, Jerusalem's vindication and glory is to be revealed before the nations, resulting in joy like that of a happy young couple (Isaiah 62). In the New Testament, Ephesians joins Revelation in picturing marriage as a sign and sacrament of Christ's union with his people. The world (or is it just the journalists?) may scorn, sentimentalize or trivialize marriage; God still celebrates it.

Hardly surprising, then, that the first 'sign' of Jesus' glory in John's Gospel takes place at a wedding, and lifts the party to new heights. This 'sign' begins a series; John underlines the second one, too (4.54), and leaves us to work out the rest for ourselves. Though the point is debated, it seems likely that he intends the seventh (or perhaps it's the eighth, the first of a new sequence?) to be the resurrection. The present

20

'sign' takes place 'on the third day', pointing forwards to that great fulfilment.

But of course Jesus' glory is fully revealed, as far as John is concerned, on the cross. There, when 'the hour has come' at last, Jesus' strange question (literally 'Woman, what is there to you and me?') is replaced by 'Woman, behold your son; son, behold your mother'. As at Cana Jesus takes the Jewish purification-water and turns it into wine, so at Calvary he takes the Jewish Passover festival and transforms it into the great revelation-in-action of God's glory and love. God has kept the best wine until now: Israel and the world look on in wonder as the true Bridegroom confounds custom and expectation, redeeming Israel and the world in a way neither would have imagined possible.

The only reason for including 1 Corinthians 12 here would have been verse 13, where Paul speaks not only of being immersed in the Spirit, but actually of drinking it. This is reflected in the choice of Psalm 36, where God 'gives his people drink from the river of his delights'. Getting drunk on the Spirit, *à la* Acts 2, is so un-Anglican that the lectionary-mongers seem to have lost their nerve and stopped two verses short. But pause to reflect on God's choice of weddings and wine as signs of glory. When we leave church, or rise from prayer (why does that phrase sound old-fashioned?), would people mistake us for wedding guests? For party-goers? Why not? Did we 'do whatever he tells' us? Did we see his glory and believe?

The Third Sunday of Epiphany

— ∾ —

Nehemiah 8.1–3, 5–6, 8–10
1 Corinthians 12.12–31a
Luke 4.14–21

Read the text, and give the sense. Both matter. The first is
given, there on the page. The second is risky, a matter of
prayer and the Spirit, a deep breath and taking the plunge.

History warns of wrong, sometimes dangerous, interpretations. But interpretation is inevitable; not to interpret is still
to interpret. History also remembers defining moments when
text and interpretation together created a new world. Ezra
and his colleagues read the law and explained it, creating not
only post-exilic Judaism but, in a measure, today's rabbinic
Judaism. Jesus read Isaiah and interpreted it, setting the stage
not only for his own career but also, in a measure, for his
followers to our own time. What could be more dramatic
than reading the law code to a community, defining them as
God's people in a new way, causing simultaneous tears and
rejoicing? Perhaps only this: reading prophecies which spoke
of future blessing, and then declaring that it was already
starting to happen.

Ezra's message called forth weeping and celebrating;
Jesus' sermon produced both antagonism and loyalty. Luke
says that Jesus was already acting 'in the power of the Spirit';
when he applied Isaiah 61 to himself he wasn't simply
promoting himself, but explaining what he had been doing.
As with other prophecies, being misunderstood came with

the package. Ezra had the governor's backing. Jesus stood alone, with Herod not far away, Rome on the horizon, and hostile listeners ready to pounce.

Whatever reception today's expositor may expect, the vocation is the same. Read the text and explain it. Expect it to create and define the community, to evoke joy and sorrow, opposition and enthusiasm. The text may be long forgotten, needing to be dusted down and re-presented. It may be well known, needing to be seen in a new light.

Paul's exposition of the unity of Christ's body provides a case in point. If it were read and expounded before the mutually suspicious churches and Christian groupings of our own day; if it were applied in the power of the Spirit to our bizarre and often anachronistic divisions; should we weep in sorrow at our failure to live by it, or throw our hats in the air at the recognition of our real identity and mutual belonging? If someone declared to us that it was time at last for this Scripture to be fulfilled, would we reject the proposal as dangerous and unworkable, or would we sign up, take the risks, and go with the new movement?

Paul grounds the unity of the Church in the one baptism into Christ's body. If we find it hard to explain the meaning of baptism today, perhaps this is because we are so used to thinking of a variety of different bodies that we can no longer hear what Paul is talking about. Where are today's Ezras, called to read and to teach? Where are today's prophets, prepared to say 'Now is the moment for this to be fulfilled'?

The Fourth Sunday of Epiphany

— ≈ —

Ezekiel 43.27—44.4
1 Corinthians 13.1–13
Luke 2.22–40

Ezekiel had seen the glory of the Lord abandoning Jerusalem and the Temple to their fate (chs 10—11). Fittingly, it is he who describes, in the strange visions of chapters 43—44, the return of that glory. Picking up where Isaiah 40 left off, he points forward to the transcendent and luminous splendour of God's presence in the wondrously restored Temple. In the last line of his book, the name of the new city is *Yahweh shammah*, The Lord is There. Jerusalem's peculiar vocation was to be the place where the God of all the earth would be revealed, lighting up the Temple, the city and ultimately the whole world with his radiant presence.

To get the full flavour of the New Testament's reworkings of this theme, you must imagine a faithful (though often faint and fearful) people living with that promise through generations and even centuries, through false dawns and dashed hopes. Think of pious and learned Jews studying Ezekiel and the other prophets, meditating, praying, waiting and wondering. Think of militant Jews getting fed up sitting around, and opting instead to prepare the way for God's glory by force of arms. And then, after all those years, think of an old man who has nurtured a vision for years, wondering no doubt if it was just a dream, and who one day lifts up his eyes in the Temple, sees a young couple with a baby, and

24

no longer doubts, but knows. And think of an old woman, frail and bent but with bright, deep eyes, who is suddenly found telling everyone that the glory has returned. A light to reveal Israel's God to the Gentiles; glory for Israel herself. It probably wasn't what Ezekiel thought it would look like, but I can see him nodding, slowly and thoughtfully, in the background, and preparing once more to fall on his face in awe and love.

The relevance of 1 Corinthians 13 to this rich theme lies in the fact that 1 Corinthians as a whole portrays the Church, corporately and individually, as the temple of the living God, and that chapter 13 is the letter's artistic and theological climax. The busy, bustling arguments of the earlier chapters, hammering out Christian practice on wisdom, personality cults, sex and marriage, compromise with paganism, and so forth, subside. Rising above them, drawing their many melodies into a majestic chorale, is Paul's poem about love: a love that he can only have learnt from the revelation of God in Jesus, a love that can only be lived by the Spirit of Jesus, a love that is as compelling to contemplate as it is difficult to practise.

The return of God's glory was never to be merely comforting. The fall and rise of many in Israel; a sign to be spoken against; a sword through Mary's soul as well. Dangerous treasure, that, to store up in your heart (Luke 2.51). The same could be said of Paul's message, too.

Ordinary Time

Proper 1

— ∾ —

Isaiah 6.1–13
1 Corinthians 15.1–11
Luke 5.1–11

'The holy seed is its stump.' Isaiah's vision in the Temple leaves him with a dreadful commission, to inform God's people of inevitable exile. The nation will be like a tree felled and burnt. But when the worst has occurred, and the smoke clears away, the stump of the tree, blackened and ugly, may again put forth new shoots. After exile there will be new life. Isaiah's original vision contains a microcosm of the entire book.

Observe how the prophet was prepared for this commission. His vision of the thrice-holy God had filled the house with smoke and his heart with shame. Fear followed swiftly, as the seraph flew to him with a burning coal, surely meaning judgement. And so it did; but that wasn't the end. 'This has touched your lips; your guilt is gone, your sin is covered.' This judgement was cleansing, purifying. So it would be with the nation as a whole. The prophet had to learn in himself the hard truth which he would then announce to the people.

Luke's story of the call of the first disciples has a similar shape, inviting us to remark on the striking new content. Instead of God's glory, shielded by seraphs, filling the house with smoke, we have a young prophet borrowing a boat, teaching the shorebound crowds, and filling Peter's nets with unexpected fish. Peter's response mirrors Isaiah's, recognizing in these events a revelation of Israel's God. But Jesus, like the seraph, does not fulfil Peter's expectations, leaving him to suffer the results of his sin. 'Don't be afraid; from now on you will be catching people alive.' The word for 'catching' in Luke's story is unusual: its metaphorical overtones are not so much of fishing, but of taking prisoners alive as opposed to killing them, hence also of restoring to life someone under the threat of death. Peter is not simply to 'fish for people', but to be God's agent in restoring people to life. Peter, like Isaiah, is to be the mouthpiece of the truth he has just learnt in experience.

Paul puts his own experience of the same strange commissioning into a theological formulation: 'By God's grace I am what I am; and his grace to me was not in vain; but I worked harder than all the rest, yet not I but God's grace that was with me.' The grace that grasped Paul reached out through Paul to grasp others with the good news of God's victory over evil in Jesus' death and resurrection. That, after all, is what we should expect, from Isaiah 6 onwards. At Calvary, the tree is cut down, its stump burnt. On Holy Saturday, the holy seed sleeps in the stump. On Easter morning, a shoot comes forth from the stump, and a branch grows out of the roots. And as God's multi-textured truth thereby takes hold of our hearts and minds, look out: that which God burns into us, we are required to pass on.

Proper 2

—— ∾ ——

Jeremiah 17.5–10
1 Corinthians 15.12–20
Luke 6.17–26

Blessings and woes: the upside-down world of the gospel, addressing, as Jeremiah had done, the heart's self-deceptions, and allowing YHWH to test the mind and search the heart.

The woes read like a list of contemporary media-starring role models. The rich: well, obviously. Those who are filled: if not rich, at least their next meal is assured, probably larger than they actually need. Those who laugh: the careless amusement of those for whom the world is not really a tragedy, merely a joke. Those praised by all: the day I write these words, another Honours List is published, giving welcome recognition to some unsung heroes and heroines, but mostly adding one more trophy to already glittering names.

Woe to them! They are probably false prophets, and will receive their reward. Jesus sounds, not for the last time, like Jeremiah himself. His agenda is designed to shock; nothing less will jolt devious hearts into thinking straight about what really matters. The blessings, equally startling, tell us, again in Jeremiah's language, how to find the stream beside which our roots will stay watered, our leaves green, and our fruit fresh. The poor; those who mourn and weep; those who are hated, reviled, and cast out because of the Son of Man.

Blessings on them! We hear the words, but most of us find that our devious heart refuses to take them seriously.

Jesus' teaching did not come out of the blue. He did not simply arrive in a town and start talking. He arrived with a previous reputation as a healer; it is historically probable that crowds gathered because of his healings, and stayed to listen to his strange oracles. This teaching was designed not simply to give generalized advice, however extraordinary, about the nature of life in God's kingdom, but to explain the secret of Jesus' power.

A church that deceives itself on such basic matters is likely also to deceive itself when it comes to the resurrection. Paul speaks of the rich/poor divide earlier in the letter. We cannot be sure that it was the rich who doubted the resurrection and the poor who believed it, though some such correlation seems at least plausible. That is how self-deceit often works.

The belief in question – not a general belief in immortality or 'survival', but the specific belief that God will give to all Christ's people a new bodily life corresponding to the transformed body of Jesus' resurrection – puts all present wealth, power and posturing into a totally different light. What passes for contemporary thought about ethics often only asks what it may be allowed to get away with: how far it can go. More self-deception. A genuinely Christian ethic would ask: granted that God is going to create a new world, and give us a newly embodied life, in the future, what sort of life is appropriate in the present? Suddenly Jesus' blessings and woes look remarkably appropriate. Easter unmasks the heart's greatest deceits.

31

Proper 3

—— ❧ ——

Genesis 45.3–11, 15
1 Corinthians 15.35–38, 42–50
Luke 6.27–38

The resurrection is central to Christianity, not just as a dogma but as a driving principle. Unfortunately, Paul's writing in this, the earliest discussion of it, is dense and difficult, and some of the regular translations don't help.

The key is Paul's contrast between perishable and imperishable. The seed and the plant are not an exact analogy for the old body and the new, but rather a way of demonstrating radical change within basic continuity.

The all-important claim is that 'God gives it a body' (v. 38). It is irrelevant to worry (as did some of the early Fathers) about how God will reassemble the exact atoms and molecules of our present bodies. They are in any case in a constant state of flux, through which matter is shared, not hoarded. Resurrection will be an act of new creation, taking up the old within it, like an architect and builder taking stones from a tumbledown old building and reusing them, enhancing their beauty thereby, within a great cathedral.

The new body, then, will be imperishable, not subject to decay or death. It will be animated, not by the 'soul' that will depart from the present body at death, but by the Spirit; that is the meaning of the 'natural body' and the 'spiritual body' in verse 44. (The common translations 'physical body' and 'spiritual body' give completely the wrong impression, implying a kind of Platonism in which physicality itself is regarded as a second-rate form of existence.)

Thus, when Paul declares (v. 50) that 'flesh and blood cannot inherit the kingdom', he is not suggesting that the resurrection body is what we would call 'non-physical'. As the rest of the passage makes clear, the present physicality, subject to decay and death, has to be transformed. In God's new creation, death is not merely to be redescribed in somewhat more optimistic language (death 'seen as' resurrection, as some have put it), but defeated and reversed. If this were not so, Paul could have answered his initial question ('what sort of body will the resurrected dead possess?') a lot more briefly.

Celebrating God's goodness in redemptive re-creation is the underlying motif of Jesus' charge to love enemies, to be merciful and generous beyond measure, and thereby to reflect the compassionate heart of the heavenly Father. To see all this as a hard challenge, towards which one struggles, is already not only to misunderstand but to disobey. Jesus envisages a life based on God's future, on the lavish and exuberant love of the Creator let loose upon the world once more in healing and grace; he urges us to let the life and love of this God flow through our lives already. We are to be resurrection people, those in whom God's future transforms the present.

That was Joseph's secret. Looking to God's future, he was able to see the present with forgiveness instead of revenge. Instead of the anger we might have expected, we find healing generosity.

The Second Sunday Before Lent

———— ∿ ————

Genesis 2.4b–9, 15–25
Revelation 4
Luke 8.22–25

The goodness and the terror of the created world dominate these readings. From the garden in Genesis to the throne-room in Revelation, all that is done reflects God's loving creativity, and his sharing of that creativity with the creatures made in his own image. God's breath in human nostrils is used to give names to the animals, and then finally to lead them in worship. Woven deep into Scripture is the human vocation, to be God's agents in bringing order and joy to the world of rivers and plants, animals and birds, and indeed to one another. Made for relationship with God, with the natural world, and with one another, we know the glory, and the high risk, of our fragile calling.

And then there is the sea: endlessly fascinating, simultaneously sulky and seductive, beckoning and threatening. The American travel writer Paul Theroux expressed bewilderment at English people, in cars or on benches, sitting looking at the sea. Why the puzzle? Like a Wagner opera, operating at levels of symbol and drama which touch the nerves other communications cannot reach, the sea reminds us of forces within and around us that have the potential both for horrible destruction and for spectacular beauty. The sea offers its own daily liturgy of chaos and creation, judgement and salvation; like all good liturgy, it draws us into its rhythm.

Genesis insists that the sea is also God's creature. It is not an alien force, a rival deity. The same is, of course, true of Satan; and the sea, already in the story of Noah God's agent of judgement, steadily becomes, in Jewish thought as elsewhere, the great symbol for the forces of dark malevolence. The Psalms celebrated God's victory over the mighty waters: referring to the Exodus, of course, but with mythological overtones wider than any single event. It was from the sea that the monsters emerged in Daniel 7, to make war on the people of God. In Revelation 4.6, with echoes of Solomon's temple, there is a sea of glass, like crystal, before the throne; chaos and evil still threaten God's plan for his creation, but the promise remains of an Exodus-like redemption (Revelation 15.2). Finally, in the new Jerusalem of Revelation 21, there is no more sea.

Jesus asleep as the sea rages around him: why (so far as I can discover) has no great artist painted that scene? It combines Jesus' serenity in the face of threatening chaos, his sharing the lot of those engulfed by it, and God's rainbow-promise that the mighty waters shall not have the last word. Where is the disciples' faith? Do they not know that Jesus is to be the agent of the new Exodus? Of the kingdom in which Israel's God will rule over the raging sea? As the waves subside, imagination makes contact with long-buried hopes and fears, and memory superimposes psalms and prophecies. Who is this, sovereign over the very symbol of untameable disorder?

The Sunday Next Before Lent

—— ～ ——

Exodus 34.29–end
2 Corinthians 3.12—4.2
Luke 9.28–43

The intriguing thing about Moses coming down the mountain with his face shining was that *he didn't know.* He had simply been talking with God; it was only when Aaron and the others met him that he realized, from their reaction, that he had been transformed. He was shining unwittingly with God's glory, and the terrified Israelites requested that he wear a veil.

The story became popular in later Jewish legend, and, with a bizarre misunderstanding, in medieval art: the Hebrew word for 'shining' was mistranslated as 'horned', and several artists painted small horns on Moses' forehead, giving him, to our later eyes, a decidedly sinister appearance. The story in Exodus is itself already somewhat comic, with Moses putting on and taking off his veil by rotation.

In 2 Corinthians 3, Paul seems to assume that Moses wore the veil when speaking the law to the people; he also suggests that the real veil lay, not on Moses' face, but on his hearers' hearts (not 'minds' as in NRSV). His talk about reflecting God's glory is exciting, but the argument is dense and difficult. The key is to realize that Paul is drawing a contrast, not between himself and Moses, but between Moses' hearers and his own. Moses failed to 'get through' because the Israelites' hearts remained hardened against the glorious

36

revelation; but the Spirit of Christ has written God's new covenant on the hearts of believers (3.3–6), giving them 'the light of the knowledge of the glory of God in the face of Jesus Christ' (4.6). As a result, when Paul addresses a group of Christians, he does so with boldness and freedom, because the glory of the gospel, which he is revealing to them, is also shining back at him from his hearers. When they look at one another, they are all gazing, as in a mirror, at the glory of the Lord.

Like Moses, the Corinthians are unaware that they are glory-bearers. They are therefore puzzled, maybe even offended, at Paul's direct and challenging style. Why doesn't he dress up his message with more flowery rhetoric? Answer: when you face a congregation of new covenant people, you can tell it like it is. 'By the open statement of the truth we commend ourselves to everyone's conscience in the sight of God.' Christians must learn to see, by faith, the glory of God shining in one another.

Here, then, is part at least of the meaning of the Transfiguration. This time, the God whom Moses met on the mountain was the incarnate one, on his way to accomplish the new Exodus (Luke 9.31). This time, the glory was to be put into action in challenging the forces of sickness and darkness. This time, the word goes out to all people: 'This is my Son, my Chosen; listen to him.' The hearts, lives and perhaps even the faces of those who hear and obey will be transformed, whether they realize it or not.

Lent

The First Sunday of Lent

———— ≈ ————

Deuteronomy 26.1–11
Romans 10.8b–13
Luke 4.1–13

These readings are not about 'temptation' so much as about true worship. Jesus recognized his temptations as distractions from worshipping and trusting the one true God. To see temptation in terms of rules we would like to break, or impulses we must learn to tame, is to succumb to a second-order temptation: to see temptation itself in terms of negatives.

The truth is very different. Every moment, God calls us to know, love and worship him, and thereby to find and celebrate our genuine humanity, and reflect his image in the world. Temptations lure us to turn away from that privilege and invitation, to lower our gaze, shorten our sights, and settle for second best or worse. The dictionary definition of the Greek word for 'sin' is 'missing the mark'. Sin, like a misfired arrow, drops short of the call to true humanness, to bearing and reflecting God's image.

Jesus maintained a single-minded devotion. His allegiance to his Father overrode immediate bodily desires; it ruled out an easy but costly short cut to his vocation (to be the Lord of the world); it forbade him, by seeking a 'proof' of his status, to challenge the word spoken at his baptism. For him, worshipping the one he knew as Father was larger and richer than all these. The real answer to temptation is not 'God will be cross if I do that', but 'if I do that, I will miss the best that my Father has for me'.

That is why the Israelites, entering the land, were to worship God with their first crops. They could not take the land for granted as an automatic right. Their celebrations were a reminder that it was theirs by God's saving grace alone (Deuteronomy 26.6–9), and a sign, through their hospitality to resident aliens (26.11), that they were channels of grace as well as recipients. Of course, they failed; Jesus' fasting in the wilderness was, among other things, a sign of corporate penitence for a thousand years of rebellion, and a prelude to the establishment of a new people whose sole identifying badge would be neither race, nor territory, but loyalty to God.

Paul indicates that Jesus has indeed become Lord of the whole world, though not by the tempter's route. His faithfulness to his strange vocation of suffering and death is now to be reflected by our faithfulness to him, summed up in our acknowledgement of his universal lordship and our belief in his resurrection from the dead. These striking claims, repeated in our own baptisms, are of course under regular attack. We are thereby regularly tempted, not merely to wrong belief, but to missing out on the best that God has for us, the genuine humanness that Jesus offers to all through the Paschal mystery. As we set out on the wilderness journey of Lent, we do well to reflect on true worship as the ground of true holiness, and true belief as its identifying mark.

The Second Sunday of Lent

—— ≈ ——

Genesis 15.1–12, 17–18
Philippians 3.17—4.1
Luke 13.31–end

The question raised by Philippians 3.17 is: how on earth can the Philippian church, Gentile Christians mostly, 'join in imitating' Paul? The chapter so far describes how Paul came to regard his orthodox Jewish background as 'rubbish', and gave it up to gain Christ. What has that to do with them?

Today's epistle urges the Philippians to adopt the same attitude to their own privileges as Paul did to his. They belonged to a Roman colony; and, though Paul could make creative use of his Roman citizenship, his gospel cut across the grain of orthodox Roman belief and practice. Fifty years earlier, the Mediterranean world hailed Augustus as 'saviour' and 'lord'. He had, after all, brought peace (of a sort) to the known world, and ruled unchallenged over an unprecedentedly large empire. Roman citizens, wherever they were, cherished both their status and their security. If enemies threatened, their saviour-lord would come from the mother city to rescue them. By Paul's day, Caesar was openly worshipped, at least in the Eastern Mediterranean.

Verses 20–21 must be read against that background. For the Christian there is only one Saviour and Lord, only one mother city, only one hope. The Philippians must be ready to abandon the imitation in order to embrace the reality. The conclusion of the argument at 4.1 (congratulations to the lectionary for getting it right), encourages them to find their identity and security in this 'Lord' and in nobody else.

They are, in consequence, to engage in the same holy boldness with which Jesus, at one remove, confronted Herod. Herod may only have been a tinpot little monarch compared with Caesar, but his sly threats were real enough. Jesus had sovereign confidence in God's overarching plan: when he declares it impossible for a prophet to die outside Jerusalem, he is not making a statement about history so much as asserting that his own prophetic vocation, which his divine commissioner would safeguard, would be accomplished there and there only. He would be enthroned, however paradoxically, in Jerusalem, and Herod would be shown up as the impostor. The way of the cross, trodden by Jesus and commended by Paul, undercuts the claims of the rulers of this world.

It thereby also fulfils the ancient promise to Abram. At the start of Genesis 15, Abram doesn't even have an heir; by the end, he has been promised both an innumerable family and a substantial territory. The former will gain the latter through the hard road of slavery and rescue, the Old Testament's way of the cross (vv. 13–16). And, as Paul encourages the Philippians to lift their eyes to the heavenly Jerusalem, so God tells Abram to look to the starry heavens to see the wide extent of his promise. No good keeping one's eyes on the present rulers of Egypt or Canaan, of Galilee or Rome; God's kingdom will come on earth as in heaven, and it will come by the way of the cross.

The Third Sunday of Lent

—— ⁓ ——

Isaiah 55.1–9
1 Corinthians 10.1–13
Luke 13.1–9

Just in case anyone thought the Old Testament was all gloomy and the New cheerful, here are two passages of dire warning from the New Testament preceded by a warm, redeeming invitation from the Old. Underlying both is God's summons to accept his mercy and his way now, while there is time: 'Seek the Lord while he may be found, call on him while he is near.' Unstated, but powerfully implied, is the message which Isaiah has in common with Luke's Jesus. 'The time may come when you will wish you had.'

Jesus' warnings about coming judgement should not be mistaken for old-fashioned hell-fire preaching. Focus on the 'likewise' in verses 3 and 5: 'Unless you repent, you will perish as they did.' Who are 'they'? The Galileans cut down by Roman swords in the Temple; the Jerusalemites crushed when the tower of Siloam fell. What does 'repent' mean in this context, then? Not simply 'give up your private sins'; rather, 'turn from your headlong flight away from God's mercy, from your quest for your own national salvation by rebellion against Rome.' Unless you give it up, Roman swords and falling stonework will be your lot, not as an arbitrary punishment from a vengeful God but as the direct result of the way you have freely chosen, following your own thoughts rather than God's thoughts. Jesus' tough little parable, then, relates directly to his own work: he has been coming to Israel, seeking fruit and finding none, and now is offering one last chance. As he says at the end of the chapter, he has longed to gather Jerusalem as a hen gathers her chicks for safety under her wings, but the offer has been refused.

Worryingly, Paul confronts Christians with more or less the same challenge. Don't think that baptism and eucharist will magically save you; they put you in the same position as the Israelites in the wilderness, and look what happened to them. Gospel symbols invoke God's presence, but doing that while misbehaving is thumbing one's nose at divine mercy. 1 Corinthians 10 joins strong sacramental and pastoral theology. When faced with idolatry or immorality, Paul doesn't pretend that baptism and eucharist don't mean anything, but nor does he suggest that they exempt one from moral obligation. Nor, however, does he suppose that Christians have to meet this challenge unaided. Amid stormy temptations, they are to cling to the faithfulness of God, who will enable them to come through.

Back, then, to Isaiah. Why does he explain the invitation to return (vv. 6–7) by saying that God thinks differently from how we do (vv. 8–9)? Presumably because no human being would have been faithful and merciful when faced with Israel's rebellion. Isaiah appeals to the transcendence of God, not to frighten, but to explain just how much more generous and merciful God is than we could ever have imagined. Not for nothing is he called, in the old sense, the evangelical prophet.

The Fourth Sunday of Lent

—— ⁓ ——

Joshua 5.9–12
2 Corinthians 5.16–end
Luke 15.1–3, 11b–end

At Gilgal the Israelites, like the prodigal, exchanged the food of the wilderness for the food of home. In a dense little scene, explicable only in its wider context, the covenant signs come rushing together: Jordan, circumcision, passover, the fruit of the land. From that moment on, without as yet a sword drawn or a city taken, the Israelites had come home.

Come home, moreover, without reproach. Scholars seem uncertain what 'the disgrace of Egypt' means, or why having the nation circumcised would roll it away. It can't mean that Israel had been in an 'Egyptian', i.e. uncircumcised, condition: the Egyptians were themselves circumcised. More likely, perhaps, that the Egyptians would have despised Israel: yes, they've escaped, but they are only dirty, uncircumcised people, so it doesn't matter. From Gilgal onwards, this taunt is removed. Israel is God's free covenant people, without reproach. No more manna, no more uncircumcision, no more wilderness: the old has passed away, all is become new, as Paul puts it in his spectacular discussion of the ministry of reconciliation.

We are inclined to get carried away in a passage like this, and to forget what it's really all about. It is an explanation of Paul's apostolic ministry. Paul stands on the promised-land side of the Jordan, refusing to look at anyone from the perspective of the 'flesh', the previous wilderness existence. What matters is Christ, and the new creation in him; because of God's action, reconciliation between Creator and creation is now a fact of history, and must be implemented. That is the thrust of the last two verses of chapter 5. Paul does not say 'we entreat *you* on behalf of Christ', but just 'we entreat'; he is describing his ministry, not appealing to the Corinthians. And 'the righteousness of God' in 5.21 is not the status of the justified sinner, but God's covenant faithfulness, which the apostles embody as well as announce. They are to be themselves people who inhabit the further side of the Jordan, living evidence that God has rolled away the reproach of his creation. They thus invite others to join them.

Reconciliation in New Testament terms means the Prodigal Son, one of the few remaining passages which almost everyone in the congregation will already know, or think they know. The story is its own meaning; no summary, no painting even, can replace it. Yet its very familiarity is a challenge: how can we bring it to life once more, prevent the sense of *déjà vu*? Try thinking it through with the Exodus symbolism fresh in mind: the young son in the wilderness, eating desert food until he comes home to the fatted calf; the father ready to roll away all reproach. But this time the reproach comes, not from outsiders, but from within. How can this reconciliation be other than scandalous? And, as at Gilgal, a strange sense of something gained and much still to achieve. What did the Prodigal Son do the next morning?

The Fifth Sunday of Lent (Passiontide begins)

—— ~ ——

Isaiah 43.16–21
Philippians 3.4b–14
John 12.1–8

Two stark characterizations from John: the full-blown devotion of Mary and the brooding cynicism of Judas. (On Mondays, Wednesdays and Fridays I think this may perhaps be the same story as that in Luke 7, where the woman is a 'sinner' and the host, and chief grumbler, is a Pharisee called Simon. Writing this on a Thursday, I acknowledge that the host in Matthew's and Mark's parallel to John is called Simon, but I still think Luke is talking about a different occasion.) Lazarus is alive again, and his sisters play out their accustomed roles, Martha serving and Mary at Jesus' feet. Modern cities fill with noise, ancient ones (in the pre-soap days) with smell; Mary's perfume wafts its welcome fragrance all through the house. Of course it's outrageous, over the top. That's the point. Brothers don't get raised from the dead every day.

But whenever people worship Jesus with everything they've got, there's always someone in the background muttering that there's no such thing as a free jar of ointment. We watch in horror at the disintegration of Judas. First, we assume, his devotion has evaporated, then his loyalty, then his honesty towards others (his thieving), then his honesty towards himself (as in the present passage, where he says one thing, no doubt telling himself he really means it, while in fact meaning another), then, not long afterwards, his ability to choose good over evil altogether. The downward slope starts gently, but gets steeper. Judas goes on choosing a world which revolves around himself, which then itself deconstructs. Judas symbolizes the way of self-destruction, just as Mary stands for the way of self-giving. Both are costly, but in utterly different ways: 'consumed by either fire or fire'.

Paul went through the process twice over. First, he gave up everything – his pride of birth, upbringing and character – in order to obey the crazy gospel of the crucified Messiah. Then, he discovered that following this Messiah meant a continual self-giving, pouring out his own energy, devotion and life itself at the feet of the one who had 'made him his own'. Jesus validated Mary's devotion by referring to his own approaching death; that same death was woven so deeply into the fabric of Paul's thinking that his life was now dedicated, as he says elsewhere, to filling the world with the fragrance of the gospel.

The contrast of Mary and Judas, the one surprising by depth of devotion, the other by depth of deceit, runs back through Scripture, as would have been plain had the reading from Isaiah gone on another couple of verses. The creator and redeemer God makes rivers flow in the desert, and paths appear in the sea. The wild animals look on and pay him homage. Israel, the people for whose benefit these mighty acts are done, looks the other way, bored and sulky. Worth taking a minute, at this stage of Lent, to reflect on what smell we're giving off.

Palm Sunday
(Liturgy of the Passion)

—— ~ ——

Isaiah 50.4–9a
Philippians 2.5–11
Luke 22.14—23.56

Isaiah 50 strikes a jarring note in the Palm Sunday celebrations. Which is just as well: we know the end of the story, the fickleness of the crowd, the turning of cheers to jeers. The only Hosannas that count are those that come afterwards, anticipating the day when every knee shall bow. Much as I enjoy Palm Sunday, I can't help remembering that, when he was riding the donkey, Jesus was in tears.

The controlling theme here is *obedience*. The strange plan of salvation is delegated to one who will hear and obey, hear and pass the message on, hear and remain loyal in listening, speaking and above all suffering. We find it hard, almost impossible, to think of God allowing, let alone requiring, suffering from his obedient chosen one(s). We react angrily to Abraham's call to sacrifice Isaac (even though it was rescinded). A colleague in a recent conference spoke of some atonement-theologies as implicating God in 'cosmic child-abuse'.

Yet the sufferings of the Servant remain haunting and evocative, part of the richest tellings of the deepest stories. They resonate with our deep sense that our world is out of joint (strange, isn't it, that those who grumble if you say

50

there's something deeply wrong with the world, on the grounds that that's negative and pessimistic, are the same ones who also grumble if you say that Jesus has saved the world, on the grounds that it's still such a mess). Redemption, if it's to happen at all, must deal with the depth of the pain.

Equally, these stories resonate with our sense, nurtured through meditating (as today) on the passion of Jesus himself, that if there is a redeeming God he must be like this: not solving the problem at arm's length, delegating it down the line, looking on impassively as someone else sorts out the mess, but strangely present, bearing the load in person, acting out the job description which had been offered to Israel, God's servant, but which Israel was incapable of fulfilling.

Pour all that meditation into a mind at once analytic and poetic, stir vigorously, and allow to settle. Result? Philippians 2.5–11: a dense, detailed, pithy vignette of Jesus as the obedient servant, now exalted (as the Messiah was to be) as Lord of the world. It is more, too: a striking, indeed stunning vignette of the God who is revealed precisely *as* the obedient servant, the God who wept on the donkey, remained obedient in Gethsemane, accepted total humiliation and death, and who thus came to the lowest point of human experience, the place where the world's pain seemed to be concentrated, that he might take it upon himself and so exhaust it. If you want to know why we believe in the Trinity, forget the Greek metaphysics, clear your mind of those muddled Hosannas, and live through Holy Week with Paul in your head, the gospel story before your eyes, and hushed wonder in your heart.

Easter

Easter Day

—— ᷒ ——

Isaiah 65.17–25
1 Corinthians 15.19–26
Luke 24.1–12

'It seemed to them an idle tale.' In Jesus' world, nobody thought of 'resurrection' as happening to one person within ongoing history. It would happen at the very end, when God would raise all his people to share in the new heavens and new earth of prophetic promise. Nothing there about a dead-and-buried person being transformed or re-embodied.

This makes it hard to imagine that the Easter stories resulted from wishful thinking, or from what is sometimes called 'cognitive dissonance', in which people restate their hopes rather than face disappointment. Plenty of people in first-century Judaism had hopes (nationalistic, messianic, libertarian) dashed again and again. None of them went around saying that the dream had in fact come true, though not in the way they had expected. Except the Christians.

What they did say was not what you might have expected. An empty tomb; a rumour of angels; disbelief and puzzlement. No heroics, no great faith, no instant sense of everything clicking into place. Rather, a new tune, starting so quietly that by the time you hear it it's already well under way, growing and swelling into music so rich, so powerful as to make you want to dance and cry at the same time. The resurrection *had already happened*, had come forward to meet them, God's future rushing like an express train into the present, into the middle of history, the middle of the world's pain, of Israel's broken kingdom-dreams. The kingdom had arrived in an unready world, like grand guests stepping out of the Rolls-Royce to find the family having breakfast in pyjamas.

The women rushing around in the early morning, Peter scratching his head staring at empty grave-clothes, might well be puzzled: this was not part of the plan. They had thought Jesus' language about his own dying, and rising again, to be a dark metaphor, indicating perhaps a great struggle against paganism or Israel's current leaders, followed by a great victory. They had not reckoned with it being literal, or with the battle being waged against the last enemy, death itself. They were going to have to get used to living in a present which was shot through with God's future, a world in which the continuing disjointedness of creation was to be seen as out of date, waiting to be brought into line with the future which had already begun to happen.

Paul wrestles with the implications of an 'end' that has already happened and an 'end' which is yet to happen, but he did not invent the idea. It came with the message of the first Easter morning. The world was now to be seen, neither as a tired old system going round and round without hope or meaning, nor as a sick joke in which intimations of immortality always ran into the brick wall of death and cynicism, but in terms of new grass and spring flowers growing through a fresh crack in a concrete slab.

The Second Sunday of Easter

—— ✥ ——

Acts 5.27–32
Revelation 1.4–8
John 20.19–end

The report of Jesus' resurrection strikes the chief priests as a threat of God's judgement. Yes and no, reply the apostles: your guilt is swallowed up in the message of forgiveness, of new Spirit-given life. But those whose way of life seems threatened by the gospel will always interpret it as bad news. Authorities regularly try to suppress or marginalize the gospel, rightly interpreting it as a challenge to their precarious position. But the resurrection is not another human scheme, one power-play alongside others. It is on a different level, God's gift to his surprised world.

It does, of course, challenge rulers who suppose themselves to be utterly supreme, answerable to nobody but themselves. This is the constant message of the book of Revelation: Jesus is the faithful witness, the first-born of the dead, the ruler of kings of the earth. One day his kingship will be universally acknowledged; for the moment, the resurrection has inaugurated him as king-in-waiting, already enthroned but yet to establish his rule visibly and publicly.

Christianity, then, did not begin as, nor is it best characterized in terms of, a pattern of spirituality (a particular way of sensing the presence of God), a code of ethics (a particular variation on the codes which are, broadly speaking, common to most religions), or even a set of doctrines. Of course, it invites people to experience God's presence, to know his will, and to believe his truth; indeed, if understood correctly, it must include all three. But it begins as a challenge to *allegiance*. There cannot be two kings of kings and lords of lords.

In the world addressed by Revelation, there was already a claimant for that title, enthroned in Rome, ruling an empire acquired and maintained by brute force. John's vision is of a different king, ruling a different empire, having gained his dominion by suffering and maintaining it by forgiveness. No wonder other priests and kings tremble at the thought. No power on earth can stand before total, divine, self-giving love.

What is more, this power is *shared*. 'He has made *us* kings and priests, serving God.' Jesus is to be imitated, and his mission implemented, by his Spirit-filled followers: 'As the Father has sent me, so I send you.' As – so: to stand before priests and rulers, to proclaim God's kingdom established through the saving lordship of Jesus, to announce the forgiveness, or the retention, of sins. Not to entice souls into private piety or otherworldly salvation, but to confront the powers of the world with the loving, life-giving power of God.

Maybe it was this challenge, implicit in Jesus' resurrection, that kept Thomas from believing. Scepticism often conceals an element of self-preservation. Belief is not mere mental assent; it is life-changing. And the life into which it changes you comes with a royal and priestly commission attached. When Jesus said 'Peace be with you', he wasn't assuring his followers of a quiet life.

The Third Sunday of Easter

—— ≈ ——

Acts 9.1–20
Revelation 5.11–14
John 21.1–19

John 21 contains in microcosmic form most of the elements of the previous narrative. We are back in Galilee, with Peter and his friends going fishing. Jesus reveals himself as he had done throughout. He feeds them by the lake. He offers forgiveness, challenge and commission.

Only now, instead of the drama moving forward inexorably to Calvary and Easter, it moves out from there. The fishing, the feeding, the forgiveness and the challenge are all shot through with a sense of something accomplished now to be worked out, something achieved that must now be implemented, something which Jesus has done which must now sweep Peter and the rest along in the tidal wave of new life, new possibilities. The scene is full of a sense of freshness and wonder: sunrise, lake and breakfast picnic hint at the transformation of creation itself.

The whole story is pervaded with this sense of transformation. 'None of the disciples dared ask him, "Who are you?", because they knew it was the Lord.' Jesus is the same, yet somehow different. He is described as a man among men, yet he has somehow been changed. The resurrection is a thoroughly Jewish belief, yet nothing in Judaism had prepared the disciples for this.

The transformation spreads through the scene. Fishing,

after a night of hard and fruitless work, becomes a sudden morning surprise. The conversation Peter needed but no doubt dreaded transformed his denials into stumbling affirmations of love and loyalty, with Jesus' questions themselves being turned into commissions: feed my lambs, tend my sheep, feed my sheep. Finally, the transformation of vocation itself: no longer is Peter to be Jesus' blustering right-hand man, ready (so he thought) to die for Jesus (13.37) out of a sense of pride and self-importance; rather, because Jesus has laid down his life for Peter, Peter will in turn glorify God by his own humbling martyrdom. What more natural, what more utterly challenging, than the simple command, 'Follow me'?

Everything is different in the light of Easter, even God. 'To him who sits on the throne, and to the Lamb, be blessing and honour and glory and might.' Jewish monotheistic worship has been transformed from within, so that the one God is now known in terms of the Lamb and his victory. And what John gives us in narrative form, the author of Revelation gives us in poetry: creation at every level now celebrates that victory and its results.

Revelation 4 and 5 are not, of course, a vision of the future. They portray the throne-room within which visions of the future will be shown to the writer, but they themselves offer a glimpse of what is going on, night and day, in the present time. The question that has faced the world since Easter is the question that confronted Paul on the road to Damascus: granted that a new, transforming reality is let loose in the world, are we prepared to join in the song?

The Fourth Sunday of Easter

—— ∽ ——

Acts 9.36–43
Revelation 7.9–17
John 10.22–30

Within the Easter kaleidoscope, the Lamb becomes the Shepherd. John 10 is already complex enough, with Jesus as both 'shepherd' and 'door', but Revelation characteristically twists the imagery round once more, and the shepherd himself turns out to be the lamb that was slain. Thus is confirmed the radical redefinition of leadership in God's economy: a meek, unwilling prophet in Exodus, a little child in Isaiah, and now a slaughtered lamb.

Jesus' shepherd-discourse takes place at Hanukkah, the feast of the Dedication, commemorating the victory of Judas Maccabeus over the Syrians, his cleansing and rededication of the Temple, and his consequent founding of a hundred-year royal house. With 'shepherd' a regular biblical image for 'king', anyone talking about themselves as the true shepherd, not least at that festival, must have been offering themselves, however cryptically, as God's anointed. But what Jesus says about the shepherd's role and task is so unlike the warlike Maccabean pattern that it becomes almost incomprehensible. Kingdoms without justice, said Augustine, are simply regimes of brigands. Jesus goes further: kingdoms based on anything less than self-giving love are brigandish distortions of the real thing.

Jesus' 'sheep' are therefore those who hear and receive his

message of a different kingdom. His life-work has revealed God at work climactically in and through him, and many have accepted his redefinition of kingship; but many do not, because they are hell-bent on a vision of the 'age to come' which will be attained through the establishment of a worldly kingdom.

We are perhaps too eager to translate the Johannine phrase 'eternal life' into something less Jewish, more Platonic, suggesting simply an endless state of disembodied post-mortem bliss. In the first-century Jewish world, the phrase meant primarily 'the life of the coming age', the new age in which wrongs would be righted, sins forgiven and God would be all in all. That is what Jesus was claiming to offer. And he was claiming that, despite the pressure among his contemporaries to seek a Maccabean-style solution to their present plight, God had ensured that some at least would follow him and find thereby the narrow way that would lead to life. In this, as in all things, Jesus and the Father were hand in glove.

It remains a mystery why one or two deaths in the early Church were perceived as intruders to be repelled, at least for the moment, while most, presumably, were mourned but accepted. Peter's raising of Dorcas stands out, fitting into the story as part of the preamble to his visit, immediately afterwards, to Cornelius, the first (or at least the first high-profile) Gentile convert. The message of new life, dramatically acted out in sharp focus from time to time, was part of the strange means by which the Good Shepherd called other sheep to join the great multitude that no one can number, those who trust him to wipe away every tear from their eyes.

The Fifth Sunday of Easter

—— ⁓ ——

Acts 11.1–18
Revelation 21.1–6
John 13.31–35

You only discover the flavour of today's Gospel if you remember that it comes immediately after Judas's departure, and immediately before Peter's rash promise to lay down his life for Jesus – and Jesus' sorrowful prediction of Peter's triple denial. Like a warm fire glowing all the brighter as the wind starts to howl and the snow to fall, Jesus' parting promise and commandment sparkle out against the dark backcloth of betrayal and disloyalty.

The promise is characteristically Johannine. Now at last God will be truly glorified. Somehow, what will happen to Jesus will both reveal and exalt the God of Israel, the one Jesus called 'father'; this will show God, so to speak, in his true colours, will unveil the divine love in all its glory. As John puts it at the start of the chapter, Jesus knew that he had come from God and was going to God, and so, having loved his own, he loved them to the uttermost. What he did on the cross was the true and complete expression of what it meant to be precisely the one who had come from God and was going back.

The command which follows is therefore anything but arbitrary. It isn't that Jesus had a particular thing about people loving each other, his own idiosyncratic addition to an ever-increasing store of miscellaneous ethical maxims. It is, rather, that just as his own life, and approaching death, were the true expression of the Father's heart, so he intends his followers to become a further, and continuing, re-embodiment of that same love. This would, of course, be unthinkable without the gift of the Spirit; hardly surprisingly, that is precisely what is promised in the rest of the discourse. The fire which Jesus has lit in the cold, dark night is to be the first in a line of beacons, stretching away into the future and out into the rest of the world, true evidences of the true God, and of the accomplishment of Jesus.

Acts highlights Peter's visit to Cornelius as one key moment in that story. Here, 'love' is not so much a feeling that binds Peter and the new Gentile converts, but the act of obedience in which Peter recognizes Cornelius and his household as his brothers and sisters in Christ, without respect of race. Another beacon: the Spirit told Peter to go somewhere he'd never have dreamed of going; the Spirit fell on Peter's hearers in the first minute or so of his discourse. And, though the Spirit is not mentioned in Revelation at the moment when the new Jerusalem comes down as a bride adorned for her husband, the uniting of God and his people, and his tender healing of all their hurts, are themselves the ultimate end of the story, the victory of love over all that distorts and defaces, damages and destroys, God's good and beautiful world. Why, in the unwisdom of the lectionary, did we have to stop at verse 6?

The Sixth Sunday of Easter

—— ∿ ——

Acts 16.9–15
Revelation 21.10, 22—22.5
John 14.23–29

No Temple, no sun or moon, and no uncleanness either. A world without evil is, to us, as inconceivable as a world without sun and moon – or, for first-century Jews, a holy city without a Temple. In the new creation, reality will be transformed so that wickedness is as impossible as sun, moon and Temple are unnecessary.

As in John's farewell discourses, the clue is the mysterious personal presence of God himself. Thus, Moses' greatest spiritual battle was not his tussle with Pharaoh and the magicians of Egypt, but with God on Sinai in Exodus 32—34.

Moses managed to persuade God – almost, one might say, against God's better judgement – that his own presence, not merely his angel, would go with Israel to the promised land, despite Israel's rebellion and idolatry. The wilderness tabernacle became a sign of this presence, making Moses' face shine when he went in; and it was eventually institutionalized in the Temple, with all the attendant dangers of presumption, of taking God for granted. Now, in the new creation, symbols give way to reality: God himself will be personally present, and the whole city will shine with his light.

This city will truly be that for which Israel longed through her years of groaning exile. Imagery from Isaiah, Micah, Zechariah and, above all, Ezekiel swirls around here, though in each case transcended: to this city the nations will bring their treasures, and from it healing and blessing will flow out to the world.

The city is not, then, the totality of God's eventual new world; it is the focal point of a world which will finally see God's light and discover his healing. The river of life-giving water, like the rivers of Eden, will flow from it, fulfilling Ezekiel's vision of a river making even the Dead Sea fresh. Worship and mission will still be realities in God's new world. But worship will be face to face, not through a glass darkly; and mission will meet no resistance, as God's healing embraces all creation.

Images of the future are vital to beckon us along the way. But they do more: they work backwards, as it were, towards us, shedding light on our present darkness. Jesus promises a peace which nothing in the present world can provide, a peace which comes from, and points to, God's future.

This is what happens when God himself, Father, Son and Spirit, comes to be at home with, and even in, those who love God and keep his word, anticipating in the present the promise of the new holy city.

On the ground, this reality regularly breaks into our plans and possibilities. Paul, frustrated at being unable to move ahead with work in Asia, is unexpectedly called across to the leading cities of Europe, and finds hearts and minds ready and waiting for the gospel. He and his colleagues, going to stay at Lydia's home, embody in themselves the promise of God's personal presence with his renewed people.

The Seventh Sunday of Easter (Sunday after Ascension Day)

—— ∼ ——

Acts 16.16–34
Revelation 22.12–14, 16–17, 20–21
John 17.20–end

If Luke had wanted to play down the trouble caused by the gospel, he would quietly have omitted the Philippi story. Healing for one person means loss of money for others, and produces political and cultural charges which, though a blatant cover for self-interest, have sufficient plausibility to result in beatings and imprisonment.

They are Jews, said the angry slave-owners. Yes, but most other Jews lived alongside Gentiles without trouble. The real problem was that Paul and Silas were teaching and representing a way of life in which Roman customs, particularly allegiance to Caesar, were not the guiding rule. As in Thessalonica, they believed in a different king, a different empire. When the gospel landed in Europe, the first thing the authorities said was 'Treason!'.

The story of the earthquake and the jailer can thus be read on at least two levels. Wherever Paul went, there were earthquakes: the Roman world, and communities and individuals within it, were turned upside down by the power of Jesus' name. A pity we miss the last paragraph, in which Paul, despite having upended their world, reminds the magistrates of their duty. This twist completes the delicate and ironic balance of church–state relations in the nascent European Church.

Omitting a paragraph because of length is one thing. Snipping out three verses because they warn that some styles of behaviour have no place in God's holy city is something else. Or do we want to avoid the scandal of the gospel, not only in the world but also in the Church? It is particularly galling to omit 22.19: cutting out the verse that tells you not to cut out verses is the ultimate in Bible-reading *chutzpah*. Don't let this prissiness distract from the picture of Jesus which these warnings surround: there is enough imagery here for a hall of mirrors, and that may be the point. The glittering and dazzling portrayal of Jesus, the Alpha and Omega, the bright morning star, is meant to lead the eye away from all other distractions and allegiances. By contemplating this Jesus we fulfil his own prayer: that we may be with him where he is, to see his glory, begotten of the Father's love. The vision of God's glory, denied to Moses, is granted in Jesus Christ.

The central characteristic of that vision is of course love: God's love for Jesus and, through Jesus, for all his people; the love of God's people for one another, creating a unity which will indeed reveal to the world the disturbing message that there is another way of being human. Disunity may perhaps be the ultimate worldliness, since it means accepting that we are defined, in the last analysis, by something other than the love of God in Jesus Christ. Let the midnight feast in the jailer's house stand for the joyful meal which will occur when all Christians realize that they belong at the same table. Now that really would be an earthquake.

Day of Pentecost

—— ≈ ——

Acts 2.1–21
Romans 8.14–17
John 14.8–17

The Israelites had been aware of certain persons in their midst, unpredictable and untameable, in whom the Spirit of YHWH dwelt. They spoke his word, led his people, encouraged, rebuked, prayed for and agonized over Israel. They were a sign of God's care and love for his wayward people. But several prophets recognized that this state of affairs could not be God's final will for his people. Jeremiah declared that all God's people would know him, from the least to the greatest. Isaiah threw open the blessings of the Davidic covenant to all who would seek the Lord. And Joel, quoted by Peter at Pentecost, declared that the Spirit of YHWH would be poured out upon people of all sorts. No longer a special élite: young and old, male and female, slave and free alike, all would be caught up by the rushing wind of the prophetic Spirit.

The first disciples were therefore as much struck by the implications of the sudden outpouring of the Spirit as by the manifestations. It wasn't the excitement of being heard speaking in a dozen different languages, dramatic though that was (and is, when it happens today); it was the fact that the Spirit was thereby showing that the long-prophesied coming day had arrived. With the death and resurrection of Jesus, the new age had dawned, and the outpoured Spirit was the confirmation. The point of Pentecost was not so much the offer of a new spiritual experience as the declaration of a new spiritual reality. God's history with the world had turned its decisive corner.

Grasped by this vision, the early Christians went back again and again to the greatest of Jewish stories, the Exodus. Paul deliberately uses Exodus-language to describe where Christians are in God's story – and at the same time to lay to rest any suggestion that because we are living in God's new day there's nothing more to work at (or the counter-suggestion that, because the world is still in a mess, Pentecost can't really have meant a new start for the world). The Church is now in the position of the Israelites in the wilderness: led by God's Spirit, assured of adoption as God's children, walking resolutely away from slavery and towards their inheritance, suffering in the present but confident of the future. And the 'inheritance', as Paul indicates in Romans 4.13 and 8.18–25, is not a single promised land but the whole redeemed creation.

The intimacy and ecstasy of the Spirit's personal in-dwelling, and the fact that with this the world has turned a new corner, lead to those clear, simple profundities which otherwise appear opaque and complex. 'Whatever you ask for will be granted.' 'Keep my commandments.' The Spirit of truth, still incomprehensible to the world, will be with you and in you, so that you may be sent into the world as re-embodiments of the incarnate Son, a sign of God's care and love for his wayward world.

Ordinary Time

Trinity Sunday

—— ⁓ ——

Proverbs 8.1–4, 22–31
Romans 5.1–5
John 16.12–15

Deep inside classic Jewish monotheism there lies a strange, swirling sense of a rhythm of mutual relations within the very being of the one God: a to-and-fro, a give-and-take, a command-and-obey, a sense of love poured out and love received. God's Spirit broods over the waters, God's Word goes forth to produce new life, God's Law guides his people, God's Presence or Glory dwells with them in fiery cloud, in tabernacle and temple. These four ways of speaking move to and fro from metaphor to trembling reality-claim and back again. They enable people to speak simultaneously of God's sovereign supremacy and his intimate presence, of his unapproachable holiness and his self-giving love.

The best known is perhaps the fifth. God's Wisdom is his handmaid in creation, the first-born of his works, his chief of staff, his delight. Through the Lady Wisdom of Proverbs 1— 8 (contrasting sharply with Mistress Folly, her parody, and her rival for human affection) the Creator has fashioned everything, especially the human race. To embrace Wisdom is thus to discover the secret of being truly human, of reflecting God's image. This is the secret of the sometimes apparently random book of Proverbs. Wisdom, like Ariadne with her thread, will guide you through the mazes and mysteries of life.

This rich seam of thought, visible at many points in pre-Christian Jewish tradition, is where the early Christians went quarrying for language to deal with the phenomena before them. Long before secular philosophy was used to describe the inner being of the one God, and the relation of this God to Jesus and the Spirit, a vigorous and very Jewish new tradition took the language and imagery of Spirit, Word, Law, Presence (and/or Glory), and Wisdom, and developed them in relation to the Jesus of recent memory and to the strange personal presence of the Spirit. It might be thought that they added a sixth to the list, namely God's Love; except that, for them, God's Love was already no mere personification, a figure of speech for the loving God at work, but a person, the crucified Jesus. Approach the incarnation from this angle, and it is no category mistake, but the utterly appropriate climax of creation. Wisdom, God's blueprint for humans, at last herself becomes human.

Thus Paul can speak repeatedly of God accomplishing his saving and re-creating work *through* Jesus, and of the Spirit as God's personal presence, bringing healing, hope and glory. The inner mutual relationships within the one God have opened up, not only to reveal God in truly human form but to invite all humans to share God's inner life. The Spirit of Truth will take what belongs to Jesus, which is itself the true revelation of the Father, and will share it with Jesus' people. The doctrine of the Trinity is not only the best we can do in speaking of the one God, but also the foundation of Christian spirituality.

Proper 4

— ⟨∽⟩ —

1 Kings 18.20–21 [22–29] 30–39
Galatians 1.1–12
Luke 7.1–10

Elijah calls for fire, but the larger story is about rain. Drought has plagued the land. King Ahab is cross with Elijah, blaming the messenger for the message. Elijah, fresh from his triumph in restoring a boy to life (ch. 17), retorts (18.18) that the trouble stems from Ahab himself, who has fostered Baal-worship in Israel. Hence the contest on Carmel. Only when YHWH is acknowledged as the one true God, and Baal-worship is stamped out, will the rains return.

The confrontation is memorable not least for the contrast of styles. There are Baal's prophets, cavorting around their altar, slashing themselves with swords and lances to raise the stakes of sympathetic magic and persuade Baal to do something, but succeeding only in provoking Elijah to splendid scorn (v. 27). And there is Elijah, symbolically evoking the story of Israel's redemption, with the twelve stones, the water, and the fiery presence of God. We think of Elijah as one of the great prophets, and forget that he stood (almost) alone against the mood of the times, constantly having to prove his credentials, constantly recalling the people to the true God.

By the first century, Elijah was seen (along with Phinehas, whose story is found in Numbers 25) as one of the great zealots. Zealous for God and the Law, he opposed paganism within Israel by all means possible, including violence. Many first-century Jews looked to him as a role model, attempting to purify the nation of their day from pagan corruption, disloyalty and idolatry. It seems that Saul of Tarsus took this line, and indeed that this was what took him on his fateful journey to Damascus, to which we shall return next week.

Galatians as a whole, introduced here with dramatic vigour, shows Paul's newly redirected zeal. In the gospel God's truth had been revealed, and he opposed all distortions of it as involving lies about God. Paul saw (v. 4) that in Jesus, and supremely through his death, the 'present evil age' had lost its grip, and that the age to come, the age of freedom and forgiveness long promised by God, had finally arrived.

His great and always paradoxical insight, expounded for the first time in Galatians, was that this action, in fulfilling the promises to Abraham, had created a single family in which all who believed in Jesus, Jews and Gentiles alike, belonged together with nothing but their faith as the badge of membership. Any attempt to co-opt the story of Jesus for a 'gospel' which left Jewish ethnic privilege intact he regarded as a spurious pseudo-gospel, and opposed with Elijah-like zeal.

Luke's account of the centurion and his servant makes very nearly the same point. Not even in Israel has such faith been found. No need to dance around and use pagan-style sympathetic magic. Jesus, like a new Elijah, raises the lad from death, demonstrating for those with eyes to see where the living God is now at work.

Proper 5

—— ⁓ ——

1 Kings 17.8–24
Galatians 1.11–24
Luke 7.11–17

Luke has, fairly obviously, told the story of the widow's son at Nain in such a way as to evoke the similar story of Elijah and the widow's son at Zarephath – who, interestingly, was already referred to in Jesus' 'Nazareth manifesto' (4.26). Luke elsewhere makes it clear that Jesus is to be seen as Messiah, and indeed more than Messiah. This does not exclude, but rather takes up within itself, the fact that he was first and foremost seen as 'a prophet mighty in word and deed' (24.19). This is one of many stories that prepares the way for that conclusion, simultaneously tying Jesus in to the long story of Israel and showing him bringing that story to its triumphant climax.

The point about such actions is not merely that they demonstrated remarkable power, but that they validated the prophet's work. The story of the Zarephath widow is one of increasing faith: she initially has enough faith in Elijah to bake him a little cake before she provides for herself and her son; she interprets the boy's death in terms of Elijah having brought judgement on her (for what reason, we are not told); but she finally acknowledges him wholeheartedly as a man of God, and his words as the true words of YHWH. The implication is that she, unlike those hardened in unbelief in Luke 16.31, now believes fully on the evidence of one being raised from the dead. In the same way, the Nain story enables Luke to point forward to his own resurrection narrative when the prophet/Messiah himself emerges the other side of death, thereby retrospectively validating all he had earlier done and said.

The centrality of Jesus, and the revelation of God's redemptive accomplishment in him, lies at the heart of Paul's passionate defence of his gospel. He insists – against, we must assume, slurs and innuendoes emanating from opponents – that his apostolic commission went back to Jesus himself, rather than being a second-order affair dependent on the Jerusalem church. Galatia cannot, in other words, appeal over his head to Jerusalem. The only person Paul answers to is Jesus himself.

The language in which Paul describes his conversion carries ironic reference to Elijah, this time to 1 Kings 19. Like the prophet, he had been very zealous for the Lord, but found himself confronted with a fresh revelation that made him go off to Arabia – to Mount Sinai, we should probably assume – so that like Elijah he might hand in his commission, might give up zeal as a bad job. However, like Elijah, he is given a new commission. A new king is to be proclaimed. The Son of God is to be revealed in him and through him (v. 16). His zeal is to be transformed and redirected. Like the widow at Zarephath, Paul sees in Jesus' resurrection the complete evidence that he has not only brought sins to light but has triumphantly dealt with the judgement that they incurred.

Proper 6

—— ≈ ——

1 Kings 21.1–21a
Galatians 2.15–21
Luke 7.36—8.3

'He loved me and gave himself for me.' These words in Galatians 2.20, coupled with those in 1.4, probably form the earliest written statement of what we know as the doctrine of the atonement. They invite comment at several levels.

First, towering over everything else, they speak of the cross as an act of love. Paul is sometimes wrongly supposed to have seen the cross solely through legalistic lenses, imagining it as an exercise in penal logic-chopping. This passage demonstrates that for him it was far more, and far deeper. It spoke of arms outstretched in love, a heart bursting for love, the self-giving of love to the undeserving beloved. It created, in the words of the late George Caird, 'a debt of love which only love could repay'.

Second, when coupled with 1.4 the phrase speaks of a once-for-all action in which Jesus, as Israel's Messiah, brought Israel and the world round the corner of history from darkness to light. Though the cross speaks to the heart of the individual believer, it does so in the context of a cosmic achievement through which the shape of reality is permanently changed. A new world has been born, with the word 'Forgiveness' pinned over its cradle. This was the work of 'the Son of God': a messianic title which, as Paul discovered, was filled with astonishing new content. Some of

Israel's ancient rulers, exemplified all too well by Ahab, were happy to kill those who stood in their way, revealing a totally misguided sense of what Israel and her kings were there for. The true King of the Jews embodies the loving presence, and dying love, of Israel's true God.

Third, as the verses immediately before today's passage make clear, the first practical implication of the cross is that the self-giving love that has created the new family must be worked out in the family's table manners. Jewish Christians and Gentile Christians no longer belong in separate categories, at separate tables. As well as being the earliest statement of the atonement, this passage is Paul's first statement of 'justification by faith'; and here it means, quite simply, that since all believers are already full members of God's people, without having to 'qualify' by keeping the Jewish law, they all belong together at the same meal.

All this is of course superbly and dramatically expressed, in narrative form, in today's Gospel. Here is the table, with the Pharisee playing host (though not very enthusiastically); here is the woman, excluded from fellowship; here is the Son of God, loving and giving himself – incurring wrath already, already sensing the shadow of the cross – and opening the new world of forgiveness. Here is the debt of love, repaid by love so extravagantly as to reveal how great the debt actually was. The somewhat troubling question is, of course: which of the two characters addressed by Jesus would be more at home in our churches this Sunday?

Proper 7

—— ≈ ——

1 Kings 19.1–15a
Galatians 3.23–end
Luke 8.26–39

Elijah went to Sinai, to hand back his commission. 'I've done all this for you, and now they're going to kill me. I've had enough.' Fear and exhaustion generated self-destructive depression. What was he expecting? A volcanic eruption, literal or theological? A new set of commandments? The renewal of the covenant with him personally, as God had once suggested to Moses?

Instead, a challenge: 'What are you doing here, Elijah?' How much of your problem is self-caused, the reverse side of zealous energy? If your weapon in God's service has been destructive anger, don't be surprised if, when things get tough, it turns back on yourself. In any case, depression, as usual, has distorted your perception of reality. God has the situation well in hand (vv. 15–18): new kings and prophets are to be anointed, and will sort things out. Elijah is not the only true Israelite. Seven thousand others have not worshipped Baal. Elijah wanted a new or renewed law. He received the command to trust and obey.

Paul was familiar with the Elijah stories, and in his pre-conversion days seems to have made them his role model, casting himself as the fiery prophet and the Christians as the new Baal-worshippers. After his conversion he, too, went off to Arabia to do business with God, and came back with a new commission, to announce the anointed one, the Messiah.

With hindsight, he saw the law of Sinai quite differently. It had looked after the Israelites, had (like a slave in charge of the children) administered rough justice to stop them going to the bad. The law had, in particular, prevented the family of Abraham compromising its unique vision and vocation by mingling with paganism.

But with the coming of the crucified Messiah all that has changed. The Messiah is now the focal point of God's people: all who believe in God's unique action through him are therefore part of the family. Abraham's promised offspring now consists of all, Jew and Gentile alike, who share this faith. (The Galatians were tempted to reinforce the superiority of Jew over Gentile; Paul, addressing this, does not develop his throwaway line, that the gospel also brings together slave and free, male and female.)

Paul even (in the next chapter) likens the rule of the Law over Israel to that of idols over the pagans. God's action in the Messiah has liberated Jew and Gentile alike from their former deadly bondage. The baptismal symbolism makes the point (3.27): coming up out of the water, both have put on identical clothes, marking their new identity. Like the Gerasene demoniac, they have watched Jesus destroy the demons which had enslaved them, and now find themselves sitting at his feet, clothed and in their right mind. Like him, too (Luke 8.39), they will now find that when they try to tell people what God has done for them, they somehow always speak of what Jesus has done for them.

81

Proper 8

—— ≈ ——

2 Kings 2.1–14
Galatians 5.1, 13–25
Luke 9.51–end

'Leave the dead to bury their dead.' One of Jesus' starkest commands, this flies in the face of the sacred Jewish obligation to attend to the burial of one's father ahead of all other duties, even saying one's daily prayers. Jesus' kingdom-announcement is so urgent, so unique, that it must either be followed, grasped and proclaimed totally or lost altogether. The family, a central and vital symbol of the people of God, is thus radically redefined. Following Jesus at once is the only thing that counts.

Elijah, by contrast, seems bent on dissuading Elisha from following him. 'Stay here; I'm going on.' But Elisha refuses: 'As the Lord lives, I won't leave you.' His doggedness is rewarded. Foxes have holes, the birds of the air nests, but prophets have nowhere to call home. Instead, Elisha inherits a double share of Elijah's spirit, the great wind of God that will blow through Israel and cleanse it from corruption, the fire that will burn away the dross.

The stories of Elijah and Elisha were alive and well in Jesus' day, and caused confusion to the disciples as well as to readers of the Gospels. When first called by Elijah, Elisha had asked permission to say goodbye to his family, and it had apparently been granted, however briefly (1 Kings 19.19–21). Elijah, faced with opposition, called down fire from heaven, but when the disciples volunteered to try the same trick they were firmly rebuked. The Spirit who spoke by the prophets is now speaking through the Son, and the wind and fire are to be found in him, in his urgent kingdom-message, in his pilgrimage to Jerusalem and in what he will there accomplish. What is now required is not the zeal that will burn up the opposition, but the Spirit of Jesus to transform those who follow him doggedly wherever he goes. 'As the Lord lives, I won't leave you'; to those who speak thus to him, Jesus will reply in the same words.

The two types of zeal emerge graphically in Galatians. The Jewish Christian 'agitators', with their zeal for the Jewish law, are causing anger and tension within the young Church. By treating the ex-pagan Christians as still outside the true family circle, they are in effect forcing them to become proselytes. But the family has been redefined, by Jesus with his radical kingdom-achievement, and now by Paul with his insistence that faith, not the Jewish law, is the badge of membership. As a result, with considerable irony, insistence on the Jewish law will result in living 'according to the flesh', in bitterness and division, putting such Christians on a level with those who follow the usual pagan 'fleshly' lifestyle. The only way forward is to inherit in full measure the Spirit of Jesus, passing beyond the divisive rule of the Jewish law, into the realm where the wind blows where it wants, and the fire of love burns away all the dross.

Proper 9

——— ∼ ———

2 Kings 5.1–14
Galatians 6.1–16
Luke 10.1–11, 16–20

Going out like lambs amid wolves hardly makes sense in any culture. Only Jesus could propose something so apparently hare-brained yet strangely powerful. Only he, knowing himself to be utterly vulnerable, yet protected by his Father, could suggest the same course to others. Despite certain opposition, misunderstanding, threats and outright rejection (the squeamish lectionary predictably soft-pedals the latter theme), Jesus' seventy chosen ones will go out in weakness, and yet in power, as a sign to Israel that the kingdom is breaking in, the kingdom at whose approach the dark enemy, the Satan himself, will fall in terror.

Behind the challenge and the commission there stands, of course, Jesus' own sense of vocation, of what was happening and was about to happen in and through his own work. Yearning for the kingdom, Israel was nevertheless not ready for the kingdom-vision he had to bring, had to enact. Every moment, though, was precious; hence the strategy of sending heralds ahead of him, to proclaim his peace and prepare his way. Jesus' mission was urgent, since those who rejected his way of peace, his alternative vision of how God would sweep through the world with justice and love, would find they had spurned their last chance. Everyone had to hear while there was time.

84

No slouch when it came to urgency, Paul challenges the Galatians one more time to think straight, to resist the blandishments of those who offered a softer, safer version of the gospel. Nothing less than the full article will do: the world crucified to me, and I to the world. If you walk by this rule, you will find peace, just as will those who welcomed Jesus' emissaries; but if you modify it you court disaster. Everything may seem to be against you. Lambs among wolves describes quite closely how many of the early converts, in Galatia and elsewhere, must have felt. Losing all to gain Christ: that was the message of the cross, of the gospel, of the new creation.

If these stirring reflections are to mean anything now, they must address the problem: what are the urgent questions upon which major issues hang at this moment? Only those who have struggled hard with such matters know how difficult it is to judge, to decide when to be 'prophetic' and speak out, how to tell the difference between a storm in a teacup and a force ten hurricane. Take Elisha, for instance; he recognized that, if Naaman's pride was humbled, and his leprosy healed, by Israel's God, he, the great enemy commander, would remain loyal to this God, and hence presumably be unwilling to fight against Israel, despite apparent compromise (bowing himself down in the house of Rimmon; do, please, read the whole story). Turn the question around, though, and look at Gehazi, Elisha's servant; for him it was all a trivial affair, something merely to be turned to his own personal advantage. Lucky the church whose prophets have their heads screwed on.

Proper 10

—— ∿ ——

Amos 7.7–17
Colossians 1.1–14
Luke 10.25–37

If you like word-development, you'll love Samaritans. Start with a geographical designation: people who live in the hill country, between Galilee and Judaea. Develop to discrimination: the pre-exilic Judaeans speaking of their northern neighbours, the people who are like us but not quite. Then post-exilic denunciation: the wrong sort, with the wrong worship, the wrong theology and the wrong behaviour. Then re-evaluation, initiated by Jesus (so far as we know, one of his most unprecedented innovations): people who might perhaps love God and their neighbour across traditional boundaries, and who might therefore come within the pale after all. Then, much later (the dictionary offers 1649 as the earliest occurrence), a real evolution: those who, not necessarily outsiders, rescue people in need. The derived sense, the shocking surprise in Jesus' day, has become, for most users, the word's only meaning.

The parable has suffered, along with the word, from being too well known. It isn't, after all, simply about helping half-dead dogs over stiles. It's about Jesus' major re-evaluation of Israel's boundary-markers. The lawyer quoted the *Shema*, the central Jewish prayer, as the litmus test for inheriting the Age to Come: love God, love your neighbour. The parable, redefining 'neighbour', doesn't conclude that the man in need was the Samaritan's neighbour, but that the Samaritan was his. The challenge is not just to copy the Samaritan, but to recognize him when he comes to our aid.

The dark side of the story is, of course, that the priest and the levite turned out not to be neighbours after all. Like those attacked by Amos, they were so interested in protecting their own status that could not see what that status – being the official representatives of the people of God – was all about, and so were actually jeopardizing it. The priest who attacked Amos ('Chapel Royal: No Prophets Allowed') was the true ancestor of Jesus' anonymous passers-by, only in his case he could not see that it was the nation as a whole that was lying half dead in the ditch, needing to be stirred into life by Amos's denunciations. When God declares that Israel doesn't measure up, and the prophet who passes the message on is labelled a conspirator, the only possible answer is condemnation.

But that isn't God's last word. When Paul greets the young church in Colosse, the feature of their new life to which he draws attention is 'your love in the spirit' (1.8). Paul, in prison (in Ephesus, in my humble but probably accurate opinion), hears from his colleague Epaphras, not that certain people have had wonderful spiritual experiences, not that they have learnt a textbook of systematic theology, but that there has come into existence in Colosse a community of people who love one another across traditional boundaries (compare 3.11). This event has the fingerprints of God all over it. For 'Samaritan', read 'Colossian'. Why not give another word a push in the right direction?

Proper 11

— ≈ —

Amos 8.1–12
Colossians 1.15–28
Luke 10.38–end

Put Paul alongside Mary and Martha, and which one does he remind you of? 'For this I toil', he writes, 'and struggle with all the energy that Christ powerfully inspires within me.' More like Martha? Yes and no. It has been customary to play the two sisters off, passive spirituality versus aggressive fussiness. Mary wins, but at a cost: as feminists point out, this model keeps both in the neat boxes devised by a male world, the one sedate and devout, the other making the tea and sandwiches.

The reality is more complex. People sat at a teacher's feet in that world, not to gaze languidly with drooping eyelids, but in order to become teachers themselves. Paul, after all, had 'sat at the feet of Gamaliel', and that hadn't made him exactly passive. Mary had crossed a boundary, entering the man's world of discipleship; Jesus had affirmed her right to be there, indeed the desirability of her being there rather than simply staying in the kitchen. Once Mary had drunk in the rich teaching of Jesus, she too would be on her feet, but not simply in the background.

Paul's energy was not simply a character trait. It was the surging new life of one who had worshipped at the feet of Jesus. Colossians, steeped in the adoration of Jesus the image, the first-born, the head, the reconciler, the fullness of

God, is also a practical, down-to-earth letter, energetically getting on with the job.

Paul was commissioned 'to make the word of God fully known' (1.25). When Amos inveighs against social injustice, economic trickery and exploitation in Israel, the most terrible of his threats (8.11–12) is that there is to be a famine, not of bread, but of the word of YHWH. A vivid picture of panic: people wandering to and fro, running this way and that, longing for the word of YHWH and not finding it. Those who turn their back on the written word, that commands justice, sabbath-keeping, and care for the poor, will find the spoken word has gone silent on them as well. Paul's gospel, against this background, is the answer to the secret but desperate longing of the heart: the image of the invisible God, the sound of the inaudible God, the touch of the untouchable God.

Which is why, we may presume, this gospel is proclaimed in the midst of, and indeed acted out in and through, suffering. When the world has gone its own way, trampling on the needy, cheating on weights and measures, casting God's wise ordering of life out of the way so that it can make another quick buck, the word of grace is bound to cause a different sort of panic. If that stuff were to get around, profits would drop. Not for nothing does Paul celebrate the fact that Christ is Lord of the principalities and powers. Sit at the feet of this teacher, and you will find work soon enough.

Proper 12

—— ⁓ ——

Hosea 1.2–10
Colossians 2.6–19
Luke 11.1–13

Part of the prophetic vocation seems to have been to carry the pain of the message in one's own soul. Thus it was, at least, with Hosea. Married to a prostitute, he felt not only the pain of Israel but also the pain of God, seeing his people cavorting off after other gods. His children were and weren't his own, just as Israel was and wasn't God's child. Self-induced judgement loomed over them, but yearning love followed as well: 'not my people' will again be addressed as 'children of the living God'.

The fatherhood of the true God undergirds Jesus' announcement of the kingdom, together with the spirituality he encouraged and the bracing moral agenda he urged. Not every parable can be pressed to yield an accurate account of God (the 'unjust judge' is the classic example), but fatherhood is Jesus' most common image for God, woven into every other story. Rooted as it is in the biblical picture of God's rescue of Israel from Egypt in the first place and from oppression thereafter, this image does not so much pin God down with a particular cultural family role as open up a window on his character. He wears his heart on his sleeve, providing for his children and coming to their rescue when they are in distress. To recognize who this God is is at once to be welcomed into a spirituality of pure trust (who was it who used to say 'I must speak to Father about this'?), even when the request is apparently unreasonable. Prayer that begins, 'Father, hallowed be your name', can continue, in that treasured mixture of intimacy and awe, into the details of the three loaves suddenly necessary at midnight.

It is because Paul had seen this God revealed in Jesus Christ that he realized, with deep sorrow, that his own fellow Jews, by rejecting their Messiah, have forgotten their true God. Despite scholarly traditions, Colossians 2 is not warning against a strange esoteric super-spirituality, but against the blandishments of Judaism itself. The emphasis of the chapter is: you have already been circumcised in Christ (2.11–12), and the law has no more condemnation against you (2.13–15). Christ's paradoxical triumph over the principalities and powers included the law itself, in so far as it set a bar against Gentiles, 'not God's people', being deemed, in Christ, 'children of the living God'. When he says (2.8) 'Don't let anyone lure you astray by philosophy and empty deceit', he is deliberately using pagan language to describe the attractions of Judaism to the pagan world: he uses the very rare Greek word *sylagogon* for 'lure you astray', with the punning hint 'Don't let anyone *synagogue* you'.

For Paul, of course, this was extremely painful. As he says in Romans, he carried the tragedy of Israel's situation in his own heart and soul. But also the joy of knowing God at a deeper level: in Christ 'all God's fullness dwells bodily' (2.9).

Proper 13

—— ∽ ——

Hosea 11.1–11
Colossians 3.1–11
Luke 12.13–21

Many years ago I preached a sermon on Luke 12. Jesus did not come, I declared, to settle our property disputes. Pleased with my own eloquence, I came home to find a note from my neighbour, pinned to the back door, telling me that my garden shed encroached on his land and that if it wasn't moved soon he would bulldoze it. He was probably in the wrong, but the irony stung too badly. I moved the shed.

But if Jesus didn't come to settle our disputes, nor does this passage simply refer to everyday stories of garden sheds. Land, and ancestral inheritance thereon, was of course one of Judaism's central symbols, then as now. Getting it right was part of obedience to God's will, and moreover focused the glittering promise of return from exile, as Hosea and so many others had promised. The God who called Israel, his little son, out of Egypt, will call his trembling exiles, from the ends of the world, back to their native land.

But God's people have always lived in the tension between vocation and the symbols which express it. Cling to the symbol, and you risk disobeying the vocation – and forfeiting the reality. The fool who pulled down his barns to build bigger ones, only to be summoned to leave it all behind, is not just a symbol for, well, a rich fool who ... did precisely that. If that were the case, the story wouldn't be a parable, but merely a moral tale. The real target was the Israel that prided herself on national security, claiming more and more territory, ancestral and otherwise, not realizing that her God was asking questions at another level altogether, summoning her back to being the light of the world, ordering her national life with justice and mercy and becoming a beacon of hope to the nations. How can being the people of God be ultimately a matter of sacred turf, if Israel is to be the light of the whole world? How can litigious and grasping behaviour reflect the generous and forgiving love of God?

The stern warnings are meant to act, as Hosea says, as the roaring of the lion that drives Israel back to her God. Paul is quite capable of the same tactic, but in Colossians 3 he takes a different route. Being dead and risen with Christ, we are to seek that which is above, not that which is on the earth. This, as the succeeding verses make clear, is not a recipe for a super-spirituality which ignores the real earthy issues. First things first: the problem is not living on earth, but living *on earth's terms*. Make this earth your god (as even Israel was tempted to do, by idolizing her God-given symbols), and you end up with lies, anger, greed and immorality, the property disputes of the present world. The Creator, meanwhile, serves notice of a higher calling: a full, true humanness, remade in his own image.

Proper 14

— ≈ —

Isaiah 1.1, 10–20
Hebrews 11.1–3, 8–16
Luke 12.32–40

Stories about a master going away and returning would have been interpreted in Jesus' world as stories about Israel's God, YHWH. He had 'gone away' at the exile, as Ezekiel describes graphically. At no point in the 'post-exilic' literature does anyone say that he has returned; but at almost every point it insists that he will. When he does, it will mean not just blessing, but judgement.

The later prophets retain Isaiah's sense that Israel's God has a controversy with his people. Things can be argued out, sins can be forgiven, but the first word may well be one of rebuke. 'People of Sodom and Gomorrah', indeed! Shock tactics to bring the people to their senses, lest God come and discover them deep in self-indulgence, violence, exploitation, and the religion that puts on airs to cover it all up. Isaiah's warnings are worryingly perennial.

The stories Jesus told about a returning master would therefore be heard primarily as stories about the expected return of God to judge his people, and they make excellent sense on that basis. The kingdom is coming, when God will return and put all things to rights; so those who follow Jesus, and are thereby constituted as the real Israel, are to trust his imminent provision rather than store up for themselves. Like servants who know what their master will want them to be doing, they obey without knowing when he will arrive.

Into this story and exhortation (Luke 12.35–38, 41–48), Luke has inserted (12.39–40) a different snippet about a different 'coming'. Now the owner is at home, and the one who comes is a thief; within Jesus' kaleidoscopic imagery, this could simply be highlighting the imminent danger as well as the reward, but it looks like a separate theme. In the application (v. 40) it is 'the Son of man' who is 'coming'. Elsewhere, the coming of the Son of Man, as in Daniel 7, is his vindicated coming *from* earth, after persecution, *to* God in heaven. But, again in Daniel 7, with that vindication goes judgement for those who have opposed God's kingdom. This dense little saying warns of imminent catastrophe: Jesus will be vindicated, but those who are not ready will find the day coming upon them like a thief in the night.

Hebrews holds up the patriarchs (and matriarchs) as examples of faith: living in the light of the future, they were ready for it when it came. The coming heavenly country is not far off and disembodied; it is the sphere, already existing and very close, in which God's purposes are stored up, like scenery ready for the stage. Citizens of this new city live already by its customs, secure in the knowledge that, though they look strange now and here, they will make sense then and there. When the master comes, he will recognize them as his own. More, he will not be ashamed, says Hebrews, to be called 'their God'. '*Their*'?

Proper 15

—— ～ ——

Isaiah 5.1–7
Hebrews 11.29—12.2
Luke 12.49–56

This Lukan passage is high on the list of Things We Would
Rather Jesus Hadn't Said. It's not gentle, it's not meek and
mild; it's not even nice. Parents and children at loggerheads,
in-laws getting across one another – what can Jesus have had
in mind?

The problem, as often, is that we fail to pick up the
biblical allusion. Micah's picture (7.6) of family dysfunction
is part of his lament about his contemporaries. Like the
suffering heroes of Hebrews 11, the prophet continues to
trust in God (7.7) and his coming rescue. He looked by faith,
Hebrews would say, to God's future, now finally revealed in
Jesus himself, the example of our faith and the object of our
hope. But to those who refuse this faith and hope, this same
Jesus declares that he has come, prophet-like, to divide Israel
down the middle. If the vineyard is yielding wild grapes,
what else is the owner to do?

People know how to read the sky, so why can't they see
what is going on under their noses? What is Jesus referring
to? Positively: his kingdom-message was bursting in with the
love and power of God, healing, rescuing, re-creating; people
who couldn't draw the right conclusions must be blind
indeed. Negatively: those who rejected his message would
come into increasing conflict with Rome, a conflict in which

there could be only one winner – not just because of the power of Rome, but because Israel would be fighting the battle without the support of her God. Jesus was urging his contemporaries to a way of being Israel which meant peace and justice. To reject his message was to choose the way of self-destruction. In reading the signs of the times, there was no room for mere optimists or pessimists. The greatest blessing and the greatest disaster ever known were both just around the corner.

The next little saying (12.57–59), sadly omitted by the lectionary, belongs exactly in this train of thought. It is another example of something usually taken as a bit of homely wisdom, when in fact it is a dark parable, like Isaiah's strange vineyard-song. Reading the times meant recognizing that Israel was about to be hauled into court; she should settle now, while there was still time, before suffering the ultimate penalty. But even as he said this, Jesus, like Isaiah, knew what the answer would be.

Why then is Isaiah's vineyard-oracle called a *love*-song? The vineyard was a well-known metaphor for a bride, to be loved, looked after, fruitful, enjoyed. Isaiah's hearers would expect a wedding song, and would be shocked. But it was a love song none the less: the lament of YHWH's grieving love over his cherished but rebellious people, a love that would be satisfied with nothing less than embodiment, to share and bear the baptism of fire, to take upon itself the bad news to make the good come true at last.

Proper 16

—— ❧ ——

Jeremiah 1.4–10
Hebrews 12.18–end
Luke 13.10–17

Moses said he wasn't a speaker. Isaiah said his lips were tainted. Ezekiel fell on his face. And Jeremiah says he's too young. One might, perhaps, be a trifle suspicious if God's call to prophecy met with too ready a response: 'Oh yes, that's fine, I think I can do a good job...'? Hmmm.

This isn't just appropriate humility (which can itself easily be counterfeited: as they say about sincerity, that when you can fake that you've really got it made, so with humility, when you can turn that on, you've really got something to be proud of). It's a matter of the sheer scale of the task, like being asked to climb the north wall of the Eiger in bare feet. It means standing trembling before the living God, in order to stand boldly before the world. Unless one has been overwhelmed by the size of this task, one hasn't been paying attention. This isn't genteel modesty. It's horror and panic.

God outflanked all Jeremiah's objections. He was marked out before conception, consecrated before birth. God's protecting presence would be with him (if 'don't be afraid' is the most frequent biblical command, 'I am with you', which regularly backs it up, is one of the most frequent of the biblical promises). God would supply him with the necessary words; the Lord of the nations would appoint him as his spokesman to the rulers of the world. Yes, there would be much negative work ('pluck up, pull down, destroy, overthrow'), but building and planting would follow. Chosen, commissioned, commanded, equipped, supported, comforted, encouraged, the young Jeremiah sets off on a career that will break him and make him.

The contrast Hebrews draws between the fearsome Mount Sinai and the joys of the heavenly Jerusalem should not make us imagine for a moment that the new covenant replaces terror with cosiness. Reverence and awe before the consuming fire is reaffirmed in the New Testament as the appropriate stance for any believer; how much more, for those called to stand humbly in God's presence in order then to speak boldly to the rulers of this age. Hebrews offers both context and hope: our life is conducted, whether we realize it or not, before the angels, archangels and all the company of heaven, and the one whom we serve has committed himself to 'shaking' heaven and earth once more, in order to establish a kingdom that cannot be shaken. We go to our Christian tasks surrounded by invisible witnesses, assured that the work we do belongs to that future unshakeable realm.

The one in whose presence we stand is now known, not just as consuming fire, but as Jesus. In every gospel reading, not least this one, we see another facet of his own prophetic call, humbly obedient to God's will, sternly opposed to the rulers of this age, gently building and planting new life, new hope. The way to discover contemporary vocation is to stand in his presence, trembling but obedient.

Proper 17

—— ⪔ ——

Jeremiah 2.4–13
Hebrews 13.1–8, 15–16
Luke 14.1, 7–14

Don't sit at the top table, declares Jesus; start at the bottom and see what happens. If this is a parable, as Luke says, it isn't advice about behaviour at dinner parties. In Luke's wider context, its meaning is cognate with Jesus' warning and summons to his contemporaries. God has promised a great wedding party, the 'messianic banquet'. But if Israel thinks she has an inalienable right to sit at the top table, she has another think coming. Pride comes before a fall, humility before exaltation. This isn't just wise counsel to an individual: it's Jesus' great challenge to the Israel of his day.

However, since Jesus Christ is 'the same yesterday and today and for ever', it is right that we apply the message to other days, other places. We dare not restrict it to the cameo portrait of prudent social humility. Jesus worked with a bigger canvas. His message, focused now on his cross and resurrection, summons the powers of the world to humility; those who think themselves great are confronted with their own true King shamefully executed, a sight which overturns all arrogance and unmasks all pretension. Faced with the crucified and risen Lord of the world, the rulers of the nations will begin with shame to take the lowest place.

Hebrews 13 outlines the lifestyle of those who have based their lives on the humiliating gospel of Jesus. Hospitality renounces pride of home and family; identifying with political prisoners renounces pride of social status. The false gods of sex and money, who puff up their devotees with a spurious haughtiness, are renounced in chastity and humble trust. Worship the true God, and share the good things you have. This humble way of living, pleasing to God, embodying the reality to which the Temple cult pointed, will call down abuse and threats from those whose own lifestyles are thereby exposed as arrogant, but this merely reinforces the fact that the present world is not our ultimate home. 'We seek the city that is to come.' In that city, pride and fear are replaced by gratitude and trust.

Half a millennium before Jesus, Jeremiah launched his first scathing rebuke to the Jews of his day. What has God done, he asks, to deserve this treatment from his own people? Not only are they elbowing their way to the top table, but when they get there they treat it as if it were their own, not God's at all – and then, having created an empty god-slot, they fill it with worthless alternative divinities. Instead of gratitude for redemption, they exhibit arrogance and abomination. Priests, rulers and prophets alike go along with it. Not only have they left the flowing spring of clear water to dig out cisterns for themselves; the cisterns they have dug are cracked and useless.

Translate this challenge, through the medium of Jesus' parable, to the world and Church of today. And make sure the medium – the way you say it – matches the message.

Proper 18

— ∼ —

Jeremiah 18.1–11
Philemon 1–21
Luke 14.25–33

Luke 14 has more than its fair share of 'hard sayings'. Hate your family; give up your possessions. A nice clear message for the end of the summer holidays. And, to back it up, a solemn warning: such carrying the cross requires clear-eyed calculation and commitment, like someone building a tower or fighting a battle. Half measures will fail, and fail shamefully.

Before we give this the salt-water treatment – first you water it down, then you take it with a pinch of salt – we should recognize its first-century local colour and focus.

Building the Temple and fighting God's battle constituted the messianic task. Herod the Great began to rebuild the Temple; by Jesus' day it was two-thirds complete. It was to be both the dwelling of God on earth and the legitimation of Herod's family as kings of the Jews. Jesus, however, had come as the true king, to build, indeed to be, the real Temple. Were his followers ready to pay the price? Jesus' contemporaries wanted to fight Rome and gain their freedom, winning God's victory over the pagan hordes. Jesus, however, had come to fight the real battle against the real enemy. Were his followers ready to enlist?

The challenge of Jesus' double project would involve cutting ties with current Jewish symbols and aspirations.

The family lay at the heart of Judaism; but Jesus was creating a new family around himself. The land, the most important possession, constituted Israel as a geographical entity; but Jesus' mission, though focused on the nation, had in view the whole of God's world. Those who followed him would therefore incur the wrath both of their Jewish contemporaries, for going soft on nationalist agendas, and of Rome, for launching a kingdom-movement. Carrying the cross was not a metaphor in Jesus' day. To apply this passage, consider the symbols and aspirations by which our own society steers its course.

God was doing at last, on a grand scale, what Jeremiah had predicted. The clay was being put back on the wheel, to be reworked into another vessel. Same clay, new pot: a vital, teasing image of the continuity and discontinuity that comes about when God's chosen and beloved people rebel. The clay cannot complain. The potter is not arbitrary or whimsical, but is responding in creative love to the failure of the first pot. (Like all images, this one eventually breaks down; but it must be allowed to make its point.)

For similar reasons, Paul appeals to Philemon on behalf of his runaway slave Onesimus. God has not finished with the lad, and is making something new of him. To recognize this will mean a huge effort of rethinking on Philemon's part, not unlike that to which Jesus was challenging his followers: instead of a piece of property, Onesimus is a human being for whom the Messiah died. Feel free to read verse 22 as well, and ponder why Paul told Philemon to prepare him a guest room.

Proper 19

—— ❧ ——

Jeremiah 4.11–28
1 Timothy 1.12–17
Luke 15.1–10

In a recent article, a priest from another tradition described the cheerful mixture of spiritualities which made up his regular personal prayer. It was a vivid and moving account of a busy man nourishing and cherishing a sense of God's presence through thick and thin. But at the end my blood ran cold. He often failed, he said; 'but since the Lord has enabled me to base myself on this structure of prayer', he concluded, 'I hope and believe He will save me, as and when He chooses.'

Well, the New Testament does speak of the witness of the Spirit, assuring us in our prayers that we are God's children and that his love will embrace us eternally. But the way he put it was misleading. How might the parable go? 'Supposing you have a hundred sheep, and a good number of them come to base themselves on a structure of feeding and resting which will be good for them; will you not bring those ones safely to the sheepfold at last?'

What was it, after all, about that one lost sheep that made the shepherd go after it? It wasn't the one with the woolliest coat. It wasn't the one with the sweet, almost human bleat. It wasn't the one that regularly nuzzled up close to his knees. It was simply the one that was lost. No qualification except a disqualification. No structure to its life, no good sense, no obedience. That was the one that got the ride home on the shepherd's shoulders. That was the one that made the angels sing for joy.

All right; of course the sheep could say, on the way home, 'I know I'm being saved, because I'm riding on the shepherd's shoulders.' But the gospel message upon which our hope is based is not about the ride home, but about the good shepherd's journey into the wilderness, a journey undertaken out of sheer love and completed with sheer joy. If this is what makes the whole company of heaven sing, then when we join with them at each eucharist we must celebrate it too. Any suggestion that we contribute something to our own rescue is like advising someone going up in a lift to take a ladder as well, just in case.

Paul saw the crazy logic of the shepherd's action. He wasn't just a lost sheep; he was a wolf, harrying and devouring the flock. But even he received mercy, so that he might serve as an example. If he could be rescued, anyone could. Rescued, though, from what? Jeremiah's classic description of life in the wilderness, rebelling against the shepherd's care and love, says it all. 'My people are foolish; they do not know me; skilled in doing evil, they have no idea how to do good.' The result: creation itself deconstructs, goes back to being 'without form and void'. The angels sing when a sinner is rescued by grace; heaven and earth mourn when God's people go astray.

Proper 20

— ∿ —

Jeremiah 8.18—9.1
1 Timothy 2.1–7
Luke 16.1–13

The first thing to get clear about the 'parable of the wicked mammon' is that it is precisely a *parable*. It is not advice about financial management: Jesus is not telling people to cheat their bosses. It makes sense within Jesus' Jewish context on the one hand and Luke's on the other.

Rabbinic parables about a master and a steward are about God and Israel. Jesus regularly charges his contemporaries with infidelity to their commission: called to be the light of the world, they have kept the light for themselves, and have turned it into darkness. One symptom of this, evidenced in the previous chapter, is that Jesus' opponents have become so concerned about keeping what they see as their master's regulations that they cannot accept that Jesus' welcome of the poor and the outcast reflects the master's real intentions. Like the elder brother in the previous parable, or the hard-hearted miser in the next one, they risk being shut out from the master's household, being put out of their stewardship. Jesus, like Jeremiah, is warning of an awesome imminent disaster, whose approach calls all standard practice into question.

What should they do? Throw caution to the winds, and embody the generous love of the master for all and sundry. The parable may hint at some local colour: the steward was

106

perhaps remitting interest (which the master should not have been levying) rather than capital. The master could not charge him with fraud without exposing himself as a usurer. But the thrust remains: judgement is coming upon God's steward-people, and it is time for them to make what arrangements they can with the wider world, with the outcasts and the Gentiles, forgetting the minutiae of the law, and the commitment to family and property. Ancestral land, no longer 'holy', has become 'unrighteous mammon', and is best used for the good of the new community, the one which the master is paradoxically calling into being through the gospel.

The moral teaching that follows (vv. 10–13) applies this more specifically. The early Church shared property, not simply as an exercise in ancient communism, but as a symbolic act: God's people were no longer defined by sacred land. Luke's fusion of this material (what was the elder brother really cross about?) throws into sharp relief his continuing challenge to the Christian community to embody God's generous welcome to all those who need the good news.

The overtones ring through into 1 Timothy. First-century Jews and Christians faced the question: granted that, as good monotheists, we must not offer sacrifice to the Emperor, what line should we take? Call down a curse on him instead? The mainstream early Church (like many Jews) said: no, we must pray for him, and for all officials. This is not just political prudence. It is based on the same covenantal monotheism that underlies Luke 16. The master loves the world outside, and wants stewards who will seek its salvation, not merely their own.

Proper 21

—— ~ ——

Jeremiah 32.1–15
1 Timothy 6.6–19
Luke 16.19–end

Among the many symbolic actions Jeremiah was commanded to perform, this one stands out as a sign, not of judgement, but of hope: hope for God's restoration the other side of judgement. Resurrection hope, if you like. He is commanded to put his money where his mouth has been (Jeremiah 31 predicts God's new covenant with Israel): in the teeth of enemy invasion and imminent disaster, he is to buy a field. I am reminded of Martin Luther, who declared that if he knew the kingdom of God was to come tomorrow, he would go out and plant a tree.

God's future, breaking into and making sense of the present, is the subject of this week's Lukan parable. Again we must remind ourselves that this is not literal teaching. Most of Jesus' hearers already believed that the wicked are punished, and the virtuous but unfortunate recompensed, in the life to come. The parable is, rather, a warning about God's imminent and this-worldly judgement on the nation of Israel for its failure to heed God's call to justice and mercy within its own society, and for its correlated failure to be the light of the world. It belongs exactly, in other words, with the other parables of Luke 14—16.

The story is a variation on a folk tale that was well known in the first-century world – with one dramatic difference. In

108

the traditional story, the request that somebody be sent back from the dead, to warn people in the present life of what is to come, is normally granted. In this case Jesus declares that his contemporaries knew enough, from their Scriptures, to see that their behaviour was out of line with God's intention, and that even resurrection will not convince them otherwise. At this point, of course, the parable does look ahead to the future life, but it is the future which will, all too soon, break into the present in the resurrection of Jesus himself. Thus the 'rich man' in the parable, like the elder brother in the previous chapter and the steward in the present one, stands for the Israel that is under judgement for its failure to recognize God's moment and fulfil God's call. Like Jeremiah's purchase of a field, even the promise of new life after judgement will not be enough to turn God's people from their present descent into ruin.

The same warning, transposed into a post-Easter key, concludes the first letter to Timothy. The life of the coming age, already given in Jesus and promised to those that are his, contains the true riches; present ones are at best something to be used to God's glory, and at worst 'the root of all evil'. If this is an overstatement, it is not so by much. Faced with the idolatry and greed riches can generate, verse 11 commands us to 'flee all this'; not merely to keep six inches away from it, but to get out and run.

Proper 22

—— ⌇ ——

Lamentations 1.1–6
2 Timothy 1.1–14
Luke 17.5–10

Paul, in prison, writes about power. Dangerous stuff, we say – tends to corrupt, and all that. Paul's setting, and the work that got him there, guards him from misunderstanding. Tyrants speak of God's power to validate their own; Paul speaks lovingly about God's power to explain why he remains in chains.

God did not give us a spirit of cowardice, he says, but a spirit of power, love and self-control – 1 Corinthians 12, 13 and 14 in a nutshell. Timothy needs reminding that he has a God-given ministry and must not be timid about exercising it. He is not in danger of enjoying God's power too much: rather the reverse. He needs to know that God delights to exercise his power through Christian ministry. But the power of the true God is never mere power; precisely because it is revealed in Jesus Christ, it is always also the power of love, and to be exercised through and in self-control (the word here means 'moderation' or 'prudence' as well as 'self-discipline').

So, Paul continues, in our suffering for the gospel we rely on the power of God. Clearly this is not a power that enables the evangelist to avoid suffering. As he says elsewhere, and as Israel learnt to her cost through the tragic experience of exile, it is a power that is made perfect in our weakness.

When we are at the end of our own resources, then God's power works through us, shedding on the world around that same grace which grasped and saved us. And, finally, God's power will sustain us to the end; when Paul says (v. 12) that God is 'able' to guard until the coming Day that which Paul has entrusted to him (presumably, his whole self), the word he uses is 'powerful'. Unlike the tyrant (in church or home, as well as in nations), Paul's appeal to God's power generates self-giving love and self-forgetful trust.

These are both in evidence in Luke 17. To begin with, one of the great lessons of Christian living: you don't need great faith, you need faith in a great God. The word translated 'mulberry tree' probably referred to the sycamore, which was believed to have especially deep roots; the stress is on the extraordinary power of God when invoked even by apparently tiny faith.

This is followed by the strange saying about worthless slaves. In a culture that all too easily regards God as a faceless and distant dictator, to stress that he doesn't need to thank us for serving him may make the wrong point; it is harder today to get people to see, as Paul says elsewhere (e.g. Colossians 1.10), that God is delighted with our weak efforts. But we certainly need to be reminded, again and again, that nothing we can do can establish a *claim* on God. No amount of prayer, generosity, suffering, organization, teaching, evangelism – nothing puts the God of grace in our debt.

Proper 23

—— ∾ ——

Jeremiah 29.1, 4–7
2 Timothy 2.8–15
Luke 17.11–19

A sharp-edged summary of Paul's gospel: King Jesus, raised from the dead, of David's seed. The word 'gospel' itself, in Paul's world, meant a royal proclamation; this explains why its heralds fall foul of the authorities. They may be chained, but the gospel itself cannot be; Paul is content with his fate, confident both of the power of the gospel and also of God's future hope for those who endure.

A ministry based on this confidence will not need to descend into disputes about words. This advice could have saved the Church much time, energy and heartache over the last two millennia. Of course, Paul did his own share of arguing; but there is a difference between disputes about words and disputes about the things the words refer to. It takes wisdom to know the difference. The one who does will be the sort of worker who can present the completed project without shame.

Preachers and teachers are sometimes tempted to use this warning about unprofitable word-wrangling as an excuse to serve up a fuzzy generalized message of goodwill, detached from the text. This is either laziness or downright rebellion. The proper alternative to squabbles over words is 'rightly explaining the word of truth'. The verb here is very rare, only occurring otherwise in the Septuagint of Proverbs 3.6

and 11.5, where upright conduct is described in the metaphor of carving out a straight road across difficult terrain. Keeping the metaphor nearly intact here, one might suggest 'leading one's hearers straight to the heart of the text'. To understand the deep meanings of a text, to see where its natural joints and divisions fall, to lay it out so that the hearers may be grasped by its message – that is the vocation that counts.

This task demands hard work. To avoid it becomes a form of ingratitude: for those who live in a world of lies and half-truths, to be entrusted with 'the word of truth' and then to fail to study it and teach it is to be like the nine lepers who, though healed, did not return to give thanks.

The Samaritan who did come back to Jesus was, of course, deeply symbolic for Luke. As elsewhere in his gospel, this is a sign of the breaking down of traditional barriers that kept the Judaean people separate from their northern neighbours, and Jews in general from pagans in general. However, even though it was indeed revolutionary to see the gospel reaching out beyond the borders of the chosen people, it was not alien to Jeremiah's strange message to the exiles. Babylon may have been the great enemy, but now that you are there you must seek its welfare. Paradoxically, the lesson that the exiles had to learn – that God was concerned for the pagan city where they lived – points forward to the explosive gospel message that would one day challenge Jews and pagans alike with the news of another country, another king.

Proper 24

———— ∾ ————

Jeremiah 31.27–34
2 Timothy 3.14—4.5
Luke 18.1–8

The passages from 2 Timothy and Luke 18 both envisage God's people hanging on, sustaining their energy and sense of direction, even though things seem to go from bad to worse. By contrast, Jeremiah 31 sees through the long night to the new dawn, the new covenant which will replace the broken accord of Sinai. For once, Jeremiah offers the good news that creates hope, giving us light in the darkness, keeping us loyal in prayer (Luke) and teaching (2 Timothy).

Those who remember Jeremiah's original commission in chapters 1 and 2 will hear, as in a great symphony, the early themes returning at last in the major key. Israel, plucked up, broken down, destroyed and overthrown, is now at last to be rebuilt and replanted. Fresh seed will be sown – a new covenant image exploited to the full by Jeremiah's greatest prophetic successor – and God will again woo his bride, will espouse her to himself in an unbreakable bond of love. Those who recognize the same themes in the New Testament – the Church as God's building, God's field, the bride of Christ – will see how thoroughly the early Christians believed that Jeremiah's great words of hope had been fulfilled in Jesus.

Why then do we find ourselves still in the position of the widow coming with dogged persistence before the unjust judge? Of course, as the parable itself makes clear (v. 8a), Jesus is not suggesting that God is like the unjust judge; the argument turns upon the implied contrast as much as upon the semi-parallel. The main thrust is the need for perseverance in prayer.

Jesus' own message looked ahead to the days that would follow his ministry, when his disciples would wait in perplexity through persecution and hardship. The encouragement is equally relevant in our own day, not least for the many Christians under persecution, but not only there. Those who face apathy rather than anger at their Christian witness need just as much to set their faces like a flint, to continue their labour of prayer come what may. And in this work they may find their constant resource in the Scriptures, and in teaching based upon them.

Perhaps not surprisingly, there is little direct teaching in the Bible about the Bible itself. The Bible gets on with being itself, with doing its job rather than with talking about the job it is doing. But precisely at the great moments of transition, one of which is marked by 2 Timothy's reflection of the end of the first Christian generation, it is essential to be reminded of that which will carry God's people through all the changes that come upon them. We who live at a time when sound doctrine is mocked as pompous dogmatism, when teachers of new myths are arising to satisfy those with itching ears, need to return to our roots in order to be reminded of the great theme that tells us who we are 'in the presence of God and of Christ Jesus'.

The Last Sunday After Trinity

—— ∼ ——

Joel 2.23–end
2 Timothy 4.6–8, 16–18
Luke 18.9–14

The harvest and the law court are the lenses through which the prophet gazes, wide-eyed, into God's future. Rain in abundance – easy to forget, in northern Europe, what a relief that would be in the Middle East – and the barns and vats will be overflowing. The sinister, almost surrealist, army of locusts which had ravaged Israel at the command of her God in the previous chapters has gone. The years that the locust had eaten will be restored to them, in a promise destined to become proverbial in its own right.

Feasting and thanksgiving will mean more than merely living happily ever after. The harvest will be literal, but will also point to the restored relationship between YHWH and his people. It will mean the people's *vindication* (v. 23); it happens in order that 'my people shall never again be put to shame' (v. 26, repeated in the following verse). In a culture where honour and shame were everything, Israel had been ashamed because the harvest had failed, hanging her head before the watching world. That, paradoxically, is the clue. Pride and wilful self-sufficiency had brought the locusts, with YHWH himself at their head (2.11); now the humble will be exalted, vindicated in the divine lawcourt. 'It was this man, not the other one, who went down to his house justified' – the one mention of 'justification' on the lips of Jesus.

People often balk at lawcourt imagery in theology, supposing it to leave us with a picture of God as a cold or legalistic judge. The language belongs, of course, in a world where true justice was as welcome (and at least as rare) as the rain needed for good harvests; where society trembled on the brink of either chaos or tyranny; and where stories of a Solomon, dispensing God's justice with clarity and wisdom, were like golden fairy tales to which the regular response would be 'If only!'. We who take justice for granted (at least, until you take part in a lawsuit yourself) can ill afford to ignore its near absence, or grievous distortions, in much of the world, both on a large and a small scale – and its constant occurrence as scriptural theme, not least in Jesus and Paul.

One of the theological tasks of our day is to learn how to tell the parable of the two men in the Temple so that it shocks and surprises our world as Jesus' story did his, opening up a vision of God's justice which is not fooled by possessions and prestige, or by social standing, but sees to the heart, and hears the genuine cry of the penitent sinner. Or, to put it another way, we need to discover how Paul's famous doctrine of 'justification', which in Romans is part of the revelation of 'God's justice', is part of, perhaps even a pointer towards, the justice that will be done by 'the Lord, the righteous judge', of whom the same Paul speaks in today's epistle.

117

Sundays Before Advent

The Fourth Sunday
Before Advent

— ∾ —

Isaiah 1.10–18
2 Thessalonians 1.1–12
Luke 19.1–10

Luke cuts Zacchaeus even more down to size, describing him with affected pomposity ('he was a chief tax-collector! He was rich!') and then pointing out that he was also a bit too small for his own good. Luke here highlights several themes which sum up what Jesus' ministry has been all about and point to the reasons for the forthcoming events.

Zacchaeus stands for the ambiguity of the Judaism of Jesus' day. Compromised with Rome, yet conscious of status; aware of a need for renewal, yet clinging to ways of living which made that renewal impossible; children of Abraham, yet lost. Jesus' response, as ever, is to come shamelessly to where the pain is: 'he has gone in to eat with a man who is a sinner' (v. 7) looks back to the accusation in 15.2, and on to the mocking on the cross, when Jesus was for the last time 'numbered with the transgressors' (22.37).

This sharing and bearing of the sinner's blame is undertaken out of a sovereign vocation. 'The Son of Man came to seek and save the lost'; and here he is, accepting Zacchaeus's confession and promise of restitution, assuring not only him but the suspicious onlookers that Zacchaeus is now a saved child of Abraham. In other words, Jesus is acting, and Zacchaeus is treating him, as if he were a priest, or, more, as if he were the Temple itself.

We should not, then, be surprised at how the chapter develops. When Jesus comes to Jerusalem, the place simply isn't big enough for him and the Temple side by side. He has staked a claim, that what the Temple stood for is now fulfilled in him. Zacchaeus has staked his own life upon that claim, and Luke invites all his readers to do the same. But to understand why salvation came to the tax-collector's house, and why it comes to ours, we need to read on, to allow Luke's final chapters to unveil the mystery which characters in his story could only glimpse.

The almost comic tone of the story, and its happy ending, cannot disguise the seriousness of the issues. Isaiah addressed Israel at a time when rebellion against YHWH was so rife that, instead of speaking to 'Israel' or 'Jacob', the words that came most naturally were 'Sodom' and 'Gomorrah', bywords for wickedness and consequent judgement. In that state, the practice of religion is worse than useless, an attempt to draw the veil of respectable practice over mouldering injustices. The only thing that matters is what Zacchaeus discovered: repentance and restoration.

Paul, standing in the same prophetic tradition but the further side of the gospel events, surveys the whole world with essentially the same message. We recoil from warnings of judgement, knowing how easily such language is abused. But judgement is the necessary obverse of justice; and if God is not interested in justice, not only Isaiah and Luke, but also Jesus himself, were all deeply mistaken.

The Third Sunday
Before Advent

—— ∼ ——

Job 19.23–27a
2 Thessalonians 2.1–5, 13–17
Luke 20.27–38

The overall theme ('resurrection') is obvious, but the detail is daunting.

It seems a shame, as the translators' footnotes say, that the Hebrew of Job 19.26 is 'incomprehensible'. The old version ('and though worms destroy this body, yet in my flesh shall I see God') is engraved on innumerable minds and hearts, courtesy of George Frederick Handel. But, though the passage doesn't predict the Christian doctrine of resurrection quite as the older translators supposed, the modified account is in some ways more moving. Job, at the end of his tether, affirms that justice will be done; that a defending counsel will live and arise (the word, in the Hebrew and the Septuagint, would have suggested 'resurrection' to readers of Jesus' day) to plead his cause; and that God himself, who for so long had seemed to be his adversary, would be on his side at the last. Take Job as an icon of the whole world, groaning in travail, longing for justice and new life, and you can translate his confidence directly into the cosmic hope of Romans 8.

And then there is 2 Thessalonians 2, with omissions that leave the 'mystery of lawlessness' and the 'restrainer' in interpretative limbo for yet another year. What we are left with is enough to be going on with: a legacy of naive literalism means that at any mention of the 'second coming' we think of clouds, raptures, and Jesus flying around like a self-propelled spaceman. Paul clearly can't be talking about such an event, since in verse 2 he warns the Thessalonians not to be alarmed at getting a letter telling them that the Day of the Lord has arrived. If this referred to a 'cosmic meltdown' one would suppose that the Thessalonians would have noticed. The truth seems more mysterious: through this-worldly events (as we would call them), God will defeat the mysterious cunning of evil, and rescue his people at last. The note of confidence in the face of superhuman adversity is what matters at the end.

And so to the Sadducees' question, and Jesus' answer – which apparently satisfied, even stunned, his hearers, but which leaves us bewildered. Surely the point Jesus was supposed to prove was not *survival* (Abraham, Isaac and Jacob are still alive somewhere), but *resurrection* (they will rise again to new bodily life)? Yes; but often enough, in rabbinic-style arguments, the game of chess is called off two or three moves early, once both parties can see how the land lies. For most Jews, with their strong theology of the goodness of the created physical world, disembodied existence could never be a final desired resting place. As long as Jesus could show that the patriarchs were still alive in God's presence, the final move ('they will therefore rise again') could be left unstated. Our apologetic, not least to worried souls within our own flocks, needs to be as shrewd, and as sharply attuned to the assumptions and questions of our time.

The Second Sunday
Before Advent

———— ⁓ ————

Malachi 4.1–2a
2 Thessalonians 3.6–13
Luke 21.5–19

Warnings against idleness seem irrelevant in our culture. Those who have work seem to have more and more of it; those who don't seem stuck in a trap. No doubt there are shades of grey, and some manage to play the system; but few today are idle by choice.

Paul's warnings, though, shed an interesting light on his teaching. The idleness against which he warns wasn't caused by his eschatological preaching (the world's going to end, so why work?). It was the result of his teaching that Christians should live as brothers and sisters in a world where siblings formed a single socio-economic unit. Part of the meaning of *agape* was the very practical (and politically subversive) one of mutual support. Now he addresses the flip side of the coin: each must contribute to the best of their ability, not simply sponge off the others. It is ironic that today these warnings might apply to welfare scroungers rather than to anything that goes on within the Church.

There is plenty of eschatological warning in the other two readings. As usual, though, we have to be careful before jumping to the wrong conclusion. Luke's Olivet discourse is emphatically and specifically about the fall of Jerusalem, not about the end of the world. As such, it may of course be taken as a model for all living that peers into an uncertain future, needing to trust in God when everything is crashing down around one's ears. The Church in many parts of the world lives with wars, rumours of wars, purges and persecutions on a daily basis; those of us who don't should read passages like this in prayerful family solidarity with those who do. A church not being persecuted should also, sometimes, ask itself why not. Martyrs and confessors around today's world will testify to us, never mind to their oppressors, that God is faithful to his promises, providing words, wisdom and above all perseverance.

And, of course, the hope of justice. The little passage from Malachi (why not read the whole chapter? It's only six verses!) may make some shudder with distaste, but the news that the God who made and loves the world will at the last put all wrongs to right is great and good news, to be clung to precisely in a world where everything seems upside down and inside out. The same sun that rises to scorch the plants that have gone to the bad is the sun that brings healing in its wings for 'you who revere my name'. This is because, of course, it is the 'sun of righteousness', or the 'sun of justice' (how often Bible translators need an English word that holds both of those together the way the Hebrew and Greek do). God's utter loyalty to his creation means that he will put everything right at the last, and when his human creatures trust his loyalty they will in turn be assured that justice will bring healing, not destruction.

Christic the King

—— ⟿ ——

Jeremiah 23.1–6
Colossians 1.11–20
Luke 23.33–43

Shepherds, shepherding stories, and shepherding metaphors
abound throughout the Bible, as one would expect in that
culture. The creative thing in Israel's traditions, though, was
the development of 'the shepherd' as a metaphor first for the
king (the lowly status of shepherds makes this daring), and
then for God himself. These traditions explode like fireworks
in the Gospels as Jesus, who probably never herded a sheep
in his life, reuses them to explain his strange activity.

Jeremiah's polemic against the wicked shepherds goes
with the preceding denunciation of the rump of the Davidic
house. Hezekiah and Josiah have not been able to save Judah
from the slide into shame, exile and devastation; the would-
be shepherds, Jehoiachin and his like, have done nothing to
look after God's sheep. In that setting, God promises to
gather his sheep once more, and to set wise and caring
shepherds over them.

Rising out of this promise, but far transcending it, is the
pledge that God will raise up a 'branch of righteousness' who
will put God's justice into effect, who will create salvation for
God's people. This Davidic king will bear a strange name:
'Yahweh is our righteousness'. He will embody God's own
promise, covenant faithfulness, justice and loyalty.

What will this look like in practice? Imagine Luke

126

answering this question by tearing down a curtain in front of a great but deeply shocking painting. Here is the king who embodies the justice, the loyalty, the salvation of God: praying for those who nail him to the cross, mocked as a false king, taunted as Jeremiah taunted Jehoiachin as though he were a mere sham, an impostor. Here he is, fulfilling God's promise to bring in his kingdom of justice and mercy, rescuing those who turn to him and his kingdom only when all other hope is exhausted. Is this, or is this not, asks Luke, what Jeremiah (and so many others) was talking about? Is this not the shepherd who would embody the saving faithfulness of God?

Colossians 1.15–20, in effect, sets all this to music. The grand poem, in which verses 15–16 balance 18b–20, with 17 and 18a themselves balanced in the middle, exploits some of the most deep-rooted Jewish language about God – that of the 'wisdom' through which God made all things – in order to talk about Jesus. He is the one through whom all things were made – and redeemed; he is the one who now embodies the ruling and reconciling work of the creator God, Israel's God. What seems bold and daring, almost oxymoronic, when we meet it in Jeremiah, is woven so closely together here as to seem almost natural. Why should not the living God come to live among us as a creature bearing God's image? Why should he not be the first-born from the dead? And why (we ask with fear and trembling) should he not unveil his royal splendour most fully when engaged in the bloody work of peacemaking?